Corporate Responsibility in the Digital Age

Ivri Verbin

Taylor & Francis Group

LONDON AND NEW YORK

First published 2021
by Routledge
2 Park Square, Milton Park, Abingdon, Oxon OX14 4RN

and by Routledge
52 Vanderbilt Avenue, New York, NY 10017

Routledge is an imprint of the Taylor & Francis Group, an informa business

© 2021 Ivri Verbin

The right of Ivri Verbin to be identified as author of this work has been asserted by him in accordance with sections 77 and 78 of the Copyright, Designs and Patents Act 1988.

All rights reserved. No part of this book may be reprinted or reproduced or utilised in any form or by any electronic, mechanical, or other means, now known or hereafter invented, including photocopying and recording, or in any information storage or retrieval system, without permission in writing from the publishers.

Trademark notice: Product or corporate names may be trademarks or registered trademarks, and are used only for identification and explanation without intent to infringe.

British Library Cataloguing-in-Publication Data
A catalogue record for this book is available from the British Library

Library of Congress Cataloging-in-Publication Data
A catalog record for this book has been requested

ISBN: 978-0-367-51668-0 (hbk)
ISBN: 978-0-367-51669-7 (pbk)
ISBN: 978-1-003-05479-5 (ebk)

Typeset in Bembo
by Apex CoVantage, LLC

To Ayelet and my children – my personal
sustainability: Yonatan, Asaf, and Alma

Contents

List of boxes	xi
Acknowledgments	xiii
Preface	xv
1 Introduction	1

PART 1
The good planet: the changing world and the changing business world — 17

2 COVID-19	19
3 The planet: climate	26
4 Sustainability and technology	33
5 Sustainability in practice	44
6 The new economy systems	58
7 Finance and investment	77

PART 2
The good challenge: future-proofing — 87

8 The wake-up call — 89
9 Whose responsibility is it? — 109
10 What does it involve? — 121

PART 3
The good process: step by step — 127

11 Define your values — 129
12 Start a dialogue — 143
13 Look after your people — 149
14 Be responsible for your supply chain — 167
15 Be responsible for your environment — 180
16 Plant roots in your community — 211
17 Revolutionize your marketing and service — 229
18 Be transparent — 245

Afterword: take the lead and go beyond — 256
About Good Vision — 258
Index — 260

Boxes

Greta Thunberg	6
Amdocs	9
Fiverr	12
Volkswagen	27
PG&E	28
Travelers Companies	30
We Mean Business	31
ALYNovation	36
BreezoMeter	36
Tesla	39
Saab	46
Siemens	62
IMPACT at INSEAD	64
Nespresso	65
Switch (Sustainable Waste into Textiles Creates Harmony)	67
LOOP™	68
Kalundborg	71
Ant Forest	77
The B Team and B Corporations	80
Cemex	82
BlackRock's Larry Fink's letter to CEOs	84
Global Risks Report 2020	98
Amazon	99
Kellogg's	101
Unilever	110
SodaStream	116

Chief sustainability officer 117
North Star Alliance 119
Recreational Equipment Inc. 124
Formulating a code of ethics: sample stakeholder
   interview questions 134
Insights 143
Enlight Renewable Energy 144
Roche Pharmaceuticals: "The Trusted Scarf" 146
Zappos 151
Becoming a more inclusive organization 155
Cassiopeia 162
Cotton 168
TerraCycle 170
Heineken 172
Patagonia 173
EcoVadis 178
Pukka 181
Interface 182
The Carbon Trust 184
CDP 185
UK legislation 188
Citi Bike 189
NetBeat™ by Netafim 200
Google Foundation 214
JGive 215
360Giving 216
Friends for Health 219
DonorsChoose 223
GiveGab 224
VolunteerMatch 225
Stella Artois 227
sweetgreen 233
P&G 234
Pepsi 235
TOMS 237
Goodvertising 238
ICL ESG reporting 249

Acknowledgments

This book could not have been written without the help of all those who have energized, challenged, and supported my work through the last decade. I begin by thanking my talented employees throughout that period, including Yigal Avrahmy, Mor Stoller, Ravid Biss, Ronel Sade, Noya Ilani, Hadas David, Liad Klang and Valentina Yakhnina, my special advisors Yair Matiyash and Liat Cohen, along with my interns Grant Campion, Brian Louis Blane, and Shane Judelman. Special thanks go to Arden Frank, who assisted with the research.

A big thank-you to Keren Tamir, who was my partner at the early days of the journey, and to my current partners in the Grant Thornton family: first and foremost to Izhar Kanne and Micky Blumental at Grant Thornton Israel for their personal and professional support, and to Paul English and Olivia Gadd from Grant Thornton International who lead the sustainability vision at our network and opened the door for me. I want to thank my colleagues at the Grant Thornton sustainability center of excellence who made this journey a global one, especially Vischnesh Chandiok from India, Markus Håkansson from Sweden, Emma Verheijke from the Netherlands, Katerina Katsouli from Greece, and Jason Levergood and Geoff Cole from the U.S. I would also like to take a moment to recognize my professors at INSEAD and at Cambridge who, although they may not be aware of the fact, helped me formulate some of the ideas behind this book.

Many people have given feedback and contributed resources to the book, among them Hila Beinish, Amos Shapira, Dalit Brand,

Levin Amb, Constantinus Bikas, Raviv Zoller, Giles Gibbons, Hila Efraty Halper, Stephan Vopel, Avi Zinger, Merav Ratan, Ruthy Rotem, Eshel Armoni, Momo Mehadav, Shira Ansky, Peter Bodin, Paul English, Hemmy Peres, and Dan Lahat.

I would also like to thank Liron Fine, who helped me to develop and edit the initial ideas, and my talented editor Dean Bargh, who made this work possible. Special thanks also go to Rebecca Marsh and Sophie Peoples at Routledge, who gave this book a most prestigious home.

Thanks and love to all our clients, who are actually the real partners in the sustainability journey.

The deepest thank-yous go to Ayelet Nachmias, the woman in my life who enables me to do what I love and to love what I do, and to my own future generation, Alma, Asaf, and Yonatan, who give me the reason to do it.

Preface

Dream big and Go Beyond

We live in a time of crisis and of change. This book is being finished in the midst of the COVID-19 shutdown, some of the ramifications of which are already apparent and will be discussed later in the book. Meanwhile, our collective failure to act decisively in combating climate change leaves the very future of human civilization in the balance.

Clearly, the time for a few incremental adjustments to twentieth-century business models – for "window-dressing" – is over. Integrated, systemic change is needed, for the future of your organization and for the future of our planet. It is not a time to be timid, but nor is it a time to be pessimistic. We need to imagine our ideal future and work out what needs to be done to achieve it – we need to "dream big."

It is too early to say as I write this whether this has been a wake-up call from Mother Nature that has helped us as members of the human race to return to our basic values and embrace principles sustainability – or whether our memory will be short and we will not only forfeit this lesson but use the pandemic to legitimize the more aggressive operation of our factories and companies in the name of "economic recovery."

But my dream goes beyond the immediate effects of the pandemic. In my dream, every organization, whether public or corporate, assumes full social responsibility as part of its organizational

DNA. The water runs clear and the air is clean because organizations' innate social responsibility will not allow them to pollute the environment. In this dream, poverty and hunger are gradually eradicated as this same social responsibility leads organizations to recognize and actively contribute to the community in which they operate. When catastrophes hit – pandemics, natural disasters – companies remember that people and planet are their most important assets.

In this dream, organizations with effective corporate responsibility programs earn more, for several reasons: their activity is performed with minimal friction, their products and services are better and more cost-effective, and, most importantly, the public understands their true value – and chooses them over other organizations.

Furthermore, I believe that not only is this dream achievable, it is already beginning to be realized. In our rapidly changing world, technology enables freedom of speech and information transparency, throwing open the curtains of secrecy that once concealed back-room deals working against the public interest. Under ever-increasing consumer scrutiny, organizations that neglect their social responsibility face relentless waves of social protest, both online and offline.[1]

Take, for example, the corporate governance scandal known as "Dieselgate," which engulfed Germany's largest car company, Volkswagen, in 2015. Because of its attempts to conceal the high diesel emissions of its vehicles, Volkswagen and its executives suffered a significant backlash, which included $15 billion in fines and settlements, a 35% decline in market value, and mass layoffs. This could not have happened in the twentieth century. First, in those days there was little social awareness about the dangers of environmental pollution, and second, in an era before the internet, smartphones, and social networks, the mechanisms for exposing and disseminating such information were very limited. In just a few decades the situation has been transformed. Public awareness of environmental issues is mainstream, corporate governance is a daily topic of discussion, and acts of concealment or fraud tend to be swiftly exposed. The demand for corporate responsibility is driven by consumers, citizens, and voters. As a result,

"In this short, readable book, Ivri Verbin offers easy-to-follow and practical advice for any organisation to change their relationship with and impact on the world. From mindset and policy to clear actions, he covers every aspect of this complex topic simply and gives great examples of how others have succeeded."
—**Peter Bodin,** *Global CEO, Grant Thornton International Limited*

"At Waze we believe that we must act as one community and take responsibility for our actions. By reading this book one can better understand the technological challenges and opportunities in promoting sustainability. This is critical information for decision makers, allowing us to make better informed decisions and be more responsible in our actions."
—**Samuel Keret,** *Director, Waze Carpool*

"Time and again we are reminded that 'we cannot control the direction of the wind, but can only adjust the sails'. Sustainability and corporate responsibility are ultimately about doing the right thing, and for CEOs like myself that means that we must be innovative, leveraging new technologies and processes to deliver value, while living up to that standard. Ivri Verbin delivers an optimistic view that this vision is not only viable and essential, but also possible."
—**Raviv Zoller,** *President & CEO of ICL, a leading global fertilizer and specialty chemicals company*

"Ivri is one of the most important voices on sustainability and corporate responsibility in our global organisation. As I would have anticipated, Ivri's book has made complex issues accessible, while demonstrating his passion and authentic desire for change."
—**Paul English,** *Global Leadership Team, Grant Thornton*

The world is at a crossroads – on our climate, inequality, global health. It really could go either way. Those companies and leaders that practice Ivri's well thought out and evidenced approach to business will help the world to beat these crises, not be the driver of them. If you have the vision to believe, read *Corporate Responsibility in the Digital Age*."

—**Giles Gibbons,** Founder, Good Business

"Ivri Verbin's publication is very timely. His point of view, based on his extensive experience working with Israeli corporations as well as governmental agencies, is of great essence to learn of the role that Israel is playing in this field. A role that will no doubt continue to expand as the Start-up Nation seeks ways to become a Social Innovation Nation."

—**Momo Mahadav,** CEO, Maala – Business for Social Responsibility in Israel

"This book combines a very sound theory with a practical guide for the successful corporation of our times, one that acknowledges the broad social and environmental role of businesses have to play. The deep knowledge and experience of the writer combined with his social sensitivity provides us with a great read, and a particularly useful and necessary compass in navigating the complex waters of the corporate world in this digital era. A stellar and truly needed book."

—**Ambassador Konstantinos Bikas**

"Ivri's book emphasizes and demonstrates to the investment community that financial success can and should help companies achieve a positive impact. In the time of the new economy and digital era, creating a positive impact is crucial for companies to reach financial success. Therefore, I think it is important for any manager or entrepreneur to read this book."

—**Chemi Peres,** President of Pitango Venture Capital

"I could not agree more with Ivri's words and therefore, think that any manager in the present or the future that is passionate about yielding a profit to its shareholders must read his book. Moving forward, all managers must take this message to heart and remember that shareholder profit is consistent with corporate responsibility."

—**Amos Shapira,** former President of El Al Airlines

Corporate Responsibility in the Digital Age

This book is a roadmap to help organizations adopt corporate responsibility and sustainability practices and be fit for purpose in a digital era. It explains why corporate responsibility is the only option in the twenty-first-century post-COVID-19 world, and guides readers through the process of transforming their organizations with continued reference to the importance of technology.

This is not a technical manual, and it is not an academic textbook: it is designed to be a quick, easily digested read. The first part looks at the current landscape – both of business and of the world in which it operates. The second part explains why corporate responsibility is the only realistic option for business in the twenty-first-century, post-COVID, and who needs to take responsibility for it. The third part is a step-by-step guide to putting principles into practice, covering: values, stakeholder engagement, employees, supply chain, environment, community, customers and marketing, and reporting and transparency. Each chapter is linked to relevant UN Sustainable Development Goals and supported by dozens of real-world examples.

By the end of the book, business leaders will have understood the scope of the challenge involved in leading a truly socially and environmentally responsible organization, and, crucially, will have understood why such a course of action is not only desirable but essential. And they will also have been inspired by a sense of purpose. The book offers direct access to the processes, insights, and techniques for installing corporate responsibility throughout organizations large and small, based on the author's many years' experience working in government and with successful large corporations. It is up-to-date and relevant, addressing the implications of COVID-19 and the modern technological "Fourth Industrial Revolution."

Ivri Verbin is founder and CEO of Good Vision and a member of Grant Thornton's international corporate responsibility team. A former advisor to Nobel Peace Prize winner Shimon Peres, Verbin is a pioneer in the field of corporate responsibility.

governments are increasingly responding to this demand and passing regulations aimed at improvement of corporate conduct. The United Nations recognizes the importance of this issue; of its 17 Sustainable Development Goals (SDGs), the majority are directly related to corporate responsibility which is why I decided to use its logos on the book cover and chapters titles.

The concept of "corporate responsibility" has been considerably revised in recent years and now encompasses much more than it did at the beginning of the millennium. At first, the term generally used was CSR (corporate social responsibility), with an assumption that the social contribution was at the heart of the matter. The European Union defined it as "The responsibility of enterprises for their impacts on society."[2] But now we understand that social contribution is just one of a number of issues at the core of the business model, alongside such concerns as product or service quality, customer service, diversity, environmental impact, and ethics. A lack of corporate responsibility leads to an absence of trust, and without trust the business sector will cease to exist. Organizations around the world who might, in the past, have remained in their comfort zone by resolving issues with a simple financial contribution can no longer do this. These days, organizations are broadening the scope of their commitment to sustainability and responsibility under the concept of the "triple bottom line": financial, social, and environmental.

Today, corporate responsibility has become a mainstream topic in most organizations, and I see this as another indication that this field is starting to reach maturity. It is undoubtedly one of the most intriguing business trends of the last two decades: a growing and dynamic field, combining strategy, organizational development, human resources, marketing – and essentially every other corporate competence. It is redefining Milton Friedman's classical economic theories. And it is not just traditional businesses that are under examination: in the current landscape, the lines between different sectors are blurring. Now, many private sector for-profit businesses have a distinct vision and social or environmental mission, while many nonprofits and foundations rely on a model of self-finance and use traditional business models.

★ ★ ★

My personal journey toward this dream began in 2001, when I served as an advisor to one of the greatest dreamers of the past century, Nobel Peace Prize laureate (and then Foreign Minister) Shimon Peres. My main task then was to coordinate cross-sector partnerships to promote regional cooperation and peace building, but then a significant door opened for me: on Peres's recommendation, I received a fellowship for the first executive education program for sustainability and cross-sector partnerships at the Cambridge Institute for Sustainability Leadership.

This program introduced me to a whole new world, which I would subsequently explore fully. In my years working alongside Peres on regional and global projects, I became aware of the scale of the power held by giant corporations such as Siemens, Novartis, Volkswagen, Inter Milan, Barilla, and so on. Peres was a visionary who spoke at length about the roles and responsibilities of the private sector in building bridges between nations. As his advisors, we were tasked with connecting the threads and promoting the organizational processes to enable such a process.

In 2002, I left the Foreign Minister's Office for the private sector in search of a field that would combine corporate activity with public and social policy and thereby serve as an extension of my political and social career. The corporate responsibility sphere was a natural choice. I enrolled in Cambridge University's first program for sustainability leaders and, together, with my business partner, Keren Tamir, we reached out to our friends at the London-based sustainability consulting firm Good Business, directed by Giles Gibbons and Steve Hilton (formerly strategic advisor to British Prime Minister David Cameron), to help us shape our work models and receive constructive feedback.

Israel, dubbed the "Innovation and Startup Nation," serves as an excellent testing ground for issues around innovation and sustainability. It is a small country with severely limited natural resources and no culture of corporate sustainability and responsibility. This is a recipe for ecological and social (and also corporate) disasters that could be well-nigh impossible to resolve. For example, contamination of a water source with industrial waste could simply mean there is suddenly no drinking water. From a business point of view, when consumer interests are disregarded, consumer protests ensue, and soon no one wants to buy your products.

As trailblazers, it was up to us to pave a way for organizational awareness and greater corporate responsibility. Many of the business models that we currently apply at scale have essentially been developed and adapted as a response to the needs we encountered along the way. In reality, all the various models are in a state of continuous assessment and improvement.

With this commitment in mind – as a company engaged in the implementation of corporate responsibility – we merged our business and sold part of our stake to a leading global accounting firm, Grant Thornton. Only through a significant collaboration with a company that deals with the core business of organizations can we lead a real revolution.

★ ★ ★

The idea of writing this book came to me many years later while I was attending the International Social Entrepreneurship Program (ISEP), an INSEAD initiative, in France. Walking among the woods of Fontainebleau is highly conducive to "dreaming big," and I realized that, if we are to make progress, my most useful contribution would be to share and disseminate all that we have learned over the years. I can add value by getting my messages across to organizations across the world to help them transition quickly and efficiently so they are fit for purpose for the challenges ahead.

As a result, throughout this book I offer you direct access to the processes, insights, and techniques we have applied in our recent projects to embed corporate responsibility in various organizations, large and small. I will gladly share this effective and valuable information – simply because to do so is our corporate responsibility.

I urge all readers of this book to dream big and make corporate responsibility a part of that dream – and of your imminent reality. It means quite simply that not only will you have done the responsible thing, but you will be one of tomorrow's survivors.

Wishing us a good vision and a better world,

Ivri Verbin
CEO, Good Vision
Grant Thornton

Notes

1 "More Americans Staying Informed; Increasing Scrutiny of Business, Government." *Sustainable Brands*, 2019. https://sustainablebrands.com/read/marketing-and-comms/more-americans-staying-informed-increasing-scrutiny-of-business-government. *The Power of Corporations in the Digital World: Deliberations of the German Initiative "Curbing Corporate Power" Concerning Regulation 4.0 with an Emphasis on Market Power and Competition Law*, 2019. https://www.oxfam.de/system/files/diskussionspapier-konzernmacht-in-der-digitalen-welt.pdf.
2 European Union, "Corporate social responsibility: A new definition, a new agenda for action." MEMO/11/730, Brussels, October 25, 2011. https://ec.europa.eu/commission/presscorner/detail/en/MEMO_11_730.

1 Introduction

I write this in an unprecedented era amidst a global pandemic – a pandemic that has hit us at a time of unpredictable change. After a long period of gradually building momentum, the rallying cries for climate and social justice have suddenly become impossible to ignore. The deleterious effects of neoliberal capitalism are becoming common knowledge, and individual organizations are under constant scrutiny in the digitally connected world. Is the old order transforming or merely adjusting? How will businesses and the global economy adjust post-COVID-19? One thing is certain: business-as-usual is a recipe for oblivion for the companies that practice it.

COVID-19 has tested many of our long-held assumptions and challenged the economic and social foundations of the neoliberal paradigm. The UK's *Financial Times*, a champion of the private sector and free markets, even began calling for an enhanced role for government and better corporate responsibility. The crisis also served as a litmus test to distinguish genuinely responsible companies from the cynical.

I contend that the sustainability revolution has much in common with previous revolutions, from the First Industrial Revolution to the Digital Revolution. Companies that do not adapt will not survive. This book provides practical tools for the required adaptation.

So how do we go about being fit for purpose in the digital, post-pandemic age of the 2020s and beyond?

Before we continue, let us take a moment to reflect that, despite the global challenges we are facing, we are in fact fortunate to be living in a period of history that is wonderful for many reasons. Life expectancy is higher than ever, many diseases have been eradicated (pandemics are not a new phenomenon), and quality of life has improved across the planet for a majority. The air is (in most places) breathable, most enjoy clean running water and safe beaches, and, with inevitable exceptions, we are experiencing an era of relative peace.

Some definitions: corporate responsibility; digital era

I look at the definitions of sustainability and responsibility in greater detail in Chapter 4, but suffice it to say at this point that sustainability, which is a holistic view of care for the planet – which means meeting our own needs without compromising the ability of future generations to meet theirs – is now interlinked with modern definitions of corporate responsibility. As we will see throughout this book, corporate responsibility is a self-regulation management approach that helps a company to be accountable to its stakeholders.[1] Since it also works toward the goals of sustainability, for the purposes of our discussions the two terms will often cross over.

While there are already shelves full of books about corporate responsibility, the ramifications of the digital age we are now experiencing are changing everything, and there is still much to be written about the subject in the context of technology. Let us now briefly focus on this topic.

We are in the midst of a "Fourth Industrial Revolution," and it is already hard to imagine a world without mobile phones. Virtual reality, machine learning, 3D printing, robotics, the "internet of things" (IoT), and blockchain are all fast becoming just as commonplace. Such technologies and applications, made possible by ever-more powerful processors, large-scale memory, and high-speed communication protocols, are enabling people and organizations to work, communicate, innovate, and add value for our stakeholders in increasingly faster and cheaper ways.

Change in both technology and ecosystems is accelerating faster than ever in human history. Today, these are not simply information technology tools but rather a social phenomenon that changes the way we think, interact, work, travel, and shop. For businesses, it alters the way – and the speed with which – we think and plan, collect and analyze data, and even report and communicate with our stakeholders.

My friend from Tel Aviv College, Professor Yesha Sivan, differentiates between infrastructure technologies – personal computers, servers, networks, WiFi, cyber-security software, GPS, etc. – and applications that allow the company to execute its business operations, such as customer relationship management (CRM), enterprise resource planning (ERP), and billing software, along with the many other applications that support organizational decision-making and analysis processes, such as data warehouses, data mining, or artificial intelligence and so on, together with tools such as portals, email, and social networks.[2]

The principle that digital technology is now integral to the very philosophy of one's business was highlighted in a McKinsey & Co. article which says that "to be meaningful and sustainable . . . digital should be seen less as a thing and more a way of *doing* things" and that it is a means of "unlocking growth now." It breaks the benefits down into three main categories: (1) creating value at new frontiers (re-examining how you actually do business); (2) creating value in core businesses (improving how you serve your customers); and (3) building foundational digital capabilities (becoming agile and fast).[3]

What is the connection between digital technology and sustainability?

Such a fundamental transformation within both the business world and society at large has huge ramifications for the meaning and practice of corporate responsibility and sustainability. As technology transforms, so does corporate responsibility, with data and know-how transferred faster and in a more transparent way than ever before – which has a dramatic effect on a corporation's relations with its stakeholders. That is why you will find, throughout this book, practical examples of the role that technology plays in implementing corporate responsibility as well as some of the challenges it presents. As a corporate responsibility expert and practitioner, I do not claim any specialized expertise in technology, but I hope in this book to persuade other non-technology-experts that we ignore its importance at our peril.

On the sustainable development front, there is no doubt that new technologies can accelerate and scale up our ability to meet the 17 United Nations Sustainable Development Goals (SDGs). The achievement of each of the SDGs – whether it be zero hunger, tackling climate change, or education and well-being – is dependent either directly or indirectly on new technologies and innovation. The success and correct application of these technologies will determine whether or not we can meet the challenges.

A World Economic Forum paper offers a careful analysis of technology's role in addressing the SDGs: the benefits and risks. On the positive side, it notes, we can already see how AI-augmented computing can help in medicine (doctors making fewer mistakes), agriculture (improved yields and minimized inputs), education (customization and dissemination), and research (climate and weather modeling, or advanced material generation for clean fuels). On the negative side, technology has the power to increase stress on society. The daily news cycles remind us of the threats facing our privacy, of crime and security issues, the growing market power of the tech giants, the risks to democracy and human rights from the misuse of technology, and the impact of automation on jobs and inequality.[4]

There is another link – which underpins the chapters in this book – between the digital transformation that companies are necessarily undergoing for the sake of their very survival and the sustainability transformation upon which many are only just embarking. I firmly believe that sustainability/corporate responsibility is a prerequisite for survival and growth, and that it is therefore imperative to begin the journey without delay.

Fifty years from now

Our greatest problems still lie in our imminent future. The COVID-19 crisis momentarily distracted our attention away from the even more momentous reality of potentially irreversible climate breakdown. Fifty years from now, will all this simply be a dying memory? Imagine a sun that is dimmer because of the pollution emitted from factories. The particles will filter out sunlight and engulf the world in a grayish fog. At night, the moon will be a faded, blurred image of itself. Clean air and water will be private goods exploited for profit and unaffordable to many. The oceans will rise, displacing millions and turning them into refugees. Natural resources will dwindle, and access to them will be the cause of bitter conflicts.

Even in the wealthier countries, daily existence will be a struggle for survival. The same will apply to businesses as much as individuals. In a world without responsibility, the strong will subdue the weak and compassion will disappear. The rich will barricade themselves behind guns, and the poor will riot.

Does this sound like a cliché of a dystopian future? Absolutely. Is it science fiction? Definitely not. Current economic and geopolitical trajectories are taking us in precisely that direction. The Industrial Revolution began barely a moment ago on the scale of human existence. But in those 250 years not only have we transformed the world and the opportunities within it, but we have played havoc with the planet's chemistry, ransacked its resources, and exterminated much of its flora and fauna. Global emissions increased from 2 billion tons of carbon dioxide in 1900 to over 36 billion tons 120 years later,[5] and species are now going extinct at 1,000 times above the baseline rate if not faster.[6] Only now are we waking up to the consequences of the transformations of the last two centuries. Environmental, social, and ethical responsibility has been a belated and reluctant adjunct foisted on corporations that have been designed only to maximize the bottom line and which have become more powerful than governments. But the question now is no longer about *whether* the outcomes described here will happen, but rather *when* and *to what extent*.

In essence, the next 50 years will be crucial in determining the trajectory of the environmental crisis. The IPCC (the UN's Intergovernmental Panel on Climate Change) in its 2019 report points to the "urgency of prioritizing timely, ambitious and coordinated action to address unprecedented and enduring changes in the ocean and cryosphere."[7] The earth has already warmed to 1°C above pre-industrial levels because of past and current greenhouse gas emissions. The IPCC is the most reliable source of scientific consensus on this issue. They warn that warming must be kept below 2°C to avoid catastrophic change across the globe, with 1.5°C the goal expressed in the Paris Climate Agreement. Yet current policies to reduce emissions are still drastically inadequate: they need to triple to meet the 2°C target and increase fivefold to keep heating to within 1.5°C.[8]

We are experiencing the effects already in extreme weather conditions and climate events. Melting glaciers, along with rising sea levels, are already endangering several Pacific island nations; global desertification is leading to a decline in crop yield; extreme temperatures are leading to an additional increase in energy consumption (for heating and cooling) in a negative feedback cycle.

Climate change is creating not only environmental challenges but also economic ones as a direct result (desertification being one example), as well as social ones: for example, we can anticipate millions more refugees displaced by rising sea levels.

But climate change is not the only challenge to be addressed in pursuit of a habitable and just world. Poverty, income inequality, resource scarcity, and gender and racial equality are all urgent concerns. How do modern corporations operate in a world increasingly clamoring not just for action on climate change – and "climate justice"[9] – but for social justice as well?

Greta Thunberg

Climate   Society

At only 16 years of age, Greta Thunberg established herself as a trailblazer of climate change advocacy. In 2019 alone she addressed the UN Climate Change Conference in Poland, launched a scathing attack on the billionaires at the World Economic Forum in Davos, traveled around the world to deliver speeches, and inspired school strikes across the globe. Her *Skolstrejk för klimatet* ("school strike for the climate") movement soon escalated: on March 15, 1.6 million people in 133 countries participated in a climate strike, followed by the even larger "Global Week for Future" in September to coincide with the United Nations Climate Summit, with possibly up to 7 million people participating across 4,500 locations in 150 countries. The "Greta Effect" has additionally inspired people of all generations to consider their carbon footprint and reduce their air travel. She continues to challenge leaders with direct and disarming honesty and clarity: "I want you to act as if the house is on fire, because it is." She expresses the anger felt by many of her generation who feel they have been betrayed by a generation who will not live to see the consequences of their actions.

Extinction Rebellion (XR) came to the forefront of worldwide attention through their demonstrations in summer 2019: another manifestation of the recourse by an increasing number of citizens to direct action through peaceful civil disobedience, inspired in no small part by Greta's leadership on the issue. It is likely that such disruption will only escalate over time.[10] There is no doubt that XR is an expression of a genuine cultural change: demonstrations are being joined by people from a wide cross-section of society, and there are signs that this cultural change is beginning to be reflected by much-needed political change.

I believe businesses are going through a period of tremendous change. Only those that realize that they do not operate outside ecological and social ecosystems will have a long-term future. And no business has been immune to the effects of the COVID-19 pandemic. The twenty-first century is a period of increasing awareness internationally of the causes and impacts of climate change and of the human and environmental costs of political and business decisions. Our interconnected world means a more informed and more organized population at grassroots level exerting pressure from below for change. The investor community is not neutral on these issues and brings a huge pressure to bear on big business. In the corporate world there is now a wealth of evidence to show that an ethical approach to business is not a luxury but a route to success.

For years, leading business strategists from Jim Collins, author of the iconic *Built to Last*,[11] to Harvard strategy guru Michael E Porter, originator of the Competitive Advantage model,[12] have tried to identify the critical factors behind companies' growth and survival. My view, which, directly or indirectly, underpins the chapters in this book, is that corporate responsibility is one of the key elements in business growth and survival in the long run.

As an example of concerted international efforts, as indicated here, in September 2015 the United Nations General Assembly adopted 17 Sustainable Development Goals (SDGs), an ambitious global agenda for the eradication of poverty, ensuring inclusive and equitable education, achieving gender equality, ensuring the availability of water and sanitation, strengthening the means of global partnerships for peace, protecting and restoring ecosystems, and more. Unlike previous agendas, the proposed SDGs have succeeded in attracting the recognition and commitment of numerous governments and organizations.

The tide has turned. The stakeholders of business – customers, employees, neighbors, etc. – will no longer tolerate irresponsibility and "greenwashing." Responsible management is not public relations. It is a vital part of any company's DNA.

Global policy is rapidly changing

The pressure of public scrutiny is growing. Such pressure is also brought to bear on governments, which in turn are imposing higher standards of accountability on corporations. In fact, two processes are happening in parallel. First, the pressure of voters on their representatives is growing. Second, a new generation, one born into a world in which environmental and social responsibility has been normalized, is being appointed to key positions. This generation now has a controlling presence in media, business, and politics – the three forces that shape our world.

If we park our inherent cynicism for a moment, we can acknowledge that there is a growing trend in many countries worldwide in which governments have become advocates of national, personal, and corporate responsibility – with all that entails. The media is quick to report on and amplify such concerns. The business sector, with which this book is concerned, is slowly but inexorably following suit.

A discerning eye will see that the global economy we thought we knew is beginning to look distinctly different. And much of that difference is about responsibility and sustainability.

The changing workplace

The workplace was already undergoing a fundamental transformation when the COVID-19 pandemic hit. Flexibility in working hours was increasing, more people were operating as freelancers, and there were more opportunities for remote work, with Millennials steadily driving the rapid adoption of technology to facilitate the flexible working trend. Then, all of a sudden, flexibility was the only way many organizations were able to keep operating. Those companies who invested in tech platforms to support remote work, such as Amdocs (see the Amdocs Box), were pulling through, while others who underestimated the importance of technology were served a reminder that their human resources were their most precious resources of all.

Amdocs

Technology   Platforms   Employees

Amdocs is a global billing company and its "Virtually Together" platform was created during COVID-19 as a space for its employees to ask questions, find useful tips and tools,

> and share perspectives and experiences. The program includes four main areas: "virtual working environment," "family and community," "well-being," and "this is how we do it."[13]

Because of this fast-forwarding, all that we thought we knew about human resources has to be re-evaluated. Companies have been forced to accept that their employees have different needs for which different solutions apply – made possible by contemporary technology. As we reimagine the way we work, meet, and shop, we have to accept that our cheese has been moved.[14]

Pre-COVID-19, *Fast Company* made some predictions about how work would change in 2020, and the pandemic has in fact made them even more relevant. First, the "gig economy" would grow, with flexible working encompassing freelancing, temping, contracting, and remote work on a project-by-project basis, or moving between employers much more rapidly. In fact, remote work has grown 91% over the last ten years, according to a Global Workplace Analytics and FlexJobs survey. Even before the pandemic hit, half of us were expected to be working remotely in some form by the end of 2020. This, of course, has major implications for HR and for onboarding and training. What companies will need to focus on is "people enablement," with a more holistic, less top-down-focused approach, establishing a fulfilling culture, creating alignment throughout the company, and providing opportunities for professional growth. A further prediction is about "HR chatbots," automated tools to deal with more low-level human resources tasks, freeing up time for more in-depth interactions. Finally, AI and machine learning will increasingly enable data-driven decisions through an automated approach:

> The idea isn't to remove the human element but to establish a more streamlined approach where AI is used as a tool to assist with and elevate current processes, elevating efficiency with tasks such as candidate screening, onboarding, and administrative tasks such as holiday requests, interview scheduling, and analytics.[15]

Back in 2010, analyst firm Gartner predicted[16] ten major workplace shifts for 2020 attributed to technology, many of which have come to fruition far ahead of time: de-routinization of work, work swarms, attention to patterns, hyperconnectedness, diversity and inclusion, augmented collaboration, and remote workplaces. Gartner predicted that half of the U.S. will work outside of traditional work environments by 2020, but in fact the number of remote workers has increased by 115% in that time.

Technological and cultural shifts are already causing the workplace to transform beyond recognition. Digital disruptors have significantly shifted the way we work, from how we communicate to where and when we get our work done. Traditional employment models are changing. Many job descriptions today would have been incomprehensible ten years ago, and new ones continue to appear. Technology is allowing people to work remotely. Some work for several companies simultaneously as freelancers or part-timers, participants in the "gig economy."

Today's employees, who increasingly comprise Millennials and Generation Z, are more concerned about their personal needs. They tend to rotate between jobs and look for meaning and added value in their workplace. Cone Communications' Millennial Employee Engagement Study[17] found that three-quarters of Millennials (those born between about 1980 and 2000) consider a company's social and environmental commitments when deciding where to work, and nearly two-thirds won't take a job if a potential employer doesn't have strong corporate responsibility practices. To a clear majority of this rising generation, such factors are *more important than financial considerations.* Meaningful engagement with corporate responsibility is therefore nothing less than a business imperative, impacting a company's ability to appeal to, retain, and inspire Millennial talent. The significance of this is inescapable when it is realized that Millennials represent an estimated half of the U.S. workforce and potentially three-quarters of the global workforce by 2025.[18] According to Alison DaSilva, Cone's executive vice president of CSR Research & Insights, "companies will have to radically evolve their value proposition to attract and retain this socially conscious group . . . Integrating a deeper sense of purpose and responsibility into the work experience will have a clear bottom line return for companies."

> **Fiverr**
>
> Technology   Platforms   New paradigms
>
> Founded in 2010, Fiverr.com is a global online marketplace for freelance services. Its name comes from the original price of "gigs" or jobs at only a "fiver" ($5.00) per task. Now you can charge more – anywhere from $5 to $995. It has the advantage of being simple to use: you can create an account and start to list gigs in minutes.[19] This platform is helping to digitize and globalize the "gig economy." Anything goes as far as offerings are concerned, with digital-based services – e.g. social media or blog posting, or influenced marketing – being common.[20] The Fiverr marketplace is dominated by young adults, with only 2% of sellers over the age of 55.

See Chapter 13 for more on employees and the changing workplace.

The responsibility revolution

For decades, the big corporations of the U.S. (and elsewhere) have been fulfilling their duty to enrich their shareholders front and center. But things are changing. In 2019, the Business Roundtable, an influential association comprising the top bosses of the most prominent firms in the U.S., issued a statement about the purpose of a corporation. It was a commitment to lead their companies for the benefit of all stakeholders, including customers, employees, suppliers, communities, and shareholders, and was signed by 181 CEOs. According to Alex Gorsky, Chairman and CEO of Johnson & Johnson and Chief of the Business Roundtable Corporate Governance Committee, "this new statement better reflects the way corporations can and should operate today." Darren Walker, President of the Ford Foundation, added:

> This is tremendous news because it is more critical than ever that businesses in the 21st century are focused on generating long-term value for all stakeholders and addressing the challenges we face, which will result in shared prosperity and sustainability for both business and society.

The truth is that one year later, research that was conducted by Professor Lucian Bebchuk and his colleagues from Harvard University has found a limited amount of change in the performance of these companies but the discourse was changed and I believe that time is needed to evaluate the evolution.[21]

These executives are rethinking capitalism's mission at a time when employees, customers, suppliers, and voters are demanding greater accountability from their leaders.[22]

But change will not just happen from the top down. We should keep our eyes on the next generation: one of the most popular courses at Harvard Business School is Professor Rebecca Henderson's "Reimagining Capitalism."

The next great revolution, the corporate responsibility revolution, is taking place right this minute. While it still feels like a refreshing breeze, the tsunami is imminent: ask any of the Volkswagen executives who were let go following the Dieselgate scandal mentioned in Chapter 3. But this is just the beginning.

The EU defines corporate responsibility as "The responsibility of enterprises for their impacts on society."[23] The corporate responsibility revolution crosses sectors and industries. It is relevant to automobile companies, pharmaceutical companies, or any type of service-providing companies. It concerns corporations, nonprofit organizations, governments, and public sector organizations.

This revolution is not directly related to technology – but technology drives it forward. It dramatically affects CEOs and leaders – but is promoted by "ordinary" people: customers, investors, consumers, and voters. It is global, on a massive scale – but it manifests locally, business by business, organization by organization. No one will be left out.

The main question of concern, no matter whether you are an owner or an employee, is: *where does your organization stand*? Are you preparing for the future? Are you still on the fence waiting to make a decision? Or is your organization part of the third group of companies and will soon disappear?

The good news is that there is still time to fix matters. And there is much to be gained.

About this book

In the first part of this book I will look at the current landscape – both of business and of the world in which it operates. In Part 2, I will explore why corporate responsibility is the only realistic option for business in the twenty-first-century post-COVID-19 world. Part 3 sets out a roadmap for corporate responsibility in a simple step-by-step manner. Each chapter is linked to relevant United Nations Sustainable Development Goals.

This is not a technical manual, and it is not an academic textbook: it is designed to be a quick, easily digested read. By the end of the book, you will have understood the scope of the challenge involved in leading a truly socially and environmentally responsible organization, and, crucially, you will have understood *why* such a course of action is not only desirable but essential. And I hope you will have been inspired by a sense of purpose: that purpose being to help your organization become part of the solution.

Notes

1 James Chen and Gordon Scott, "Corporate social responsibility (CSR)." *Investopedia*, February 22, 2020. https://www.investopedia.com/terms/c/corp-social-responsibility.asp.
2 Yesha Sivan and Raz Heiferman, *Doing Digital*. Tel Aviv: i8 Ventures, 2018.
3 Karel Dörner and David Edelman, "What 'digital' really means." *McKinsey*, July 2015. https://www.mckinsey.com/industries/technology-media-and-telecommunications/our-insights/what-digital-really-means.
4 Celine Herweijer and Dominic Kailash Nath Waughray, "How technology can fast-track the global goals." *World Economic Forum*, September 24, 2019. https://www.weforum.org/agenda/2019/09/technology-global-goals-sustainable-development-sdgs.

5 Hannah Ritchie and Max Roser, "CO_2 and greenhouse gas emissions." *Our World in Data*, October 2018. https://ourworldindata.org/co2-and-other-greenhouse-gas-emissions.
6 "How many species are we losing?" *WWF*. http://wwf.panda.org/our_work/biodiversity/biodiversity.
7 "Choices made now are critical for the future of our ocean and cryosphere." *IPCC*. https://www.ipcc.ch/2019/09/25/srocc-press-release.
8 "Countries must triple climate emission cut targets to limit global heating to 2C." *The Guardian*, September 23, 2019. https://www.theguardian.com/environment/2019/sep/23/countries-must-triple-climate-emissions-targets-to-limit-global-heating-to-2c.
9 "Principles of climate justice." *Mary Robinson Foundation*. https://www.mrfcj.org/principles-of-climate-justice.
10 Damien Gayle, "Extinction rebellion activists stage protest at Bank of England." *The Guardian*, October 14, 2019. https://www.theguardian.com/environment/2019/oct/14/extinction-rebellion-activists-stage-protest-at-bank-of-england.
11 James C. Collins and Jerry I. Porras, *Built to Last: Successful Habits of Visionary Companies*. New York: Random House, 1994.
12 Michael E. Porter, *Competitive Advantage: Creating and Sustaining Superior Performance*. New York: The Free Press, 1985.
13 https://www.amdocs.com/community/virtually-together.
14 *Who Moved My Cheese* by Spencer Johnson (G. P. Putnam's Sons, 1998) is a parable about the pitfalls of unadaptable thinking and an entreaty to accept and prepare for change.
15 Bas Kohnke, "Four ways work will change in 2020." *Fast Company*, December 20, 2019. https://www.fastcompany.com/90444541/four-ways-work-will-change-in-2020.
16 Thomas Wailgum, "Your workplace in 2020: Gartner's predictions." *Computerworld*, August 4, 2010. https://www.computerworld.com/article/2519849/your-workplace-in-2020-gartner-s-predictions.html.
17 "Three-quarters of millennials would take a pay cut to work for a socially responsible company, according to the research from cone communications." *Cone Communications*, November 2, 2016. https://www.conecomm.com/news-blog/2016-cone-communications-millennial-employee-engagement-study-press-release.
18 Peter Economy, "The (Millennial) workplace of the future is almost here: These 3 things are about to change big time." *Inc.*, January 15, 2019. https://www.inc.com/peter-economy/the-millennial-workplace-of-future-is-almost-here-these-3-things-are-about-to-change-big-time.html; "Generations-demographic trends in population and workforce: Quick take." *Catalyst*, November 7, 2019. https://www.catalyst.org/research/generations-demographic-trends-in-population-and-workforce/.
19 Cindy Fahnestock-Schafer, "The truth about Fiverr: Good, bad and ugly." *Tough Nickel*, February 25, 2018. https://toughnickel.com/self-employment/truth-about-Fiverr.

20 Ginger Dean, "15 ways to make money on Fiverr." *Forbes*, August 29, 2016. https://www.forbes.com/sites/gingerdean/2016/08/29/15-ways-to-make-money-on-fiverr/#272a27875cda.
21 https://corpgov.law.harvard.edu/2020/08/19/was-the-business-roundtable-statement-mostly-for-show-3-disregard-of-legal-constraints/
22 Alan Murray, "America's CEOs seek a new purpose for the corporation." *Fortune*, August 19, 2019. https://fortune.com/longform/business-roundtable-ceos-corporations-purpose. See also Maggie Fitzgerald, "The CEOs of nearly 200 companies just said shareholder value is no longer their main objective." *CNBC*, August 19, 2019. https://www.cnbc.com/2019/08/19/the-ceos-of-nearly-two-hundred-companies-say-shareholder-value-is-no-longer-their-main-objective.html.
23 "Corporate social responsibility: A new definition, a new agenda for action." *EU Memo*, October 25, 2011. https://ec.europa.eu/commission/presscorner/detail/en/MEMO_11_730.

Part 1
The good planet
The changing world and the changing business world

2 COVID-19

This book was completed in the midst of the COVID-19 crisis. It is clear that the effects of the crisis will be felt for years to come, but even in early August 2020 some implications were becoming known.

In May 20, we at Grant Thornton conducted our annual Survey (IBR) of mid-market businesses of more than 10,000 businesses across 29 economies about sustainability and Covid 19, and we have founded that although 61% agree that the "public expectations of what companies should be doing around sustainability will rise as a result of the Corona virus," 57% agree that "the economic hit from the Corona virus will inevitably make sustainability less of an internal priority for companies." This gap will continue or even create tension between stake holders' expectations and companies' response and between long term and short term is integral in any discussion about corporate sustainability.

Businesses of all sizes suffered, although there were, as always, some winners. Some were fortunate to have the right product at the right time (big tech) and some were smart enough to respond quickly and appropriately (some food retailers and restaurants). For tourism and the hospitality industry in general, it was calamitous, with airlines, hotels, and events badly affected.

Some effects were immediately felt and had major implications for business. An obvious one was a more sophisticated and flexible use of technology. We won't forget what we learned during self-isolation, the habits and the technical skills: tech has taken a quantum leap forward with regards to its role both in business and in society. Millennials and Gen Zs were already taking us toward a workplace characterized by flexible working and videoconferencing (see the Introduction and Chapter 13), but that became commonplace almost overnight. COVID-19 is removing artificial barriers to moving our lives online: many people have realized that the only thing stopping them from working efficiently at home and saving two hours a day of commuting was the permission to do so and the right app. It will be hard in the future to deny employees such an option. "In other words, it turns out, an awful lot of meetings . . . really could have been an email. And now they will be."[1] Expect a big upturn in anything tech-based that facilitates remote interaction, such as VR and telemedicine.

Another characteristic Millennial trend that has been accelerated is the decline of individualism as a guiding philosophy. As we self-isolated, we found ourselves paradoxically more connected than ever, communicating more often with those who are physically distant. The common enemy helped remind us that we have more uniting us than dividing us. There is a direct link here with consumerism, rampant forms of which have long been linked with a culture of individualism. Will restraining our consumption finally be seen as a reasonable price to pay to ward off future pandemics and climate disaster? As we reconsidered who we are and what we value, we became more communal:

> we will be better able to see how our fates are linked. The cheap burger I eat from a restaurant that denies paid sick leave to its cashiers and kitchen staff makes me more vulnerable to illness, as does the neighbor who refuses to stay home in a pandemic because our public school failed to teach him science or critical thinking skills.[2]

On a broader scale, in what was being defined as a "posttruth age," we remembered to listen to experts: public respect for expertise – in public health at the very least – was partially restored. Similarly, we witnessed a revived trust in government institutions: and big government was suddenly back in vogue as huge central, concerted fiscal and other emergency measures were seen as the only sane responses. "The world needs strong public–private partnerships to help contain the spread of this deadly virus," said Eduardo Martinez, president of the UPS Foundation.[3] The political shockwave that such a crisis causes will be felt for years, although it is too early at the time of writing to describe the long-term effects. However, as with the world of work, the genie is out of the bottle and won't be put back. We now know that what we were told was impossible and unaffordable is eminently possible after all. Universal basic income is now a serious policy idea, as is mandatory paid sick leave in the U.S. In the UK, the homeless, whose numbers were rising rapidly, were immediately found shelter. Evictions for rent defaults were suspended. What will be the political consequences of poorer populations finally realizing that their needs were dismissed only because it wasn't politically expedient to attend to them?

The coronavirus crisis is putting corporate responsibility to the test as never before. There are stark warnings from Naomi Klein, a seasoned campaigner against the rampages of disaster capitalism, who fears the same forces may prevail, to "shower aid on the wealthiest interests in society, including those most responsible for our current vulnerabilities, while offering next to nothing to most workers and small businesses."[4] But she acknowledges that we have a choice in such a time of unprecedented change. There are always "ideas lying around" in such a time, to quote Milton Friedman, ideas whose time has come, so are the ones we choose going to be "sensible, fair and for our protection or predatory and calculated"? That still remains uncertain.

The saying "when the going gets tough the tough gets going" was never more true. Like other cases the Covid crises differentiates between authentic responsible companies and those who use it mostly for public relations.

The opportunity presented itself for a renewal of priorities, and the way large companies responded to this crisis will define them for years to come. Already both heroes and villains are emerging. On March 26, 2020, Danone guaranteed its 100,000 employees contracts and income until June 30, gave them all COVID-19 health coverage, and provided bonuses for those who need to work on-site. Luxury conglomerate LVMH quickly repurposed its French facilities to make disinfectant gel – facilities that normally produce perfume and cosmetics for top brands.[5] Virgin Atlantic, however, attracted criticism by asking its employees to take eight weeks of unpaid leave, not long after having appealed to the UK government for support from the public purse.[6] And the profiteers will not be kindly remembered. Harel insurance, one of my first clients, has stopped payments from its clients that were in quarantine and could not use their cars. Some found opportunities where others saw only crisis. Food retailers quickly set up "we will pack for you" services to limit the handling of products. ChowNow, an online food ordering platform, offered takeout and home delivery, and the Walgreens chain expanded its prescription-delivery services.[7]

How companies behaved toward their employees proved to be a key indicator of how their reputation was going to fare in the future. Atta Tarki, Paul Levy, and Jeff Weiss noted in the *Harvard Business Review*, "Those who manage the economic effects of this crisis in a clear and compassionate way create more value for their companies and will come out of this pandemic stronger than ever before."[8] According to Mark R. Kramer, senior lecturer at Harvard Business School, "What companies do to help their laid-off employees – above and beyond what is required or expected – will be remembered and repaid in increased loyalty, higher productivity, and a lasting reputational benefit for many years to come."[9]

Other signs of an ethical response included: making sure smaller suppliers were paid even ahead of time, supporting health care providers, and foundation aid for community support, such as food pantries, free clinics, and other nonprofits to address the immediate needs of the communities in which the company operates. Businesses were asked to walk the talk and take charge; this was not a time to look solely at the bottom line: "Companies write off the costs of restructuring, product failures, or acquisitions that go wrong all the time. Everyone will understand writing off losses due to the coronavirus pandemic," wrote Kramer.[10] Rather, this was a time to accept that you are highly likely to take a short-term hit, no matter what, and that your long-term survival is predicated on how your reputation emerges at the end of the crisis. A considered, well-communicated approach with the good of the wider community as a priority was required – which is corporate responsibility in its essence. Even those companies that stood to gain from the crisis wisely considered their approach. Walmart in the U.S. was predicted to need possibly 150,000 new hires to meet demand, but it nonetheless planned to provide a cash bonus to hourly workers for their "dedication to serving customers in a time of an unprecedented national health crisis." Furthermore, it pledged to keep prices fair, divert products to areas of the country where they are needed most, combat price gouging by third-party sellers, and make sure employees stayed home if unwell. This was in addition to a $25 million commitment to support organizations responding to the outbreak.

As one commentator asked,

> Rather than tweak the old rules to help business stem losses, what if our business leaders use this opportunity to develop new decision rules – to enable a more resilient and generative relationship between business and workers, business and communities, business and natural systems?[11]

She went on to ask whether this could be a revaluation of the "take, make, dispose" model and finally a shift to the design principles of a circular economy (discussed in Chapter 6).

There were implications for supply chains, as dependence on globalized supply chains was thrown into question, to be balanced against the inevitable increased costs of switching to a more robust domestic supply chain. Priorities were interrogated within the investment community, with the PRI (Principles for Responsible Investment) stating, "Responses will need to support other priorities critical to public well-being and long-term economic strength, such as combating inequality and enabling the low-carbon transition."[12]

One less-discussed facet of the crisis was the light that it shed on our other major crisis: the climate. The coronavirus-induced global economic downturn was predicted to cause CO_2 emissions to drop in 2020 for the first time since the financial crisis of 2009. However, the reduction was expected to be no greater than 5%. The alarming conclusion from this figure is that it required a global pandemic with thousands of deaths, massive unemployment, and economic dislocation to reduce emissions by such a small amount. This is a stark wake-up call about the scale of the climate challenge and the efforts needed to solve it.[13]

Notes

1 Katherine Mangu-Ward, "Regulatory barriers to online tools will fall," in "Coronavirus will change the world permanently. Here's how." *Politico*, March 19, 2020. https://www.politico.com/news/magazine/2020/03/19/coronavirus-effect-economy-life-society-analysis-covid-135579.
2 Eric Klinenberg, "Less individualism," in "Coronavirus will change the world permanently. Here's how." *Politico*, March 19, 2020. https://www.politico.com/news/magazine/2020/03/19/coronavirus-effect-economy-life-society-analysis-covid-135579.
3 Dave Reynolds, "Coronavirus aid from U.S. groups arrives in China." *Share America*, February 6, 2020. https://share.america.gov/coronavirus-aid-from-u-s-groups-arrives-in-china/.
4 "'Coronavirus capitalism': Naomi Klein's case for transformative change amid coronavirus pandemic story." *Democracy Now*, March 19, 2020. https://www.democracynow.org/2020/3/19/naomi_klein_coronavirus_capitalism.
5 Sarah Kent, "LVMH to manufacture disinfectant gel in French factories to help prevent a hand-sanitizer shortage." *Business of Fashion*, March 15, 2020. https://www.businessoffashion.com/articles/news-analysis/lvmh-to-manufacture-disinfectant-gel-in-french-factories-to-help-prevent-a-hand-sanitizer-shortage.
6 Sharon Marris, "Coronavirus: Virgin Atlantic asks staff to take eight weeks of unpaid leave." *Sky News*, March 16, 2020. https://news.sky.com/story/amp/coronavirus-virgin-atlantic-asks-staff-to-take-eight-weeks-of-unpaid-leave-11958150.
7 Judith Samuelson, "Covid-19 is a chance for business leaders to rework their pact with society." *Quartz*, March 25, 2020. https://qz.com/work/1825292/will-coronavirus-prompt-business-to-rework-its-pact-with-society/.

8 Atta Tarki, Paul Levy, and Jeff Weiss, "The coronavirus crisis doesn't have to lead to layoffs." *Harvard Business Review*, March 20, 2020. https://hbr.org/2020/03/the-coronavirus-crisis-doesnt-have-to-lead-to-layoffs.
9 Mark R. Kramer, "Coronavirus is putting corporate social responsibility to the test." *Harvard Business Review*, April 1, 2020. https://hbr.org/2020/04/coronavirus-is-putting-corporate-social-responsibility-to-the-test.
10 Ibid.
11 Samuelson, *op. cit.*
12 "How responsible investors should respond to the COVID-19 coronavirus crisis." *Principles for Responsible Investment*, March 27, 2020. https://www.unpri.org/covid-19.
13 Jennifer T. Gordon, "The implications of the coronavirus crisis on the global energy sector and the environment." *New Atlanticist*, March 24, 2020. https://www.atlanticcouncil.org/blogs/new-atlanticist/the-implications-of-the-coronavirus-crisis-on-the-global-energy-sector-and-the-environment/.

3 The planet
Climate

Every year new records are being set for carbon emissions, greenhouse gases, and extreme temperatures resulting from climate change. Over half of these emissions are the result of anthropogenic activities such as deforestation, burning coal, oil and gas for industry and transportation, and the continued destruction and contamination of natural habitats. Over the next century, long-lasting changes in global climate will have severe impacts on ecosystems and human well-being. Countless studies confirm this worrying trend, and the matter requires a significant and systemic change in every organization.

The organizational risks of failing to respond will be severe.

Climate change: impact on business

Much has been said about the impact of climate change on the business sector. The World Economic Forum's 2019 Global Risk Report[1] describes the failure of climate change mitigation and adaptation as one of the most significant risks to our society and businesses. Global consulting giant McKinsey & Co. has identified the six types of risks climate change poses to businesses, some related to the value chain and others to external stakeholders.[2]

Infrastructure, factories, and supply chain operations are susceptible to extreme weather events, such as fires, floods, and hurricanes, which are becoming more frequent and more severe. For example, in 2011, parts of Thailand experienced its worst floods in over 70 years as a result of heavy rains and tropical storms. The floods hit industrial areas – and immediately disrupted the global supply of electronics and car parts. Production for the world's largest computer manufacturers (Acer, Samsung, Lenovo, and Apple) was suspended, as it was for large auto manufacturers such as Toyota and Honda. It took almost two months to clear the water from the factories, significantly disrupting these organizations' supply chains and bringing economic and organizational costs estimated at nearly $44 billion.

Historically, companies have been used to paying little or nothing at all for their environmental (and social) capital and for their use of the natural environment – including carbon emissions and waste. But the rules of the games are changing. Increasing price volatility of raw materials and other commodities also poses risks. The high-tech and renewable energy industries, for example, face price risks in the competition for scarce minerals used in the production of hard drives, televisions, wind turbines, photovoltaic systems, and electric vehicles. But water prices can also rise due to drought, and of course energy prices are not stable, being exposed to geopolitical fluctuations or even new climate-related regulations.

Volkswagen

Reputation   Climate

Volkswagen, still recovering from its "Dieselgate" scandal and in order to hedge against rising fossil fuel prices, is investing over €1 billion in renewable energy projects, with the aim of powering its factories mainly through on-site energy production. Gradually, in step with other car manufacturers, Volkswagen is redesigning most of its range to incorporate more sustainable engines, whether hybrid or electric.

Finally, there are market risks related to core products. Alternative cooling technologies, for example, could replace air-conditioning systems. Ski resorts can no longer count on snow or cold weather. Such effects could range from a slight decrease in market share to a complete loss of business.

Some level of climate change is unavoidable, and indeed we are already experiencing it. As such, our response must involve the two-pronged approach of both mitigation and adaptation. Mitigation means reducing emissions and stabilizing greenhouse gas levels, and adaptation means adjusting to climate change and reducing our vulnerability to its effects. Adaptation is manifested in large-scale infrastructural changes (protecting buildings from rising sea levels or improving road surface quality to withstand higher temperatures) as well as in behavioral changes (conserving water, proper management of climate risks, etc.).[3] Corporations can assess, communicate, and mitigate their CO_2 emissions as well as their climate-induced risks to meet international investors' demands. Consultants can assist companies in doing this in a cost-optimal manner by conducting detailed risk–cost–benefit assessments to inform investments and to optimize the return of these for each company.[4]

PG&E

Risk   Climate

For an example of the impact of climate change-related events on the insurance sector, look no further than the California wildfires of 2018. The state investigator CAL Fire ruled that PG&E's (Pacific Gas and Electric Company) equipment was at least partly responsible for damages caused by 11 out of the 16 fires. That added up to a potential liability of more than $17 billion, $11 billion of which

> was ultimately covered by insurance.[5] So strategies for that sector will need to look at minimizing future fire damage liabilities. That's quite a challenge, however, given the likelihood that climate change has permanently increased fire risk in the state's most vulnerable areas. And any buildings to emerge in the same locations will look like a serious reoccurrence risk.

Additional risks face a company's external stakeholders, one of which is market fluctuations. Because of climate-related exposure such as carbon pricing, supply chain disruption, or product obsolescence, capital costs increase. Ratings risk varies widely between and within industries, yet even companies with carbon-intensive activities can begin to manage it. Currently, more than 4,000 organizations report their exposure to the CDP (previously known as the Carbon Disclosure Project), which is undoubtedly a first positive step in addressing the issue.

In many industries, government plays a crucial role in setting the rules of the game. With climate change, many of these rules are changing, and with government action comes regulatory risks, which include greater bureaucracy, added costs, delays in specific business operations, subsidized competitors, or even the withdrawal of existing subsidies.

Reputation risk is also potentially huge. In the context of climate change, reputation risk is the probability of loss of profitability due to the either a company's operations or the positions that it takes which are seen by the public as harmful. Reputation risk can be direct, stemming from a company-specific action or policy, or it can be indirect, in the form of public perception of an overall industry. Reputation issues can manifest as consumer boycotts or local community protests which threaten a company's social license to operate. They can damage the regulatory environment and investor relationships, or render the company less attractive to future employees.

What can be done? Prepare.

> ### ˙elers Companies
>
> Risk   Climate
>
> The Travelers Companies, Inc., is one of the largest providers of personal and commercial property and casualty insurance products in the United States. Specific actions that it has taken to adapt to climate change include reassessing coastal underwriting practices, updating catastrophe modeling, offering "risk control" services, redesigning pricing, and encouraging disaster awareness and preparedness among homeowners and commercial customers.

Several rating agencies, such as Standard & Poor's[6] and Moody's,[7] are already looking at assessing the climate risks facing companies and countries, thereby better informing investor groups about their exposure to such risks. Indeed, as early as 2015, the global consulting firm Mercer developed a climate-change investment risk assessment process called TRIP (Technology, Resource availability, Impact and Policy). The "policy" aspect is "broadly defined as all international, national, and sub-national targets; mandates; legislation; and regulations meant to reduce the risk of further man-made or 'anthropogenic' climate change."[8]

The 2°C challenge

As mentioned in the Introduction, the Paris Agreement of December 2015, signed by 195 countries, aimed to limit the global temperature rise this century to no more than 2°C above pre-industrial levels. Under this agreement, each country determines and reports on its own contribution to mitigating global warming. We at Good Vision joined the hundreds of organizations around the world who accepted the "2°C Challenge"[9] declaration, urging governments to cooperate and take action at a national level to transition to green growth and reduce the processes and activities that cause climate change. It is an initiative of the Corporate Leaders Network for Climate Action (CLN), which advocates for strong policy measures on environmental issues and includes business leaders from a range of sectors around the world, including energy, finance, retail, and mining.

We Mean Business

Climate   Leadership

While climate change is the most pressing issues of our time, it also presents one of the century's greatest opportunity for businesses. We Mean Business is a global nonprofit coalition that works with the world's most influential companies to actively combat climate change, with 1,176 global companies agreeing that to ensure sustainable economic growth and a universally prosperous future, the world must transition to a zero-carbon economy. Through partnerships with nonprofits including BSR, the Carbon Disclosure Project, and the B Team, We Mean Business works from the level of leadership to drive policy change and advance the transition toward a carbon-neutral economy, asserting that "A collaborative partnership between business and government can ensure the transition is achieved at the speed and scale required, securing future profitability for business and delivering national and international decarbonization commitments." By encouraging governments to establish policies with bold targets and clear timelines that enable and support climate action from a corporate level, We Mean Business believes that the transition to net-zero carbon by 2050

> can be achieved. The nonprofit enables and encourages business to take tangible actions such as adopting science-based emissions reductions targets, committing to 100% renewable power, growing the world market for sustainable fuels, reducing short-lived climate pollutant emissions, and improving water security.[10]

Notes

1. "The global risks report 2019." *World Economic Forum*. https://www.weforum.org/reports/the-global-risks-report-2019.
2. "How companies can adapt to climate change." *McKinsey & Co.*, July 2015. https://www.mckinsey.com/business-functions/sustainability-and-resource-productivity/our-insights/how-companies-can-adapt-to-climate-change.
3. "Responding to climate change." *NASA*. https://climate.nasa.gov/solutions/adaptation-mitigation; "Long-term investors: Are you aware of your climate risk exposure?" *Mercer*, 2015. https://www.mercer.com/content/dam/mercer/attachments/global/investments/long-term-investors-are-you-aware-of-your-climate-change-risk-exposure-mercer-2015.pdf.
4. "How business can meet the challenge of climate change." *Science Nordic*, September 26, 2017. http://sciencenordic.com/how-business-can-meet-challenge-climate-change.
5. Alanne Orjoux, "PG&E settles with insurance companies for $11 billion in California wildfires, utility says." *CNN*, September 13, 2019. https://edition.cnn.com/2019/09/13/us/pge-california-wildfires-settlement/index.html.
6. Jessica Williams, "How environmental and climate risks and opportunities factor into global corporate ratings: An update." *S&P Global*, November 9, 2017. https://www.spglobal.com/en/research-insights/articles/environmental-and-climate-risks-factor-into-ratings.
7. "Moody's approach to climate risk." *Moody's Investors Service*, November 2018. https://www.mainstreamingclimate.org/wp-content/uploads/2016/10/Moodys-Presentation-Climate-Risk-Trends.pdf.
8. "A guide to climate change investment risk management for US public defined benefit plan trustees." *Mercer*. https://www.mercer.com/our-thinking/climate-change-investment-risk-management.html.
9. www.2degreecommunique.com.
10. https://www.wemeanbusinesscoalition.org/.

4 Sustainability and technology

The role of technology

It is banal to say that technology continues to change. What must be borne in mind is that the pace of technological change is *accelerating* – exponentially. As long ago as 2001, futurist Ray Kurzweil wrote that every decade our overall rate of progress was doubling, "We won't experience 100 years of progress in the 21st century – it will be more like 20,000 years of progress (at today's rate)."[1]

It is now becoming clear that new technology is one of the key factors in enabling truly transformative change. There are myriad opportunities to be found here for those with awareness and vision, but the challenges represented by an exponential growth in technology encompass dozens of issues going forward, from the future workplace to the planetary ecosystem. This book will investigate some of the interlinkages between technology and corporate responsibility both with regard to the opportunities but also the threats. And we will find examples of how technology can scale projects to new levels and bridge gaps.

Technology and COVID-19

As we have seen, the COVID-19 pandemic has put businesses to the test. Alongside an appropriate ethical response, an agile technological response has characterized those businesses that seem most likely to survive in the face of such uncertainty. A common misinterpretation of Darwin's maxim "survival of the fittest" is the assumption that "fittest" means "strongest," when it was intended to mean "most adapted to the situation" ("fit" in the sense of "fit for purpose").[2] Here are some examples of businesses that have exploited technology to adapt quickly and intelligently.

Virtual travel very quickly became an appealing offering to the grounded and confined. Vacation destinations around the world offer live cams and feeds, with virtual museum tours and live streams from zoos being especially popular.[3] The restaurant sector was one of the hardest-hit during the pandemic, and ingenious strategies were needed just to keep trading. San Francisco's Creator, famous for its robot-made hamburgers, devised a safe, contact-free way of delivering food, with a sealed entrance and a pressurized transfer chamber. Guests order through an intercom and pick up hermetically sealed meals through the conveyor window.[4] Virtual Dining Chicago is an online means of sharing the latest news on take-out options and ways to support local bars and restaurants during isolation.[5] In New York, you could choose a local restaurant, bar, or cafe as a virtual venue on the goodhang site, invite friends to a chat, and support local establishments with gift card purchases and GoFundMe donations. Said goodhang founder Janvi Jhaveri, "We built goodhang to help people connect (safely and virtually via Zoom) while supporting the small businesses they normally would be convening in."[6]

Zoom

As the dining and entertainment industries stared into the abyss, virtual meeting software Zoom suddenly became part of everybody's vocabulary – up from 10 million users in December 2019 to 200 million in April 2020. Virtual interaction had already been growing as a technology of choice among an increasing number of Millennials in the workplace (see the Introduction and Chapter 13), but it became mainstream overnight. The immediacy of Zoom's interface was its key competitive advantage – along with being free to use and accommodating up to 100 users. It also quickly became an interesting case study about the intersection of technology and corporate responsibility as its inherent weaknesses emerged, with controversy about its security and privacy. Princeton University computer science professor Arvind Narayanan even referred to it as a "privacy disaster" and "malware."[7] The issues included sending data to Facebook without notifying users and falsely describing itself as "end-to-end encrypted." And we now have the term "Zoombombing" to add to our vocabulary, a practice in which trolls gatecrash meetings. The debate underscored the inherent tension of balancing mainstream needs with robust security. Zoom's huge spike in use highlighted problems that were already familiar from platforms such as Twitter, YouTube, and Reddit, which are inherently designed to allow strangers to interact, and yet anti-abuse features were added only after Zoom launched and complaints arose.[8]

Tech4Good

There is a growing trend in which technology is seen as a means to do good – as a goal rather than as a by-product of profit-making. This process is under way now, in all areas of technology, yet it is still in its infancy.

In Israel, the "startup nation," there is a growing community of impact ventures, particularly within the technology sector. An impact program in that country is Tech4Good, which invests in technological startups focused on addressing social and environmental problems worldwide. These startups are, among other things, creating accessibility solutions for people with disabilities and developing technologies that enable those living below the poverty line to enjoy products and services that improve their quality of life.

ALYNovation

Technology   Health

Doctors at the ALYN Pediatric Rehabilitation Hospital in Jerusalem had been working for many years to develop innovative assistive solutions for children with disabilities. Eventually, they were persuaded to join local startups to cooperate in an initiative to convert their designs for international commercial use: the result was ALYNovation.[9]

As time passes and technology evolves, traditional boundaries dissolve, and creativity becomes attached to values. The business world will look very different in ten years' time.

BreezoMeter

Technology   Environment

The startup BreezoMeter was founded in 2014 by three entrepreneurs[10] who had all originally decided to move their families to the city in Israel with the cleanest air quality. However, this was far from straightforward as relevant air pollution information was hard to come by. This gave them the idea of establishing a company that could provide such insights.

Air quality is a real and serious problem. According to the World Health Organization, over 80% of the world's urban population live in areas in which air quality guidelines are not met; air pollution kills over 7 million people annually and affects over 90% of the world's population.[11]

BreezoMeter's mission is to improve the health and quality of life of millions of people by providing accurate air quality data. Its current platform is based on monitoring data from public agencies such as Israel's Ministry of Environmental Protection, along with meteorological data, satellite imagery, and even traffic reports. With this combined information, the company's algorithm can monitor air pollution levels in a given street. The company is currently developing a small sensor data collection platform, an additional data source that will offer an even higher resolution of air quality data in urban areas, down to just 30 meters.[12]

Furthermore, BreezoMeter's data on air pollution and allergens is available via API to businesses in the smart home, automotive, and smart city industries. The company recently partnered with one of its investors, Hella Ventures, to develop a new automotive product called AirShield addressing the health risks that drivers and passengers face as a consequence of air pollution.

Where are the tech giants?

There are countless small and agile technological startups like BreezoMeter (see the BreezoMeter Box) which were conceived in the spirit of corporate responsibility or else adapted to it. However, the internet and technology giants, despite their seemingly infinite resources, do not always seek a direction or strategy to implement corporate responsibility in proportion to their size and means. Clearly, considering their vast impact on modern society, if such companies wanted to do so, they could make the world a better place: in the social and communal spheres in which they operate, these companies possess powerful tools which they could use to create a more egalitarian, open, and inclusive society.

With great power comes great responsibility, as the saying goes, and we might expect them to act with caution and consideration toward the citizens of the world, a large majority of whom are essentially their customers. However, this is not what we are seeing. In fact, in recent years, we have allegedly borne witness to the improper use of such power, especially where data security and privacy are concerned[13] as it was partially argued at the congressional hearing on July 29th 2020.

In fact, the behavior of the tech giants allegedly diverges from the trajectory we are used to seeing in more "traditional" businesses, which, on attaining prominence and power, would generally direct some of their newfound resources toward matters of sustainability and responsibility. Maybe our latter-day tech giants have grown too rapidly to have reached the phase in which they adopt the responsible strategies of a mature corporation. Their founders, after all, still have no grandchildren.

During the COVID-19 crisis we saw how one-off charitable donations don't substitute for true corporate responsibility in this sector, with Mark Zuckerberg supposedly failing to burnish his damaged reputation with a donation of $25 million to fund research into potential treatments. British data journalist Mona Chalabi posted a TikTok video demonstrating that the donation amounts to only 0.03% of the Facebook CEO's estimated net worth. The video went viral on Twitter and sparked online discussion about wealth and charity.[14]

Sustainability as a driver of innovation

There is a direct link between sustainability and innovation, and smart companies realize this. In fact, in a few you'll find the chief sustainability officer is also the chief innovation officer, ENEL being an example.

With two-thirds of companies now incorporating sustainability as one of their core missions, it is critical for sustainability to be in alignment with their R&D. Annemarie Meisling, Head of Sustainability at Danish bioscience corporation Chr. Hansen – the world's most sustainable company in 2019, according to the Corporate Knights Global 100 Index[15] – explains that their innovation pipeline is measured against the UN Sustainable Development Goals (SDGs), ensuring that their sustainability department works closely with R&D.[16]

Marie-Claire Daveu, Chief Sustainability Officer at global luxury giant and pioneer of luxury sustainable fashion Kering, explains the link between a CSO and innovation: "a successful CSO has to be a visionary thinker, a creative problem-solver, an operational implementer and collaborative leader."[17] She further maintains that sustainability functions as a driver of innovation, creativity and value creation, and no longer simply as an ethical necessity. Daveu stresses the growing importance of the Kering group's Materials Innovation Lab, which provides its fashion houses with sustainable fabric and textile samples and promotes sustainability among suppliers.[18] Dalit Brand-Levine, from Sano Brunos Enterprises, with whom we work on integrating sustainability, has indicated that in order to achieve optimum synergy, sustainability considerations should be systematically integrated into the innovation process at a very early stage.

Disruptive innovation

As technology advances at a dizzying pace, a new form of innovation is emerging. A disruptive innovation is one that bursts forth rapidly, upending a traditional market and leading to the creation of a new one. A classic example is Netflix, which gained an early foothold in the streaming of movies and destroyed the DVD market. Such disruptions are happening at an increasing rate and are affecting both the "new" and "old" economies.

Tesla

Technology   Innovation

Tesla is an excellent example of a disruptive innovation. For years, despite considerable efforts, no major auto manufacturer was able to introduce and market a range of alternative-energy vehicles at affordable prices. But in Palo Alto, California, in 2003, two teams of engineers were competing to create an electric vehicle and founded a company together.

When they were joined by an electric motor manufacturer, Tesla was born.[19]

The most prominent among the company's young and energetic founders was Elon Musk, a young physicist who was only 31 at the time. Musk, now the company's CEO, sparked the public's imagination with an esoteric electric sports car called the Roadster. Unlike the Toyota Prius and other hybrid vehicles – the "greenest" cars on the market at the time – Tesla was specifically designed as an electric car with a battery which was built into the chassis and took up less space, thereby offering its vehicles a significant competitive advantage.

Tesla's technology offered both social and environmental benefits, very quickly emerging as a luxury brand and status symbol that is both green and sexy (as opposed to green and technical). Today, Tesla is focusing its technology on making electric cars more affordable – inspiring other car manufacturers to do the same.

Technology and responsibility

The ethics of technology – how to use it responsibly – is going to be one of the key issues of the coming years. Science fiction writers have had much to say about it, but now it is facing us in the real world. A line from the 1993 movie *Jurassic Park* has now become a popular meme: "your scientists were so preoccupied with whether or not they could that they didn't stop to think if they should."

One of the most controversial topics is the ongoing development of artificial intelligence (AI). On one hand AI and machine learning can be instrumental in promoting sustainability by supporting sustainable procurement, energy saving etc but on the other hand it will inevitably come to pervade many of our workplaces, so the question is: how can it be a tool for mutual advantage to both corporations and stakeholders? "Technological social responsibility" is a new corporate strategy, developed by Eric Hazan, which aims to provide infrastructure to guide the technological revolution for the benefit of all. TSR calls for "a conscious alignment between short- and medium-term business goals and longer-term societal ones."[20]

All new developments bring both positive and negative consequences. The misuse of AI to fatten the wallets of business leaders and shareholders at the expense of jobs, privacy, data security, and safety is a serious threat to society as we know it. The responsibility of ensuring that technology continues to be harnessed in service of increasing welfare, leisure, and health rather than being an engine of stress, inequality, and risk aversion ultimately falls upon the corporation. McKinsey research shows that companies such as Walmart, SAP, and Facebook are already accepting this responsibility by training their employees to operate in an automated work environment and preparing them for AI disruption. If technology is used in such a way that a gentle transition and management of declining labor is facilitated by raising skill levels and generating a more "fluid labor market," the potential remains to double the growth in welfare and raise GDP gains to unprecedented levels.

In order for this bountiful future to be made manifest, three fundamental corporate functions must be implemented, so Hazan's research indicates. First, key leaders must make their boards and shareholders realize the long-term societal and financial benefits for their businesses. Second, companies should proactively re-skill their workforces in order to manage a fluid integration of machines and human functionality, minimizing forced unemployment. Lastly, companies must fully adopt the concept of shared value by promoting educational opportunities to generate mutual benefits for corporations and stakeholders.

If societal considerations are not factored in with corporations' technological advancements, income growth will slow, inequality will increase, unemployment will be a major threat, and both health and leisure opportunities will decline. Such an impoverished society is less likely to support profitable businesses.

Notes

1 Ray Kurzweil, "The law of accelerating returns." March 7, 2001. https://www.kurzweilai.net/the-law-of-accelerating-returns.

2 Darwin actually borrowed the term from Herbert Spencer and used it in the fifth edition of his *On the Origin of Species* to mean "better designed for an immediate, local environment."
3 Jennifer Kester, "20 virtual travel experiences to try." *Forbes*, March 24, 2020. https://www.forbes.com/sites/forbestravelguide/2020/03/24/20-virtual-travel-experiences-to-try/#17f205296b82.
4 https://www.creator.rest/covid19.
5 https://www.virtualdiningchicago.com.
6 Eve Turow-Paul, "How restaurants are innovating during the COVID-19 pandemic." *Forbes*, March 23, 2020. https://www.forbes.com/sites/eveturowpaul/2020/03/22/how-restaurants-innovating-during-the-covid-19-pandemic/#14e42e772c2b.
7 Kari Paul, "'Zoom is malware': Why experts worry about the video conferencing platform." *The Guardian*, April 2, 2020. https://www.theguardian.com/technology/2020/apr/02/zoom-technology-security-coronavirus-video-conferencing.
8 Lily Hay Newman, "The Zoom privacy backlash is only getting started." *Wired*, April 1, 2020. https://www.wired.com/story/zoom-backlash-zero-days/.
9 Shoshanna Solomon, "ALYN sets up tech center to invent new ways to help special needs kids." *The Times of Israel*, May 16, 2017. https://www.timesofisrael.com/alyn-sets-up-tech-center-to-invent-new-ways-to-help-special-needs-kids.
10 Ran Korber, CEO; Ziv Lautman, Marketing Director; and Emil Fisher, CTO.
11 "Air pollution." *World Health Organization*. https://www.who.int/airpollution/en.
12 https://breezometer.com.
13 Zak Doffman, "1.5m users hit by new Facebook privacy breach as extent of data misuse exposed." *Forbes*, April 18, 2019. https://www.forbes.com/sites/zakdoffman/2019/04/18/facebook-illegally-harvested-data-from-1-5m-users-as-it-leveraged-its-data-machine/#26c624696a2e; Craig Timberg, Renae Merle, and Cat Zakrzewski, "Google for months kept secret a bug that imperiled the personal data of Google+ users." *The Washington Post*, October 8, 2018. https://www.washingtonpost.com/technology/2018/10/08/google-overhauls-privacy-rules-after-discovering-exposure-user-data.
14 Margot Harris, "A controversial TikTok visually illustrates Mark Zuckerberg's coronavirus donation in comparison to his total wealth." *Insider*, March 30, 2020. https://www.insider.com/mark-zuckerbergs-coronavirus-donation-as-percentage-of-wealth-tiktok-2020-3.
15 "Chr. Hansen remains in world elite of most sustainable companies." https://www.chr-hansen.com/en/media/2020/1/chr-hansen-remains-in-world-elite-of-most-sustainable-companies.

16 "Behind the 'most sustainable company in the world': Chr. Hansen." *FoodNavigator.com*. https://www.foodnavigator.com/Article/2019/02/15/Behind-the-most-sustainable-company-in-the-world-Chr.-Hansen.
17 "Could you cut it as a chief sustainability officer?" *Odgers Berndtson*, October 8, 2019. https://www.odgersberndtson.com/en-gb/insights/could-you-cut-it-as-a-chief-sustainability-officer.
18 "The rapid rise of the chief sustainability officer." *Odgers Berndtson*, October 8, 2019. https://www.odgersberndtson.com/en-pt/insights/the-rapid-rise-of-the-chief-sustainability-officer.
19 The company is named after Nikola Tesla, a legendary physicist and electrical engineer and a contemporary of Thomas Edison.
20 Jacques Bughin and Eric Hazan, "Can artificial intelligence help society as much as it helps business?" *McKinsey & Co.*, August 2019. https://www.mckinsey.com/business-functions/mckinsey-analytics/our-insights/can-artificial-intelligence-help-society-as-much-as-it-helps-business.

5 Sustainability in practice

Unsustainable use of resources and environmental degradation are the two biggest challenges when it comes to changing the relationship we have with our planet. Developed countries produce over 1,300 lbs of waste per capita annually – an astonishing amount which causes soil and groundwater pollution, odor nuisance, air pollution, and methane gas emissions. Waste generation is increasing by 5% annually, with landfills filling rapidly.

What is sustainability?

Dr. Lia Ettinger, my colleague from the Heschel Center for Sustainability, claims that "sustainability is a democratic and optimistic perspective that places human dignity and liberty at its center, based on a deep understanding that we are all a part of the fabric of life that nurtures and sustains all living creatures on earth. Sustainability is rediscovering the value of things we depend upon." This is indeed a "green" (or environmental or ecological) definition, but it is only one aspect of sustainability. As an organizing concept and as a social agenda, sustainability attempts to express the deep and inseparable link between environment, society, economics, and politics. Injustice, oppression, and inequality are all factors in the creation and aggravation of the environmental crisis, and in a negative feedback cycle, the crisis exacerbates these conditions.

The classic definition of sustainable development is "development that meets the needs of the present without compromising the ability of future generations to meet their own needs."[1] Sustainable development includes aspects of economic welfare, social equity, and a limit to environmental damage, avoiding depletion of the resources on which we depend. As a result, such development can be maintained, unchanged, over time.

A sustainable society means a democratic economy that provides adequate living conditions for all its citizens within an equal, robust, and involved society – a society that includes strong and diverse communities within a healthy, stable, and productive environment. A sustainable society is not only for the here and now, but also for generations to come.

The business world cannot stand idly by and claim that it is not involved, is not affected, or has no effect. On the contrary, the private sector is among those most affected and plays a decisive role in our ability to lead a sustainable society; the greater the contribution to the problem, the greater the responsibility for its mitigation.

The triple bottom line

Within the corporate world, the potential for change was kickstarted by the concept of the "triple bottom line" (TBL), coined by John Elkington over 25 years ago. In traditional business accounting, the "bottom line" refers to the overall financial profit or loss. But, in recent years, environmental and social organizations have pushed for a broader definition of the bottom line, to encompass full-cost accounting. For example, if a corporation declares a financial profit, yet thousands of deaths and illnesses have resulted from its asbestos mine, or its copper mine pollutes a river, then taxpayer money must be spent on health care expenses and river water treatment. In conventional accounting, these are "externalities" and do not feature in the corporate accounts. But success or failure clearly cannot be measured only in terms of financial profit and loss: it must also be measured in terms of the well-being and health of the billions of people on the planet and the environment on which we all depend. The TBL concept therefore adds two new "bottom lines," environmental and social, alongside the economic impact of the company's performance.

Today, Elkington proposes that the TBL framework must be strategically recalled and fine-tuned: the changes of the past 25 years mean new thinking is required. From the outset, the TBL goal was a system change – a transformation of capitalism. It was never intended to be just an accounting system; it was designed to create a "genetic code" for tomorrow's capitalism, with a focus on breakthrough change. The corporate responsibility efforts we are currently witnessing are, on the whole, not providing the systemic rewiring that Elkington envisaged. To create real change, a new wave of TBL innovation and a wider implementation is needed. The current TBL reporting frameworks will not suffice as long as they lack the necessary pace, scale, or far-reaching resolve. Elkington hopes that, 25 years from now, we will be able to look back to this "recall" as the moment we began truly working toward a groundbreaking triple bottom line with a new genetic code that will push our economies forward.[2]

Saab

Ethics

The code of ethics of Saab, the Swedish aerospace and defense aircraft manufacturer, is a fine example of TBL thinking. "We care for the environment. Wherever we act,

> we shall contribute to sustainable development. This means that we shall reduce environmental risks and minimize our footprints in the environment. Caring for the environment is a natural part of Saab's daily business. We expect . . . Saab employee[s to] actively seek information about environmental impacts of our operations and products and consider the possibilities to reduce environmental risks and our environmental footprints in any business or activity you come across."[3]

The plastic problem

One of the biggest problems we have caused for ourselves is the ubiquity of single-use plastics. Environmental impacts include use of nonrenewable natural resources, production and transportation processes that require energy and emit greenhouse gases into the air, interference with and destruction of biodiversity and ecosystems, and ocean waste. Today, 90% of coastal waste is plastic, and 32% of this statistic is single-use plastic such as packaging. This is without taking into consideration the health effects. Ingredients in plastic such as DDT, polychlorinated biphenyls (PCBs), bisphenol A (BPA), polybrominated diphenyl ethers (PBDEs), and a variety of phthalates are toxic and can cause diabetes, cancer, fertility issues, and abnormal hormonal activity. As plastic breaks down in our oceans, tiny plastic particles called "micro plastics" enter the food chain – and ultimately, us.

Global initiatives

Over 60 countries have recognized the environmental and humanitarian consequences of plastic consumption and have passed laws to restrict or prohibit the marketing and sale of disposable plastics. Alongside national legislation, many large companies are making efforts to tackle this problem acknowledging responsibility for their impacts. Development of biodegradable substitutes is being accelerated, and plastic lifecycles are being transformed to eliminate transport to landfill of untreated plastic waste. Companies such as Starbucks and McDonald's, who rely heavily on plastic, have invested in R&D to explore plastic alternatives. Unilever is working to uphold its 2017 commitment to make all plastic packaging recyclable, reusable, and compostable with 25% made from recycled plastic content. To achieve this, it has invested in new business models around refills and reusable packaging, cutting waste (see also the LOOP example in Chapter 6). Other major companies who are developing initiatives and taking responsibility include Nestlé, Ikea, Evian, Marriott, United Airlines, American Airlines, Whole Foods, Hyatt, and Disney. Other initiatives to increase plastic recycling are plastic exchanges such as ocean works which expand the supply of recycled plastic as raw materials for different industries.[4]

What does sustainability look like in practice?

All companies in all sectors have impacts and implications for sustainability. For the purposes of this chapter we will take a closer look at some examples. Three sectors with massive pre-COVID-19 environmental footprints are fashion, tourism, and meat. Here we will briefly look at some of the implications of acknowledging the challenges and beginning to address them.

Sustainable fashion

Billions of items of clothing – necessary and not so necessary – are produced, distributed, and thrown away each year. The fashion industry is growing, but its negative environmental and social impacts are outpacing its slow and gradual efforts to improve. So says *Pulse of the Fashion Industry*,[5] written in collaboration with the Boston Consulting Group and the Sustainable Apparel Coalition, which reports on sustainability in the fashion industry.

There is therefore plenty of opportunity for leadership on this issue. Since 2017, **Delta Galil**, a global textile company and one of our clients at Good Vision, has been working to reduce its environmental footprint, mainly through the internalization of technology. For example, it is pioneering the technological development of more sustainable textiles. Traditional recycled polyester made from plastic bottles creates high levels of GHGs with its energy-intensive yarn production process, so Delta has partnered with Antex to create a recycled PET polyester from off-grade polymers, resulting in fewer GHG emissions. It has also developed a nylon from recycled fishing nets, a biodegradable nylon, a biodegradable polyester, and fabrics from bamboo. Its "Eco Dye" is an additive that saves 30–40% of dye process time which means savings of 30% in energy and water.

But innovation in sustainability is not only for large companies. Among the hundreds of new technologies emerging is one developed by Marina Ross, my friend from INSEAD, in which functional and nano-coatings, created by her nano-tech company **Hydrop**, improve the eco-friendliness of textiles.

As we will see in Chapter 14, cotton has a big environmental impact. Seven hundred gallons of water go into producing a simple cotton T-shirt and 2,000 gallons for a pair of jeans. The **Better Cotton Initiative** (BCI), a global nonprofit organization and the largest cotton sustainability program in the world, has a mission to "make global cotton production better for the people who produce it, better for the environment it grows in and better for the sector's future."[6] In order to make "better cotton" a sustainable mainstream commodity, BCI works with various stakeholders and large-scale corporations like Gap Inc., Adidas, Nike, Fast Retailing, PVH, Ralph Lauren, Burberry Inditex, and H&M to "promote measurable and continuing improvements for the environment, farming communities and the economies of cotton-producing areas."

Levi's, Burberry, PVH, and Kering are among the industry leaders who signed the **Science Based Targets** initiative in July 2019 with the goal of reducing greenhouse gas emissions at the supplier end. Establishing sustainability best practice in supplier plants is one of the biggest issues facing the industry worldwide.[7]

An average consumer throws away 70 pounds of clothing per year, with the amount of textile waste totaling an astonishing 13 million tons annually. Of all this waste going to landfill – for various other reasons as well, including overproduction and brand identity protection – 95% of it could be reused or recycled.[8] Notably, in 2017, **Burberry** was condemned for destroying unsold clothes, accessories, and perfume worth £28.6 million to protect its image and maintain its exclusivity[9] (although it is not the only well-known label to do this). It soon announced an end to that practice – and the production of items made from real animal fur. As this shows, rising consumer awareness and demand for environmental and social ethics means companies will increasingly be held accountable for their actions. Burberry CEO Marco Gobbetti now offers a new definition of "modern luxury": it means "being socially and environmentally responsible."[10]

In recent years, renting and resale models have gained market traction, offering customers the post-purchase satisfaction but at a lower cost, both financially and environmentally. These models create greater circularity within the fashion supply chain and reduce fashion waste. According to Claire Bergkamp, director of innovation and sustainability at Stella McCartney, reselling and rental are disrupting the fast fashion model.[11] In a 2017 survey, consultancy Kantar Futures found that "Consumers are placing greater importance on the long-term benefits of a product, rather than cost-saving options that are seemingly more disposable."[12]

Sustainable tourism

Tourism and hospitality are the sectors most immediately and obviously affected by COVID-19, being intrinsically linked to nonessential travel. Tourism is about movement, and transport acts as a vector for the distribution of pathogens. Restrictions on nonessential travel meant that airlines grounded planes, drastically slashed flights, or suspended operations completely, with nearly eight in ten flights globally being canceled. The United Nations World Tourism Organization (UNWTO) declared that "tourism has been the worst affected of all major economic sectors."[13]

Tourism revenues fell by 95% in Italy and 77% in Spain in March 2020, according to the banking group UBS. To understand the impact on economies more broadly, the tourism industry pre-pandemic accounted for 10% of global GDP – and much more in some countries, such as Greece (20%) and Portugal (18%), according to the World Bank.[14] The WEF at the time, quoting the World Travel and Tourism Council, estimated the coronavirus epidemic was putting up to 50 million jobs in the global travel and tourism sector at risk, with travel likely to slump by a quarter over 2020 and Asia being the most affected continent.[15]

Air travel is a major contributor to greenhouse emissions. A 2018 study published in *Nature Climate Change* showed that emissions from tourism add up to 8% of the global total, with flying making up the largest share of this. So, "when the world stays home, the planet benefits."[16]

As such, our expectations around foreign leisure travel are a major challenge in reorienting human behavior to combat climate change post-COVID-19. According to an article in the *Journal of Sustainable Tourism*,

> The COVID-19 pandemic should lead to a critical reconsideration of the global volume growth model for tourism, for interrelated reasons of risks incurred in global travel as well as the sector's contribution to climate change . . . an opportunity to critically reconsider tourism's growth trajectory, and to question the logic of more arrivals implying greater benefits.

The article argued for "change on a broader level that will lead the global tourism system reoriented toward the SDGs, rather than 'growth' as an abstract notion benefitting the few."[17]

So the field is wide open for innovative solutions post-COVID-19. What role can technology play? Some airlines are making progress in research into making flight less impactful, such as biofuel and electric-powered aircraft. "There's still a lot of potential fuel economy that could be gained from redesigning aircraft to be more efficient," said Colin Murphy, deputy director of the Policy Institute for Energy, Environment, and the Economy at the University of California, Davis.[18]

At the 2nd World Conference on Smart Destinations, held by the UNWTO in 2018, Secretary-General Zurab Pololikashvili opened the conference with these words: "Technology helps us to manage our social, cultural, and environmental impacts better. Moreover, if well managed, tourism can act as an agent of positive change for more sustainable lifestyles, destinations, and consumption and production patterns." The conference discussed and introduced technological advances like big data and geo-localization to shape new tourism models based on innovation, technology, sustainability, and accessibility.[19]

One way to change our approach to travel as individuals, is through "slow travel" and "self-powered travel." For example, Authenticitys, a platform that connects visitors with local experiences, offers a "Urban Regeneration E-Bicycle Tour" in Madrid.[20] And, when we do fly, we can purchase carbon offsets.

In South Africa, an economy already in deep trouble at the time of writing, a rise in "value-driven tourism" is predicted. According to Wayne Troughton, managing director of HTI Consulting, a development consultant for the hospitality sector across Africa and the Middle East,

> It's becoming clear to us that value-driven products, especially in the accommodation sector, like aparthotels or traditional hotels offering far more amenities over and above their core offering for the price of a room, will be better positioned to meet these travelers' needs.[21]

Another inspiring example of the integration of sustainability is Amsterdam's Conscious Hotels, pioneers in eco-friendly tourism.

The tourism industry was already a target of criticism before the pandemic, with poor environmental awareness meaning inefficient use of resources, environmental damage, and disruption to the lives of residents and local communities. The UN, the OECD, and the UNWTO have set sustainable tourism as a key objective for the upcoming years, with the UNWTO launching an online platform to provide resources for meeting the SDGs in tourism. The Tourism4SDGs.org website has a wealth of information including updates on sustainable development efforts around the world in such areas as accessible tourism, biodiversity and wildlife, climate change, ecotourism, waste management, and water management.

The question remains whether we can take the opportunity to make decisive changes about the direction of our economies. Some argue that airlines should be allowed to fail and governments "should prop up only those sectors that will help secure the survival of humanity and the rest of the living world."[22] Yet the forces of business-as-usual are powerful. At the time of writing, for example, $25 billion had already handed out by the U.S. government to support failing airlines.[23]

Sustainable food

The food industries – agriculture and meat – that sustain our growing global population comprise about 10% of global GDP, according to the World Bank, or about US$8 trillion globally,[24] and are responsible for 26% of global emissions, use half of all habitable land, and consume 70% of global freshwater resources, according to Our World Data. When these numbers are broken down, meat production has the greatest impact: 31% of food industry greenhouse gas emissions are from livestock and fish farming. Raising livestock requires twice as much land as is needed to grow crops for direct human consumption. Large slaughterhouses also contribute to the devastating effects of deforestation and habitat destruction. The UN Food and Agriculture Organization (FAO) estimates that 45% of deforestation in Argentina between 1990 and 2005 was due to livestock farming. Many now argue that a plant-based diet is the only way to ensure adequate food for all members of a growing global population.[25] The industry itself is slow to react, with just 5% of the world's largest meat companies having undertaken analysis of climate change impacts on their business.[26]

Technology is playing an increasing role here. Both as a response to these issues and to growing demand for vegan food, entrepreneurs and innovators are creating plant-based and lower-impact alternatives. Beyond Meat, a California-based startup, has taken the market by storm with its plant-based products, now available in 58,000 grocery stores, restaurants, hotels, and universities. Even fast-food moguls like KFC, Burger King, and TGI Fridays have bought into meat alternatives. Beyond Meat's products not only resemble real meat, but require 99% less water, 93% less land, and 46% less energy, making their greenhouse emissions 90% lower than those of livestock production.[27]

Lab-grown meat offers a similarly reduced impact, using 99% less land and emitting 80% fewer greenhouse gas emissions than traditional meat. Israeli startup Future Meat Technologies is currently leading in this innovation with its cost-efficient and sustainable business model. It is expanding rapidly, having raised $16.5 million in funding, $14 million of it from S2G Ventures, which also helped finance Beyond Meat's IPO.[28] They see lab-grown meat as the future and are quickly working to bring their production to scale, planning to release their hybrid products at a competitive cost level from their pilot production facility by 2021 and then a second line of 100% cultured meat products at a cost of less than $10 per pound by 2022. With such competitive pricing, the market for meat substitutes is expected to reach $2.5 billion by 2023.[29]

Food waste is far more of a prevalent issue than we realize. It occurs at every phase in the agriculture supply chain: from the field to distribution centers, supermarkets, restaurants, food processing plants, and homes. While 40 million Americans struggle with hunger, 1.3 billion tons of food – equivalent to about US$680 billion – is wasted every year, according to the UN Food and Agriculture Organization. Food and agriculture giants like Chobani, Chipotle, and Maersk Ventures have now all established food waste as a priority on their agendas. Private investors are concurrently noticing this massive inefficiency in the industry, channeling US$125 million into startups that are addressing this very issue.[30]

One of the recipients of this finance is Wasteless – an Israeli startup with offices in New York, Tel Aviv, London, and Amsterdam, and operations in the U.S. and the UK – which received $2 million in private investment in 2018. Wasteless aids supermarkets in their battle against food waste using dynamic pricing. Its AI price engineering algorithm creates "smart prices" for grocery stores by continuously analyzing customer shopping patterns and product shelf life in order to learn from product pricing policies and optimize the present value of a product's revenue from its expiration date. Supermarkets are thus able to increase revenue, increase margins, improve freshness, and reduce food waste.

Notes

1 World Commission on Environment and Development (WCED), *Our Common Future* (the Brundtland Report). New York: Oxford University Press, 1987.
2 John Elkington, "25 years ago I coined the phrase 'triple bottom line.' Here's why it's time to rethink it." *Harvard Business Review*, June 25, 2018. https://hbr.org/2018/06/25-years-ago-i-coined-the-phrase-triple-bottom-line-heres-why-im-giving-up-on-it.
3 *Saab Code of Conduct*. https://www.yumpu.com/en/document/view/28482430/code-of-conduct-saab.
4 www.oceanworks.com.
5 https://globalfashionagenda.com/pulse-2019-update/#.
6 *Better Cotton Initiative*, "About BCI." https://bettercotton.org/about-bci.
7 Rachel Cernansky, "How fashion is helping suppliers fight climate change." *Vogue Business*, July 23, 2019. https://www.voguebusiness.com/technology/fashion-brands-climate-change-science-based-targets.
8 Csilla Herbszt, "How much waste does the fashion industry produce?" *The Pretty Planeteer*, June 24, 2019. http://theprettyplaneteer.com/fashion-industry-waste.
9 "Burberry burns bags, clothes and perfume worth millions." *BBC News*, July 19, 2018. https://www.bbc.co.uk/news/business-44885983.
10 Elizabeth Paton, "Burberry to stop burning clothes and other goods it can't sell." *New York Times*, September 26, 2018. https://www.nytimes.com/2018/09/06/business/burberry-burning-unsold-stock.html.
11 "Can the 'broken' fashion industry become more sustainable?" *BBC News*, November 27, 2018. https://www.bbc.co.uk/news/business-46347337.

12 Rebecca Marston, "Stella McCartney and Ellen MacArthur call for fashion sustainability." *BBC News*, November 28, 2017. https://www.bbc.co.uk/news/business-42150572.
13 https://www.unwto.org/tourism-covid-19.
14 Jon Henley et al., "Covid-19 throws Europe's tourism industry into chaos." *The Guardian*, May 2, 2020. https://www.theguardian.com/world/2020/may/02/covid-19-throws-europes-tourism-industry-into-chaos.
15 Joan Faus, "This is how coronavirus could affect the travel and tourism industry." *World Economic Forum*, March 17, 2020. https://www.weforum.org/agenda/2020/03/world-travel-coronavirus-covid19-jobs-pandemic-tourism-aviation.
16 Chloe Berge, "How can we be sustainable post-Covid 19?" *BBC*, April 16, 2020. http://www.bbc.com/travel/story/20200415-how-can-we-be-sustainable-post-covid-19.
17 Stefan Gössling, Daniel Scott, and C. Michael Hall, "Pandemics, tourism and global change: A rapid assessment of COVID-19." *Journal of Sustainable Tourism*, April 2020. https://www.tandfonline.com/doi/full/10.1080/09669582.2020.1758708.
18 Berge, *op. cit.*
19 "Technology guiding the way to sustainable tourism?" *Authenticitys*, November 24, 2018. http://www.authenticitys.com/blog/technology-guiding-the-way-to-sustainable-tourism.
20 https://www.authenticitys.com/en/e/urban-regeneration-e-bicycle-tour/.
21 Vicky Karantzavelou, "Covid-19 impact could be huge opportunity for value-driven tourism products like aparthotels." *Travel Daily News*, May 5, 2020. https://www.traveldailynews.com/post/covid-19-impact-could-be-huge-opportunity-for-value-driven-tourism-products-like-aparthotels.
22 George Monbiot, "Airlines and oil giants are on the brink. No government should offer them a lifeline." *The Guardian*, April 29, 2020. https://www.theguardian.com/commentisfree/2020/apr/29/airlines-oil-giants-government-economy.
23 Oliver Milman, "Pandemic side-effects offer glimpse of alternative future on Earth Day 2020." *The Guardian*, April 22, 2020. https://www.theguardian.com/environment/2020/apr/22/environment-pandemic-side-effects-earth-day-coronavirus.
24 Ingrid Fung, "The present and future of food tech investment opportunity." *TechCrunch*, October 22, 2019. https://techcrunch.com/2019/10/22/the-foodtech-investment-opportunity-present-and-future/.
25 Sarah Gibbens, "Eating meat has 'dire' consequences for the planet, says report." *National Geographic*, January 16, 2019. https://www.nationalgeographic.com/environment/2019/01/commission-report-great-food-transformation-plant-diet-climate-change/.

26 Catherine Early, "Meat sector has 'head in sand' over climate disruption, investors warn." *BusinessGreen*, March 12, 2020. https://www.businessgreen.com/news/4012233/meat-sector-head-sand-climate-disruption-investors-warn.
27 Daniella Genovese, "What is beyond meat?" *Fox Business*, February 20, 2020. https://www.foxbusiness.com/lifestyle/what-is-beyond-meat.
28 "Funding will be used to build the world's first cultured meat pilot production facility." *Globes*, October 10, 2019. https://en.globes.co.il/en/article-israeli-co-future-meat-raises-14m-1001303399.
29 Amelia Lucas, "Beyond Meat's vegan burger is heading to HelloFresh meal kits." *CNBC*, August 19, 2019. https://www.cnbc.com/2019/08/19/beyond-meats-vegan-burger-is-heading-to-hellofresh-meal-kits.html.
30 Dana Gunders, "More than $125 million poured into food waste startups in 2018." *Forbes*, November 14, 2018. https://www.forbes.com/sites/danagunders/2018/11/14/more-than-125-million-poured-into-food-waste-startups-in-2018/#4f396def6d03.

6 The new economy systems

When discussing the global economy, we find ourselves reaching for terms such as "capitalism," "socialism," "liberalism," "industrialized and developing countries," "customs barriers," or "globalization." All these concepts occupy key positions on the global interests map: they are the principal forces acting on our lives at this current point in history, and they essentially dictate economic discourse – for the time being. However, it is my assertion that they are only secondary to the real economic struggle facing humanity in the coming century.

What is that struggle? Put simply, it is the struggle to create a dignified existence for over ten billion people, in an overpopulated world, relying on limited and dwindling natural resources and struggling with global epidemics. This enormous challenge will shape the lives of our children and grandchildren. Will our descendants be born into an apocalyptic or a post-apocalyptic world? Or into a green and sustainable world?

Economic discourse needs to find ways to look beyond these concepts that we inherited from the twentieth century and focus on new economic approaches that promote the importance of sustainability. I remain optimistic about our ability to do this, and already we are seeing some highly encouraging trends. New economic models are emerging that can serve as a basis for a new philosophy of business operations. Although not all will be applicable to every organization, the intriguing ideas and proposals they offer can nonetheless operate as a source of inspiration.

The sharing economy

A "sharing economy" is a means by which resources and surpluses can be used efficiently. It is being made increasingly feasible through technological innovation.

A well-known example is Airbnb, a global company operating an online platform that allows people to rent out their properties when not in use. What was once a vacant home when its owners were away on vacation now becomes an income-generating asset. Another recognizable example is Uber, a ride-hailing service that allows drivers to use their own vehicles to pick up passengers. Instead of leaving the car parked in the garage, the owner can use it as a source of income and as a competitive factor in the transportation market. Lesser-known examples are the private car rental venture Turo or the house-swap platform Home Exchange. A growing number of companies are challenging the traditional models of resource distribution and creating new and collaborative models through platforms that purportedly allow end-users to independently manage the market.

One of the key factors in establishing a sharing economy is trust among participants. In an era in which trust in the business sector has progressively fallen, paradoxically, the model of a sharing economy is dependent on establishing a climate of trust among users – otherwise you would never enter an unknown Uber vehicle or open your home to strangers on Airbnb. In his book *The Sharing Economy*,[1] Professor Arun Sundararajan suggests that, as the sharing economy develops, as a manner of crowd-based capitalism, it may be able to diminish its reliance on interpersonal trust by adopting blockchain technology, the crowd-based process behind Bitcoin which uses cryptography to verify transactions.

The importance of an expansion of digital capabilities in ushering in cultural and behavioral change cannot be overemphasized. Such an expansion is what will enable the creation of massive networks that are accessible, transparent, and able to provide an immediate response. It is also what will underpin the existence of collaborative economic ventures based on the "wisdom of the crowd," both as participants and as reviewers.

Criticism of this phenomenon can be heard on both social and environmental grounds. From a social point of view, as it was in the congressional hearing in July 2020, the way in which technology giants such as Google and Facebook gather and allegedly use personal data is neither transparent nor democratic; and, due to the tremendous power these companies wield, they are open to charges of manipulation of opinion, as was claimed regarding the 2016 Trump election campaign. Also, companies such as Uber, it is claimed, are eroding labor rights: the employee contracts within such models offer no employment security, no limits on working hours, no pensions or other benefits, and no mechanisms for negotiations. Another weakness of the model is that it can be hijacked by those other than the private individuals for whom the platform was intended. Agencies and owners of multiple properties are exploiting Airbnb's features, turning some city streets into "de facto hotels."[2] In New York, it is estimated that at least one-third of Airbnb apartments are owned by commercial operators,[3] circumventing maintenance and employee regulation and paying less tax than in traditional hospitality models.[4]

From an environmental point of view, it is argued that any beneficial environmental impact – for example, with the Uber model – is marginal: fewer people may own vehicles, but the total distance they travel increases as a function of the ease with which they can rent or hail a vehicle.[5] As an alternative to private ownership of cars, it is hard to predict whether a car-sharing service will lead to an increase or decrease in amount of car travel, so the environmental impact could be positive or negative, depending on distances traveled. A company primarily marketing to and attracting non-car-owners is unlikely to be net-green, whereas one that incentivizes people to sell their cars and actually travel less is more likely to be net-green. This is a key point that will not be lost on new generations of climate and environmental activists: any corporate environmental communications strategy selling "green" products will at some point find itself judged against the ineluctable fact that all products have environmental impacts – and the greenest option will always be *no product at all*. This is a profoundly anti-consumerist message to take on board and therefore is unpalatable for many businesses. Perhaps the smartest companies, and the ones most likely to still be around in 20 years' time, are those with net-zero or net-positive targets built into their philosophy.

From pipeline to platform

Economists are now referring to a "Fourth Industrial Revolution." This revolution will fundamentally change the way we live, work, and relate to each other. Fundamentally different from previous industrial revolutions, it involves new technologies, across disciplines and sectors, that fuse the physical, digital, and biological worlds. They will even challenge our concept of what it means to be human.[6]

One important feature of this new paradigm is the development of the platform business model: seven of the ten most valuable companies globally are now based on a platform business model. McKinsey & Co. estimate that, by 2025, 30% of global economic activity equating to $60 trillion could be mediated by digital platforms[7] – and yet it has been estimated that only 3% of established companies have adopted an effective platform strategy.[8] An online platform provides the infrastructure and rules for a marketplace, which brings together producers and consumers. Each player in this modern ecosystem plays one of four main roles: producer, consumer, provider, and owner. Platform businesses bring together producers and consumers in high-value exchanges. Their chief assets are information and interactions, which together are also the source of the value they create and their competitive advantage. In this two-sided market, as the number of participants on each side grows, this value increases: a phenomenon known as a "network effect." Companies that do not learn how to create these platforms or learn the new rules of strategy will be unable to compete for much longer.

Examples of platform businesses are Uber, Alibaba, and Airbnb, the spectacular growth of which abruptly upended each of their industries. Apple understands these new rules of engagement very well: the iPhone and its operating system has been conceived as more than just a product or even a conduit for services. Apple sees its iPhones as a means of connecting participants in two-sided markets – app developers on one side and app users on the other – generating value for both groups.

> **Siemens**
>
> Technology Platforms
>
> You don't have to be a new company to participate in the platform revolution. Siemens, which was founded in 1847, in 2017 launched an open, cloud-based "internet of things" (IoT) B2B operating system which it markets as a "scalable cloud Platform as a Service (PaaS)" to industrial companies. It collects and analyzes data from production processes and from service delivery, thereby enabling companies to optimize their processes and develop new data-driven business models – such as automated production and vehicle fleet management. In this way Siemens helps its corporate clients embrace new data capabilities, including the development of customer-specific business models and integration of different IT systems.[9]

The impact economy

We will encounter impact investing in the next chapter. According to McKinsey,[10] an impact economy is distinguished from a traditional capitalist economy that prioritizes only financial returns. Sir Ronald Cohen, one of the impact pioneers and the author of *Impact*, defines it as the potential of an action to improve lives and the planet – impact economy, consumers and shareholders challenge entrepreneurs and executives to show that they generate their profits in a manner that contributes to the public good. This approach to doing business is already being enacted by some organizations on several levels – in their strategic choices, in managing their supply chains, in allocating funds to investments – and by some municipal authorities. But we have yet to see it embraced comprehensively by entire industries or national economies.

To create an impact economy, a larger scale of public figures, institutions, and governments must be involved to establish practices, policies, and standards that value the pursuit of social and environmental impact as highly as the pursuit of profit. Investors, asset managers, philanthropists, and entrepreneurs must work together to efficiently allocate funds, refine business models, and create supply chain transparency while consumers use their dollars to support businesses who create and measure positive impact. Through the joint effort of these stakeholders, the impact economy can reach maturity, increase in scale, and improve productivity. According to McKinsey, these are the three major developments that would contribute to the full development of the impact economy:

1 Instituting public policies that provide incentives and disincentives and create certainty.
2 Achieving a broad commitment to mutually reinforcing operational, measurement, and reporting norms for fund managers, social entrepreneurs, and impact-economy intermediaries.
3 Creating an industry body that promotes policies and standards of excellence and moves all participants to adopt them.[11]

In more practical words, Sir Ronald Cohen argues in his book on impact (2019) that we must shift to measuring outcomes, not activities. Instead of measuring an organization's time and dollars spent, and countries and people reached, let's measure the actual improvement made to lives and the environment.

The impact economy is poised to disrupt some of the main paradigms of conservative companies as well as being a catalyst for the introduction of a new model of purpose-led company – the so-called social enterprise (see later in this chapter), committed to delivering social value through market-based practices.[12]

> **IMPACT at INSEAD**
>
> Technology   New paradigms
>
> What do the CEO of software giant SAP, a social entrepreneur from Lebanon, the CEO of a Moscow technology company, and an Israeli CEO have in common? They all appeared at IMPACT week, a social-business entrepreneurship initiative held in Fontainebleau, France, home of the world-renowned business school INSEAD. Indeed, today, many business schools, including Harvard Business School and Oxford Saïd Business School, are integrating sustainability and social issues into their core programs.
>
> As a long-time participant in the corporate responsibility field, I was also invited, alongside social-business entrepreneurs from around the world.
>
> The ISEP INSEAD Social Entrepreneurship program is aimed at better understanding the interfaces between business and society, commonly referred to as the "impact industry." The program participants have led a number of projects, mostly based on technology and innovation. Notable ones include: a British shoe company that developed a shoe that stabilizes Parkinson's disease tremors; a company that integrates nanotechnology into textiles to reduce the need for ironing or frequent cleaning (thus saving energy); and a Portuguese venture called Viarco,[13] which enables color-blind individuals (a significant 5% of the world population) to distinguish between colors.

The circular economy

At Shimon Peres's funeral in Jerusalem, I was privileged to chat with HRH the Prince of Wales, who is the patron of the Cambridge Sustainability Network, of which I am a proud member. It came as a surprise that the first thing that he asked me about was the status of the circular economy in Israel. It is an area in which he believes he has a lot to offer.

The World Business Council for Sustainable Development (WBCSD) defines the circular economy as follows: "the goal of circular economy is to retain as much value as possible from resources, products, parts and materials to create a system that allows for long life, optimal reuse, refurbishment, remanufacturing and recycling."

A circular economy is nothing less than a redefinition of the entire production process. Whereas a traditional model sees companies make products and sell them to customers, who ultimately throw them away, a circular economy turns this process into a loop. By-products and waste are no longer seen as waste, but as a resource. Any actual waste is reduced to an absolute minimum, with both biological (compostable) and technical (non-compostable) materials reused to their maximum potential.

In 2015, the European Union rolled out an action plan to accelerate Europe's transition toward a circular economy, in which every EU Member State was required to adopt and implement the concept. The first stage of this plan is aimed at substantially reducing the amount of material going to landfill, instead turning waste into resources by separating, recycling, and reusing. The second stage concerns the redesign of products and materials for circular use, so that they can be more easily reused or turned into an energy source. An important part of this is substitution of plastics.

Nespresso

New paradigms   Circular economy

Circular economy principles can be implemented in many ways. In January 2018, Nespresso Israel began a collaboration with a winery to provide them with the waste coffee from used capsules. The coffee is composted and used to fertilize the vineyard.[14] Beyond the purely economic value, both companies recognize the shared value created for the consumer and the environment. Coffee is well known to be an excellent fertilizer additive, so this serves as a great example of viewing what was once waste as a resource for another industry.

A circular economy can be, and often must be, achieved incrementally – and the steps taken will often look simply like good business or good logistics. Nespresso in the Middle East also launched an at-home pod collection for recycling, in which trucks delivering the new pods pick up the used ones on the return journey rather than coming back empty; and they do a pickup only if it is associated with a drop-off. This cuts back on empty truck journeys and unnecessary emissions, helping to progress a little further toward closing the loop.[15]

In this new paradigm of "one man's trash is another man's treasure," all waste is re-evaluated, with its recoverable materials identified, and put to good use either by the company itself or by a third-party manufacturing process. The benefits of this approach also include newfound collaboration between different companies and industries, and previously unclaimed revenue.

In January 2019 the World Economic Forum published its second *Circularity Gap Report*.[16] It noted that the world economy is currently only 9% circular – exactly the same figure as the previous year, with only minimal resources flowing back into the economy after use; as the WEF says, "our global engine is stuck in reverse."[17] There is clearly much opportunity for growth; and innovation and creativity are key elements in bringing the circular economy to your own business. The opportunities to close this circularity gap are endless – and it is an opportunity to be part of a future that is free of waste as we know it.

We are just beginning to confront the reality that the old linear economy of making, selling, and discarding is not even strategic, never mind sustainable. The surface has barely been scratched in terms of ways the circular economy can be implemented, so there is a highly competitive advantage in bringing these concepts to your company early on. We are looking at a future in which all parts of the production process are efficient, and this includes reimagining what the end-of-life of a product looks like.

> **Switch (Sustainable Waste into Textiles Creates Harmony)**
>
> New paradigms   Circular economy
>
> Global textile company Delta Galil collaborated with Lenzing AG and Lenze to create a benchmark garment with a transparent and eco-lifecycle from birth to rebirth. The "Switch" T shirt uses Lenzing's Tencel™ and Refibra™ technology, taking waste from the factory floor to create new fabrics and thereby creating a circular economy for fabric.[18]

This new way of thinking and making is strategic for several reasons. For one, there is a shift in attitude among customers across the board with regard to their own consumption habits. There is a general increase of awareness about issues related to landfill and contamination: consumers know about the rising quantities of plastic accumulating in the oceans and ever-growing mountains of waste on land. The so-called Millennials are now a hugely significant demographic: by 2025, they will represent 75% of the global workforce.[19] As their spending power has increased, new trends in consumer behavior are being seen, with 73% prepared to pay more for sustainable goods.[20] According to the *Environment*

Journal, "Millennials will be heavily involved in the way the world achieves its circular economy aspirations."[21]

In terms of resource management, implementing a circular economy principle into your company represents forward-thinking. No matter your industry, the materials we take for granted today may not always be so easily available. Various models show how long natural resources can be sustained at the current rate of use, but they all point to one inescapable fact: many natural resources are finite. It makes sense at every level to integrate a robust policy of reuse and recycling into our processes now.

LOOP™

New paradigms   Circular economy

Unilever, in a major coalition with other large companies – other manufacturers, a retailer, a courier, a resource management company and a recycling company – is aiming to develop supply chains that are more circular from design through to consumer use. Its circular platform, LOOP™, is described as "a whole new way to shop, where you buy products in packaging that can be returned and refilled," likening it to 1950s milk delivery. Often cited as a prime example of a sustainable practice that used to be commonplace but has been abandoned, in some countries milk used to be delivered to your door in glass bottles. Empties were left on the doorstep, collected and exchanged for full ones, washed, and refilled. LOOP aims to facilitate a shift away from single-use disposable packaging (discarded or put in the recycling after use) to durable packaging (reused). Its model, like so many innovative consumer-focused initiatives, is online. Consumers buy either directly from the LOOP website or from a partner retailer and receive their product in a reusable tote (eliminating single-use shipping materials like cardboard boxes). Once they have finished the product, LOOP picks up the tote from their home, replenishes as needed, and delivers the refilled shipping tote to the consumer. The products themselves are in refillable packaging, with initial trials including the brands AXE, Dove, Hellmann's, Love Beauty and Planet, Love Home and Planet, REN Clean Skincare, Rexona, Seventh Generation, and Signal. As the company states on its website, "We can't create a circular economy for consumer goods in isolation. . . . To deliver the necessary change, at scale, we must work with others on a complete transformation of how we think, use and dispose of packaging. "These efforts demonstrate the ability of a circular economy to become commercially viable. The next step is to educate consumers and shift behavior.[22]

Cradle to Cradle

Circular systems of production first gained attention through a concept known as "Cradle to Cradle." Architect Walter Stahl coined the phrase based on the argument that modern industry follows a linear course, which can be described as "Cradle to Grave": items are produced using limited resources and in polluting processes; they start their lives with a defined purpose and, once they have served that purpose, they become waste and are discarded. But the idea of "waste" does not exist in nature: one organism's waste products are valuable nutrients for another. With ecosystems fine-tuned by natural selection, nature's recycling systems are flawless.

The Cradle to Cradle (C2C) model, which became widely known when German chemist Michael Braungart and U.S. architect William McDonough published their manifesto on the subject,[23] promotes the idea of repurposing products as a basis for creating new ones, whether biological or technical. The reuse of a product or its raw materials allows for a circular production cycle, but this should also be accompanied by an extension of the product's life through repair or maintenance.

To enable this to happen, we must first produce a product that is truly sustainable (i.e. fully reusable or recyclable). Sadly, there are still few such products in production today. Many of those products that are presented as being recyclable will in fact at end-of-life undergo a process of *downcycling* (creating a lower-value product). In a Cradle to Cradle model, products are designed in such a way that they can undergo *upcycling*, meaning their raw materials maintain their quality and can serve as a basis for creating high-quality products.

A product that wishes to carry the C2C certification[24] needs to fulfill five criteria: material health and safety; fitness for use in a circular economy; use of renewable energy in the production process; water stewardship (sustainable use and treatment of water in the production process); and social fairness, meaning responsibility toward employees, the environment, the community, and other stakeholders.

The concept was also explored by the international organization The Natural Step (TNS),[25] established in Sweden in the late 1980s by Dr. Karl-Henrik Robèrt, a pediatric oncologist whose research raised the question of whether we should treat the cancer cells themselves or the factors that contribute to the disease. Approaching problems from this more holistic standpoint led Robèrt to develop a framework that detailed the conditions required to sustain Earth and its resources for the benefit of humanity and the environment.

According to the TNS framework, a sustainable organization must meet four system conditions. First, it must not use Earth's expendable resources at a rate that exceeds their rate of regeneration. Second, it must not afflict the environment with a concentration of toxic substances at a rate that exceeds their rate of dispersion. Third, it must not contribute to the physical degradation of nature or of natural processes through deforestation or building on areas that serve as natural habitats. Finally, it must not contribute to the creation of conditions that undermine people's basic needs, such as a secure environment and sufficient wages to sustain them.

This framework has been endorsed by *Science* magazine as a scientifically sound approach for defining a sustainable organization (as opposed to other definitions, such as the one set out by the Brundtland Commission, which set a philosophical foundation rather than a practical one).[26] According to the TNS framework, given a company's current economic needs, short-, medium-, and long-term strategies should be devised with the aim of gradually becoming a sustainable organization.

Industrial symbiosis

Under the "circular economy" umbrella, we also meet the concept of "industrial symbiosis." Here again, the analogy of natural systems is the inspiration, and the focus is the design of sustainable industrial parks or the optimization of systems in which different companies interact. Industrial parks are created as eco-industrial clusters, in which manufacturing companies – critically, those that can feed off each other to form a material and energy loop – are located. Instead of these companies operating independently, they collaborate in a "symbiotic" relationship following the example of a natural ecosystem where everything is reused. Here, too, one industry's waste products (material, water, energy) is used as a resource for another in the same zone.

This is a brilliant idea, and feasible in practice. Such collaborations are already helping to significantly reduce waste, with over 50% in savings being achieved in some industries. Ultimately, the greatest winner is the environment, benefiting from significant reductions in the resources consumed by industries as a whole.

Kalundborg

New paradigms   Industrial symbiosis

Kalundborg, Denmark, is a leading example of industrial symbiosis, bringing environmental planners and researchers on pilgrimages from all over the world. Take a deep breath, because the symbiosis in Kalundborg encompasses almost every aspect of the lives of its 15,000 residents.

It begins with the local power station. The excess heat from the station is used to warm local fish farms and most of the area's homes and businesses. The excess steam from the plant is piped to the nearby oil refinery and to a production plant operated by the multinational biotech company Novo Nordisk. Air filters on the power plant's smokestack turn sulfur dioxide into gypsum, which is then sold to a neighboring plasterboard factory, which dries it in kilns fired by the excess flare gas piped over from the refinery.

The power station, in turn, uses the refinery's wastewater for cooling purposes. The biotechnology company transfers the residues of fermentation processes to the local farmers to use as fertilizers. Sludge from the county's wastewater treatment plant is sold to a local soil clean-up company, which uses it to grow pollution-eating bacteria that clean contaminated soil. Even the fly ash from the power station is sold to local cement companies.

There is no doubt that this serves as an inspiring model for the future, in which we entirely rethink our attitudes to natural resource use.

Social enterprises

A social enterprise is a business that uses commercial methods to accomplish social goals. The business model and the relationship between business objectives and social goals vary from organization to organization, but one of the prominent differences between a traditional business model and a social one is attitude to profit. Social enterprises are not an alternative for government funding or traditional nonprofit organizations; rather, they offer an additional framework for expanding the possibilities of social action. Over the years I have been privileged to judge numerous social entrepreneurship competitions, and it has become clear that there are endless new models for such enterprises, on a par with those for for-profit technological ecosystems.

There are several social enterprise models. The first gives absolute priority to the social cause, making it the core of the enterprise and disregarding business considerations. These include sheltered workshops and rehabilitation programs for special-needs individuals. A second model defines its social purpose as a key commitment yet places importance on generating revenues. These enterprises often include initiatives to empower weaker populations. A third model still makes its social purpose a priority but must generate sufficient income for long-term survival, financing itself with income from its business operations. These initiatives include empowerment of special-needs populations through training and real work experience. Another model affords business and social objectives equal importance. These are social businesses: established to promote social goals, often designed to empower special-needs populations through vocational training and regular employment, or businesses promoting recycling initiatives. The final model is driven by business objectives, with all operations aimed at generating income for the organization – for example, selling gift baskets, clothing, or crafts. Social enterprise can also be developed as part of a regular business, such as in the case of Ben and Jerry's PartnerShop®, a form of social enterprise in which nonprofit organizations leverage the power of business for community benefit.

Here, too, technology has allowed complex hybrid models to emerge. A lower entrepreneurial threshold now allows companies of any size to bring a mobile application or other social-related software to market. New "Tech4Good" startups are emerging every day, and many charities and foundations are now using these technologies to advance their potential. The Tech4Good awards recognize organizations and individuals who use digital technology to improve the lives of others and make the world a better place. The 2018 winner was "Be My Eyes," a free app addressing accessibility by helping the blind in situations where a pair of eyes is needed. It connects blind and low-vision people with company representatives and sighted volunteers for visual assistance through a live video call. A previous winner, "The Small Robot Company," is reimagining farming in the robotic age. With its service offering of small, precise, and efficient robots, it plants, feeds, and weeds arable crops autonomously, with minimal waste.

Michael Porter's "shared value" is of interest in this domain. The Harvard strategist's model integrates many corporate responsibility principles, the most significant one here being the requirement to add value for all stakeholders.[27]

An example of the business opportunities in this area is the Bottom of the Pyramid (BOP) concept which has emerged from the growing consumer market in India, China, and various African nations. The rationale is that, by addressing the need for accessible products and services of people who earn less than $100 a month, additional consumer demand can be created while also improving livelihoods. The key to this includes the use of innovative financing and providing basic services and products at very low prices.

Notes

1 Arun Sundararajan, *The Sharing Economy: The End of Employment and the Rise of Crowd-Based Capitalism*. Cambridge, MA: MIT Press, 2016.
2 "How Airbnb has been hijacked by agencies making a huge profit." *The Times* (London), August 3, 2019. https://www.thetimes.co.uk/article/investigation-how-airbnb-has-been-hijacked-by-agencies-making-a-huge-profit-nvw082sl0.
3 Luis Ferré-Sadurní, "Inside the rise and fall of a multimillion-dollar Airbnb scheme." *New York Times*, February 23, 2019. https://www.nytimes.com/2019/02/23/nyregion/airbnb-nyc-law.html.
4 Alexandrea J. Ravenelle, *Hustle and Gig: Struggling and Surviving in the Sharing Economy*. Oakland, CA: University of California Press, 2019.
5 Ross Kerber, "Can Uber and Lyft help combat climate change? Green investors are not convinced." *The Independent*, April 3, 2019. https://www.independent.co.uk/news/business/analysis-and-features/uber-lyft-climate-change-ipo-environment-global-warming-a8852396.html.
6 Klaus Schwab, *The Fourth Industrial Revolution*. New York: Currency, 2017.
7 *McKinsey & Co.*, "Digital insights: Winning in digital ecosystems." January 2018. https://www.mckinsey.com/~/media/McKinsey/Business%20Functions/McKinsey%20Digital/Our%20Insights/Digital%20McK

The new economy systems 75

    insey%20Insights%20Number%203/Digital-McKinsey-Insights-Issue-3-revised.ashx.
 8 Jennifer L. Schenker, "The platform economy." *The Innovator*, January 19, 2019. https://innovator.news/the-platform-economy-3c09439b56.
 9 *Accenture*, "Five ways to win with digital platforms." 2016. https://www.accenture.com/us-en/_acnmedia/pdf-29/accenture-five-ways-to-win-with-digital-platforms-full-report.pdf; *Siemens*, "MindSphere." https://new.siemens.com/uk/en/products/software/mindsphere.html.
10 David Fine, Hugo Hickson, Vivek Pandit, and Philip Tuinenburg, "Catalyzing the growth of the impact economy." *McKinsey & Co.*, December 2018. https://www.mckinsey.com/industries/private-equity-and-principal-investors/our-insights/catalyzing-the-growth-of-the-impact-economy.
11 Ibid.
12 Shrupti Shah, Ross Rocketto, and Rob Terrin, "What Is the Impact Economy Anyway?" *Forbes*, August 5, 2013. https://www.forbes.com/sites/forbes-personal-shopper/2020/04/03/8-of-the-best-beard-oils/#5c8966411a51.
13 "ColorADD: The color alphabet." *Viarco*. https://www.viarco.pt/en/coloradd.
14 "The coffee capsules that will fertilize the vines." *Extra*, January 2018. http://www.extra-mag.co.il/the-coffee-capsules-that-will-fertilize-the-vines [in Hebrew].
15 "How to recycle your Nespresso capsules." *Nespresso*. https://www.nespresso.com/uk/en/recycling.
16 "Circular economy strategies would tip balance in battle against dangerous climate change." *Circle Economy*, January 22, 2019. https://docs.wixstatic.com/ugd/ad6e59_ba1e4d16c64f44fa94fbd8708eae8e34.pdf.
17 "The world is 9% circular: The circularity gap report 2019." *Circle Economy*. https://www.circularity-gap.world.
18 *Delta Galil*, "2017–2018 corporate social responsibility report: 40." https://deltagalil.com/media/DeltaCSR-2019.pdf.
19 Peter Economy, "The (Millennial) workplace of the future is almost here: These three things are about to change big time." *Inc.*, January 15, 2019. https://www.inc.com/peter-economy/the-millennial-workplace-of-future-is-almost-here-these-3-things-are-about-to-change-big-time.html.
20 Melanie Curtin, "73 percent of millennials are willing to spend more money on this one type of product." *Inc.*, March 30, 2018. https://www.inc.com/melanie-curtin/73-percent-of-millennials-are-willing-to-spend-more-money-on-this-1-type-of-product.html.
21 Tim Price, "'Generation green': How millennials will shape the circular economy." *Environment Journal*, November 13, 2018. https://environmentjournal.online/articles/generation-green-how-millennials-will-shape-the-circular-economy/.

22 "We're introducing reusable, refillable packaging to help cut waste." *Unilever*, January 24, 2019. https://www.unilever.com/news/news-and-features/Feature-article/2019/we-are-introducing-reusable-refillable-packaging-to-help-cut-waste.html.
23 Michael Braungart and William McDonough, *Cradle to Cradle: Remaking the Way We Make Things*. New York: North Point Press, 2002.
24 Certification is granted by MDBC. See https://mbdc.com.
25 *The Natural Step*. https://thenaturalstep.org.
26 "Sustainable development is development that meets the needs of the present without compromising the ability of future generations to meet their own needs" (World Commission on Environment and Development [WCED], *Our Common Future* [also known as the Brundtland Report]. Oxford: Oxford University Press, 1987).
27 Michael E. Porter and Mark R. Kramer, "Creating shared value." *Harvard Business Review*, January–February 2011. https://hbr.org/2011/01/the-big-idea-creating-shared-value.

7 Finance and investment

The financial sector remains the principal growth engine of the global economy. Trillions of dollars which move rapidly from one market to another set priorities and change the world order.

In recent years, key global players (the United Nations, the European Union, the World Bank, etc.) have identified the critical role of financial markets in tackling climate change at a global and national level. A 2017 review identified over 300 regulations and policies related to "green finance," in addition to thousands of "green" financial products. In fact, the London Stock Exchange alone lists more than 70 green securities and bonds related to renewable energies and measures addressing climate change.[1]

Ant Forest

Technology   Climate

The Ant Forest application has recently won the "UN Champions of the Earth award"[2] for encouraging its half a billion users to reduce their carbon footprint and for planting around 122 million trees. The app enables companies and individuals to monitor their environmental impact in real time. At its core is the idea that by using algorithms and big data, it is possible to positively influence behavior. The users reduce energy use by modifying their day-to-day behavior and "grow" virtual trees, which are later translated into real trees planted in some of China's driest areas.

ESG investments and impact investments

There are two main investment types that focus on the triple bottom line: ESG investments and impact investments.

ESG (environment, social, and governance) investment focuses on how a company operates, and it basically measures the level of company responsibility and sustainability. It is essentially perceived as part of mainstream investing. According to Investopedia, ESG criteria are a set of standards for a company's operations that socially conscious investors use to screen potential investments. Environmental criteria consider how a company performs as a steward of nature. Social criteria examine how a company manages its relationships with its employees, suppliers, customers, and the communities in which it operates. Governance deals with a company's leadership, executive pay, audits, internal controls, and shareholder rights, which means that it is huge in scale – accounting for over $30 trillion in total worldwide, according to the Global Sustainable Investment Alliance.[3] Impact investing, on the other hand, is a tool used by early-adopter investors. It is much smaller in scale and focuses on creating solutions to a particular challenge – for instance, buying bonds that finance gender-equal affordable housing or tackling climate change.

Impact investment

Impact investing is a term created by a group of foundations and investors convened by the Rockefeller Foundation in 2007. The Global Impact Investing Network (GIIN) defines this term as "investments intended to create positive measurable social and environmental impact alongside a financial return." The definition is broad enough to contain a variety of investments. The concept equally prioritizes both profit and social impact and is the foundation of a larger idea: the impact economy (see Chapter 6).

Impact investments constitute a growing trend among investors looking to combine financial investment with a social contribution. Such investors seek socially conscious businesses, technologies, and startups that are both profitable and address social and environmental challenges. Businesses that try to solve the social and environmental challenges of our times in a profitable way are known as social enterprises (see also Chapter 6). In recent years we have seen this phenomenon flourish and grow. According to a report published by UBS, 38% of family offices are engaged in impact investing, while almost every bank and investment house can offer its customers an impact investing portfolio, with a focus on sectors such as education, health, environment, or agriculture.

There are four types of impact investment. The first is an investment model first developed in England in 2010 called Social Impact Bonds. The second model is where impact funds invest with the intention of generating a financial return alongside a measurable social and/or environmental impact. The funds often represent investors who wish to combine their philanthropic objectives with their capital investment.

Acumen Fund, founded 15 years ago by Jacqueline Novogratz, a former Wall Street investment banker, has already granted over $100 million in credit facilities for social and environmental initiatives. Additional impact funds have been established by banks such as Credit Suisse and BNP Paribas, providing approximately €1 billion a year to social business ventures through their offices around the world. Interestingly enough, the default rates for loans under such funds is similar to that of other credit channels. Many pension and investment funds have also developed a variety of impact investment instruments, to meet the growing demands of their members and investors.

The third type of impact investment is in B Corporations or "B Corps": companies or corporations that engage in revenue-generating activities alongside creating a positive impact on society and/or the environment (in other words, using a social enterprise model: "B Corps" are called such when certified by the nonprofit B Labs). The fourth type is risk insurance investing: a unique initiative created by an Australian insurance company which places 25% of their institutional clients' premiums into investments with an additional social objective.

Although impact investments are still regarded as niche solutions, albeit in the vanguard, we can also observe significant change among mainstream investors. Private mutual funds, such as pension funds, and public funds, such as the IFC (International Finance Corporation) and the World Bank, are increasingly incorporating ESG criteria into their investment decisions. Such changes are on the scale of trillions of dollars a year.

There are different types of investors, each with their own preference. Yet they all share one thing in common: the use of professional instruments. Serious impact investors work according to clear, specific methodologies and standards. A company cannot simply announce, "We're social: invest in us." Investors will always seek to understand what change the company is promoting, what problem it claims to address, through which measures, and for how long. Investors talk in numbers, in quantities, and in targets. Just as traditional investors demand a business plan and investment returns, impact investors expect to quantify the value of their investment, both economically and socially.

The B Team and B Corporations

Leadership

The B Team is a nonprofit initiative founded by Sir Richard Branson and formed by a group of global business leaders to conceive an improved means of conducting business that considers the well-being of both people and planet. Business motivated solely by profit – "Plan A" – is no longer an option. "Plan B" – in which the private sector redefines its responsibilities and achievements according to the social, environmental, and economic benefits and protection it provides – is the only way to move forward. The B Team focuses on creating tangible and positive action by establishing challenges that stimulate and scale the development of systemic solutions where businesses can collectively make a difference. Civil society leaders, system experts, sustainability pioneers, economists, entrepreneurs, and business leaders have all joined forces under the B Corp movement to advance this initiative, including Ford Foundation, Kering Group, Guilherme Leal, Strive Masiyiwa, Joann McPike, the Tiffany and Co. Foundation, The Rockefeller Foundation, Unilever, Virgin Unite, Derek Handley, and One Young World. These distinguished business forces are leveraging their power to raise the general quality of life, enable scientific and technological progress, and create "an unprecedented era of sustainable, inclusive prosperity for all." Moving forward, The B Team's immediate focuses are to

> continue to build business support and leadership that positively influences government action on realizing company ownership transparency and ending anonymous companies, develop business leadership to shape the development and adoption of greater transparency in public procurement through open contracting and work with business and investors to better understand the business case for private sector support for civil rights and to develop approaches for private sector leadership.[4]

The growth of impact investing

Impact investing is now a global industry: a $100 billion ecosystem of financial instruments, platforms, organizations, credit funds, and others that enable social business ventures to rapidly grow and develop. Alongside the impact entrepreneurs, an additional level of intrapreneurs (entrepreneurs from within) has emerged. These social intrapreneurs cultivate social values from within the organizations for which they work using existing corporate platforms and networks.

Many financial institutions have announced that their investment process will include a social impact assessment in the near future, whereas some, such as members of GIIN (Global Impact Investing Network),[5] are already doing it. This is positive and optimistic news because it indicates that investors around the world are increasingly coming to understand that their capital has the power to enact change, and they have chosen to make a difference.

In recent years, the traditional lines between the corporate and social sectors have become blurred. While many businesses are seeking a social or environmental vision and mission, nonprofits are making use of standard business practices and even generating profits. Some social initiatives are evolving and developing within traditional businesses to provide an added value to their customers and to the public in general.

Cemex

Technology   Society

The Mexican building materials company Cemex provides accessible construction services to low-income families. The company has established a network of small branches selling cement and other building materials in underprivileged

> communities, allowing families to build their own homes while greatly expanding its customer base.[6] It was able to reduce prices mainly because of technological improvements to its production, inventory, and distribution systems.

Improving investor relations

Corporate responsibility increasingly serves as a doorway (or gatekeeper) to investment funds and private equity devoted to environmental and social causes. Such parties select their investment portfolio based on criteria around social or environmental responsibility. Billions of dollars are identified with environmental and ethical investments, primarily through pension funds and institutional investors. Currently, global financial analytics companies such as Bloomberg, MSCI, FTSE, and others provide environmental, social, and governance (ESG) data to investors around the world to assist them in analyzing social and environmental risks in their portfolios.

In fact, in 2018, Larry Fink, founder and CEO of the world's largest asset management company, BlackRock, sent a letter to CEOs of public companies urging them to take responsibility and make a positive contribution to society. This represented a powerful wake-up call for the CEOs. In early 2019 BlackRock reiterated its call to action, stressing "the inextricable link between purpose and profits."

As capital markets shift to include responsibility and sustainability as mainstream issues, a company's investor relations department must stay informed and work together with the sustainability department so that they can provide answers to investors' requests for information in aspects with which they had previously been unfamiliar.

Inspiring new initiative in this context is the Impact-Weighted Accounts Project at Harvard Business School, under the leadership of Professor George Serafeim; its mission is to drive the creation of financial accounts that reflect a company's financial, social, and environmental performance. In order to create accounting statements that transparently capture external impacts in a way that drives investor and managerial decision-making.

BlackRock's Larry Fink's letter to CEOs

Investment   Leadership

"The money we manage is not our own. It belongs to people in dozens of countries trying to finance long-term goals like retirement. And we have a deep responsibility to these institutions and individuals – who are shareholders in your company and thousands of others – to promote long-term value.

"Climate change has become a defining factor in companies' long-term prospects. . . . But awareness is rapidly changing, and I believe we are on the edge of a fundamental reshaping of finance. . . . And because capital markets pull future risk forward, we will see changes in capital allocation more quickly than we see changes to the climate itself. In the near future – and sooner than most anticipate – there will be a significant reallocation of capital. . . .

"As I have written in past letters, a company cannot achieve long-term profits without embracing purpose and considering the needs of a broad range of stakeholders. . . . Ultimately, purpose is the engine of long-term profitability."[7]

ESG disclosures and regulation

U.S. Supreme Court Judge Louis Brandeis was famous for saying that "sunlight is the best disinfectant." Indeed, sustainability reporting has become a norm for many publicly listed and private companies (see Chapter 18). Nonprofits and public entities have also started to disclose ESG information to their stakeholders. In fact, most organizations now face some level of investor, customer, and/or supplier demand for increased transparency about ESG issues, particularly around supply chain integrity, board diversity, or climate change adaptation. In 2018, 85% of all S&P500 companies produced some type of ESG disclosure.

There has also been growth in ESG-related regulation and disclosure requirements – totaling 1,052 requirements (80% of which are mandatory) in 63 countries. From 2017, the European Union non-financial reporting directive (NFRD)[8] has required companies that operate in EU Member States and meet certain criteria to prepare a statement containing information relating to environmental protection, social responsibility and treatment of employees, respect for human rights, anti-corruption and bribery, and diversity on boards. Regulatory bodies and stock exchanges are also responding to growing investor demands for uniform ESG information linked to financial performance.

How can we get better access to such investors? This is not a trivial task. Investors generally search for data and indications about the company and its conduct, its corporate governance, and the way it manages risks. Financial institutions mostly have an almost identical and routine method for analyzing financial reports; but social reports are a different matter.

As someone who has compiled corporate responsibility reports and performed assurance on these reports for numerous banks, I can bear witness that there are a great deal of procedural and practical variances in the nature and method of data collection. Furthermore, the rank and position in the company of the responsible function, as well as their proximity to management, can affect the contents of the report, as I will elaborate in Chapter 18.

Notes

1 *Green Finance Institute*. https://www.greenfinanceinstitute.co.uk.
2 "Chinese initiative Ant Forest wins UN Champions of the Earth award." *United Nations Environment Programme*, September 9, 2019. https://www.

unenvironment.org/news-and-stories/press-release/chinese-initiative-ant-forest-wins-un-champions-earth-award.
3 Global Sustainable Investment Alliance, "2018 global sustainable investment review." https://www.ussif.org/files/GSIR_Review2018F.pdf.
4 *B Teams*. https://bteam.org/.
5 *Global Impact Investing Network*. https://thegiin.org.
6 *Cemex*. https://www.cemex.com.
7 "A fundamental reshaping of finance?" *BlackRock CEO Larry Fink's Annual Letter to CEOs*, 2020. https://www.blackrock.com/corporate/investor-relations/larry-fink-ceo-letter.
8 *Directive 2014/95/EU*. https://eur-lex.europa.eu/legal-content/EN/TXT/?uri=CELEX%3A32014L0095.

Part 2
The good challenge
Future-proofing

8 The wake-up call

The principal objective of any business is profit maximization. This has always been the key to its existence, the reason for its establishment and for investing in its shares. It is often argued that corporate responsibility represents an unacceptable divergence from this underlying *raison d'être*. In fact, Milton Friedman expressed this idea eloquently in his oft-quoted 1970 article for the *New York Times*.[1] But in recent years, and especially post-COVID-19, things have changed. As noted in the Introduction, even the voice of the free market, the UK's *Financial Times*, thinks there should be more regulation and government intervention. It is increasingly being acknowledged that a company that embraces corporate responsibility essentially expands the circle of those who profit from the company. Corporate responsibility is a declaration that the company generates value to other stakeholders besides its shareholders. More immediately, there are many examples throughout this book showing how responsible business is profitable business. We have already seen in Chapter 4 how sustainability can be a driver of innovation. In Chapter 15 you will see how environmental responsibility generates organizational and financial dividends. Reducing the consumption of nonrenewable resources is an area offering significant financial savings as a result of environmentally responsible behavior that integrates environmental considerations into corporate strategy and everyday activity.

While the dangers of ignoring the current imperatives are very real, in fact, the benefits of corporate responsibility can be substantial for a company, realized in the medium and long term (and sometimes also the short term) in real dividends. And, of course, no company can survive without a successful bottom line.

Why change?

Every so often a CEO or chair of a company asks me, "How will corporate responsibility really help my organization?" This is a perfectly reasonable question. After all, true engagement with corporate responsibility necessitates a fundamental change – and organizations, as we know, do not particularly like change. They have worked hard to get where they are, reaching a break-even point after having invested heavily and finally achieving success. So why change? If it's not broken, why fix it?

Yet the corporate graveyards are full of "successful" companies that have subsequently dissolved for one reason or another. Suffice it to mention Nokia and Kodak – companies with a once-healthy bottom line that are now relics of the past. Why? Because there was a fundamental change in the market, and the organization did not react in time. Such changes could be technological, in public opinion, or a local or global regulatory change. Corporate responsibility integrates all these aspects – with one factor empowering another.

There is a certain paradox here. On the one hand, the more established an organization, the greater its capabilities, and the greater its ability to respond to change. It possesses the resources, the prestige, and the executive talent to potentially make the right decisions. On the other hand, these same advantages also represent its Achilles heel. It is intellectually and logistically challenging for a large organization to make changes. Changes mean short-term expenditure, which in turn means irregularities. Shareholders need to be persuaded, and sometimes this alone can be disenabling. Understanding corporate responsibility means understanding future risks and getting used to the notion that business is no longer going to be "as usual."

So far, so good?

A man falls from a high-rise building. As he passes the tenth floor, someone yells from the window, "How's it going?" The man yells back, "So far, so good! There's even a refreshing breeze and the view is amazing!" But reality, of course, will soon strike.

This is a fairly good analogy of the current situation. A series of revolutions has already begun, directly affecting organizations around the world: the "internet of things" (IoT), blockchain technology, social phenomena such as the shared economy, or environmental phenomena such as circular economies, as discussed in Chapter 6. In fact, between the time these lines are being written and the time you read them, various other revolutions will have inevitably entered the fray – but many organizations have yet to make physical contact with them. The effects of these revolutions are waiting for them, ten stories down. Nokia executives found themselves in exactly this situation with the launch of the first iPhone. What first seemed like a refreshing breeze quickly turned into a destructive hurricane. Nothing was broken – but everything definitely needed fixing.

Throughout this book, we investigate some of these changes (and there are some surprises in store), but in the meantime let's look at the organizations themselves. They can essentially be divided into three main groups.

The first group, which is growing rapidly, consists of organizations that choose to implement changes today to meet their needs tomorrow. To borrow a concept from the field of building maintenance, these organizations opt for the most advanced (and cheapest) solution: predictive maintenance. They analyze today the changes that will become necessary in the future and implement them gradually without time or budget constraints. This is the optimal approach. Not only are the changes at this stage relatively minor, they can be applied without disrupting the organization's daily operations. The process is implemented in baby steps, with regular monitoring and improvement, and when the effects of the new reality reach the bottom line, these organizations will be ready for them.

This leads us to an unexpected bonus: every change brings along new business opportunities and the bigger the change, the bigger the opportunities. The internet changed the world and brought with it the accessible information revolution. One company, for example, understood that the internet brings with it the opportunity to organize and provide access to all this information, and to profit from relevant advertisements. That company is called Google. A few years later, Web 2.0 brought about the social media revolution. While Google was preoccupied with establishing its engulfing dominance on information, another company saw an opportunity in the people who consume and create it. That company is called Facebook. Through the course of the internet revolution, another company realized that the real power lies in available and personal communication. It predicted the trend and developed the perfect mobile phone, completely different from what was available at the time: captivating, stylish, and an endless cash cow through the sale of apps, services, and other content. That company is called Apple. And we have not even mentioned Amazon, eBay, PayPal, or Alibaba.

The second group of companies consists of those who perform breakdown maintenance. These companies will perceive the change as it occurs, and will be agile enough to understand and exploit it. The price, of course, will be high. They will need to abandon costly production lines and make painful changes in personnel. These changes may affect shareholder value.

These companies will survive, and some will even thrive after making the necessary changes. Microsoft, for example, was compelled to transform its Office software business from a product/perpetual license sales model to a cloud-based subscription model to premium customers. The basic Office operations system is now available online for free. This was not an easy change for the company. Samsung is also an example of such a company. It was among the first to understand the deluge in demand for touchscreen mobile phones such as the iPhone. In one fateful decision – which we will discuss later – it abandoned the old technology and changed its production lines at tremendous cost. Ultimately, this decision paid off, and today the company sells its touchscreens to – Apple, of course. However, one can only speculate how much more Samsung could have gained if it had anticipated the touchscreen revolution first. And what about Google? It took the company years to develop an operating system – Android – that could compete with the simplicity of the iPhone. How much market share did it lose? How much revenue from app sales? And how much would Microsoft be worth today if only its executives understood that the real economic implications of the internet revolution rest in advertising? After all, Microsoft held undisputed dominance over everything related to home computing.

This leads us to the third group of companies, the one of which no one should want to be a member. This group consists of companies that failed to predict the looming changes, did not prepare in time, and, as a result, simply disappeared. Perhaps the most resonating example of such a company is Nokia. It was incredibly successful, a leader in its field, filled with confidence and sure in its path. It had access to the most advanced technology and carried an image of invincibility.

When Apple introduced its iPhone, Nokia chose to ignore reality. People all around the world craved the "magic," easy-to-use, touchscreen phone; yet Nokia insisted on adhering to its existing operating system. It had all the means to remedy the situation – but it insisted that nothing needed fixing. After all, everything was fine until now, wasn't it?

In this chapter we will focus on why corporate responsibility is no longer optional and how it is the best and probably the only means of **future-proofing your business**. Just as the companies highlighted here failed to predict the new technology wave and were left standing, so those companies that ignore the sustainability revolution will find themselves on the sidelines, or worse.

Social license to operate

Much CR literature of recent decades breezily proclaimed the "win–win" of doing the right thing while increasing your bottom line – the so-called "business case." An inevitable criticism of this outlook is the underlying implication that good behavior is only recommended so long as it increases profits. But the key phrase emerging from this literature – and more relevant today than ever – is "social license to operate." Bluntly, companies that don't meet the behavioral expectations of a wide range of stakeholders risk extinction just as surely as those who cannot make money.

In the past, companies could operate as if in a vacuum. They underwent no moderation except from local authorities and certainly neither needed nor sought any abstract form of "public approval." Chemical plants polluted, mining companies extracted, refineries refined, and the larger and more predatory a company was, the less responsive it was to the public.

In recent years, the tides have turned. Now, even the corporate dinosaurs find that they risk a tidal wave of harmful negative public opinion in response to unacceptable behavior.

The Flint water crisis emerged in 2014 when drinking water for the city of Flint, Michigan, began to be sourced from the Flint

River instead of Lake Huron and the Detroit River, to save money. Due to insufficient water treatment, lead leaching from pipes into the drinking water exposed over 100,000 residents to the harmful toxin. After a pair of scientific studies proved lead contamination was present in the water supply, a federal state of emergency was declared in January 2016. Flint residents were instructed to use only bottled or filtered water for drinking, cooking, cleaning, and bathing. As of early 2017, the water quality was back at acceptable levels, but residents were still being instructed to use bottled or filtered water until all the lead pipes have been replaced, which could take at least three years.

Another example occurred in 1986 when a massive ammonia tank was installed in the Israeli port city of Haifa, in the heart of a densely populated area. This was a very questionable decision, as any malfunction or leak could result in a frightening number of casualties. Nonetheless, the tank remained in operation for years without interference, serving as it did the marked commercial interests of powerful industrial groups. That was a different world in those days. Corporate responsibility was essentially science fiction, and "social license to operate" was not one of the rules of the corporate game. The hundreds of thousands of local residents were simply unaware of the constant danger in their midst. Remaining uninformed, they exerted no pressure on their elected officials, who in turn took no legal action to remove the hazard. However, as public awareness took hold, demands rose for the removal of the tank. In a predictable response, the chemical company employed a team of lobbyists, experts, and lawyers and even launched various legal measures to keep the tank where it was. However, their efforts gradually collapsed against the intensity of public pressure. Ultimately, in 2018, the company was compelled to empty the ammonia tank and provide suitable alternatives.

A social license to operate is no longer optional, whether the company is customer-facing or B2B. It can belong to one of three categories: "Useful," a "Necessary Evil," or "Harmful." It has a choice, and the category it finds itself in will be determined by its corporate responsibility policies.

Of course, many companies operate in industries that are undeniably challenging in terms of environmental pollution or other such factors. A mining company, for example, will operate huge furnaces and heavy mechanical equipment, and will also be a big energy consumer. That is the business model, and it cannot be changed. So where does their social license to operate come from? They demonstrate responsibility in those areas where change is possible. Perhaps the fuel used to power the furnace could include the by-products of other companies. Or there could be a profound commitment to the local community and a concern for its welfare. But first and foremost, it will be through dialogue and transparency, which will help build trust and reach understandings with relevant parties.

Companies with an established social license to operate can operate more freely and more profitably. And this is not the sort of license that can be "bought" with a cynical attitude. An organization that demonstrates corporate responsibility would not exploit the social license it had earned: such a license is a thing of immense value and will viewed as such by the company staff; also, it would be self-defeating.

Manage risks responsibly

Risk is where threat (external or internal) meets organizational vulnerability with no suitable measures and controls in place for its mitigation. There are various types of risk: financial, technological, environmental, or medical. In many cases these are interlinked, as we have seen with COVID-19; and in recent years, we are witness to the rise of social risks. Risks and/or opportunities related to environmental, social, and governance (ESG) criteria – which comprise a set of standards for a company's sustainable and ethical operations – may also be referred to as sustainability, non-financial, or extra-financial risks.

So what is social risk? It occurs when the threat of social stakeholders meets organizational vulnerability – for example, customers (stakeholders) protesting against a price increase. This risk is increasingly present, because in an era of social networks such protest is easier to mobilize than ever before and at no actual cost. Every company needs to protect itself from this type of risk, and this is something that can be achieved. Risk management is now understood by most businesses, largely as result of prior experience, as a strategic concern; and they understand that it is in their power to influence a wide range of actions and decisions.

Yossi Ginossar, my risk management mentor at Grant Thornton, refers to risk management as a critical aspect of business management. It enables organizations to systematically and proactively manage risks related to their operations by identifying and assessing risks and creating an appropriate response to mitigate the organizational threat associated with each risk.

Here, too, corporate responsibility plays a crucial role, since risk management is about establishing better decision-making processes. A company that strives to decrease its environmental and social impacts or acts fairly and responsibly toward its stakeholders is inevitably exposed to fewer risks. With friction-causing factors reduced, the threats of lawsuits, media scandals, etc., diminish. Indeed, one of the most significant risks in the financial system is conduct risk, and this created the opportunity for a remarkable interface between our abilities as ethical consultants and the risk management capabilities at Grant Thornton.

Enterprise Risk Management (ERM) is a principal method for expanding a company's understanding of the risks it faces. Expanding ERM to include ESG criteria can help the company avoid risks while creating new opportunities. The right strategy will make the company more agile and competitive. How is this done?

In 2018, the Committee of Sponsoring Organizations of the Treadway Commission (COSO), a joint initiative dedicated to the development of frameworks on Enterprise Risk Management and governance, launched a new risk management standard. The COSO Enterprise Risk Management Standard[2] formally determines that aspects of corporate governance, including social and environmental issues, must be accounted for in corporate risk management – and thus organizations should prepare accordingly in order to prevent such risk-related losses.

The COSO initiative, although brought into being away from the limelight, represents a turning point in social, environmental, and corporate governance practices in organizations around the world. It serves as an official recognition of the need to address such risks through a preventative systematic approach.

The bottom line is that a risk management process is complemented by a strong corporate responsibility policy. Such a policy controls and mitigates economic, environmental, and social risks.

Global Risks Report 2020

Risk

The 2020 Global Risks Report, published by the World Economic Forum and designed for organizations to use a reference point to identify critical risk issues internally and externally, declares unification of political and economic forces critical to combat threats to the climate, public health, and technology systems. In this its 15th edition, 800 global decision-makers and experts were asked to rank their concerns in terms of both likelihood and impact. They agreed that the top risks expected to increase in 2020 were: economic confrontations and friction between major powers, domestic political polarization, extreme heatwaves, destruction of natural ecosystems, cyber-attacks targeting operations and infrastructure and data/money theft, protection of trade and investments, populist and nativist agendas, recession, and uncontrolled fires. For the first time in the report's history, the environment was reflected as a major concern as "environmental threats dominate the top five long term risks by likelihood and occupy three of the top five spots by impact."[3]

You are being watched

We live in an era driven by the "wisdom of the crowd," where the greatest actual force comes from the general public, consumers, and inhabitants. The "silent majority" no longer keeps silent. The internet, social networks in particular, enables the voice of the individual to be heard – and amplified by thousands of others. It is no longer possible to silence individuals who voice a truth with which others can identify. The truth can no longer be easily suppressed.

And what does the individual really want? It always comes down to the same basic needs: clean air, freshwater, an environment free from pollutants, a life of well-being and comfort, and a safe and secure future for the children. The silent majority has always wanted this, but now they are far better informed about who is most likely to enable this; or, rather, who is impeding it. And they will vote with their wallets.

Amazon

Tech giants   Reputation

By 2019, Amazon had paid only £61.7 million in tax in the UK, despite having amassed over £7 billion in revenue in that country in that time.[4] In 2017, Amazon was ordered by the EU to repay €250 million to Luxembourg, after that country granted it state aid which meant that it paid four times less tax than local rivals in a move that was subsequently judged to have been illegal.[5] Add to this its reputation for poor labor practices, as well as its impact on local independent bricks-and-mortar businesses, and it is clear to see why it remains the target of campaigns to boycott it. A campaign for an "Amazon-free Christmas" in 2014, in which over 11,000 people signed a pledge, saw the retail giant miss out on around £2.5 million worth of sales over the festive season.[6] More recently, "Prime Day" boycotts have aimed to hit it on what should be one of its biggest turnover days.[7]

Amazon seems to be withstanding the negative publicity quite robustly.[8] But it will be interesting to see how long the allegations of poor corporate responsibility and impugnment of its social license to operate can be sustained. Amazon relies on its cheap prices and frictionless shopping experience: it has harnessed tech to lock its customers in – not through brand loyalty but through pure convenience. According to a Wharton School of Business professor, "If the boycott reflects a movement – rather than a moment – it can change the world around it."[9]

In early 2020, Jeff Bezos committed $10 billion to addressing climate change in an initiative he called the Bezos Earth Fund. He called for collective action from companies of all scales, nation states, global organizations, and individuals, with funding allocated to scientists, NGOs, and activists addressing climate change. The value of the fund is ten times the amount foundations worldwide gave in total in 2018, yet it is merely a drop in the bucket of Bezos's personal wealth. So, although this action is a massive boost for climate justice and sets a precedent for business leaders around the globe, it drew criticism from those who question why Bezos chose to create this trust rather than pay more taxes, or higher wages, or address Amazon's massive and controversial carbon footprint, or improve its working conditions, or cease making deals with oil and gas moguls.[10] It therefore stands as an object lesson that philanthropic giving does not substitute for sound corporate responsibility in your operations.

Negative publicity continues to adhere to Bezos and Amazon. It was reported in April 2020 that not only had the COVID-19 pandemic benefited the Amazon CEO but the additional $24 billion accrued to that point since the shutdown had propelled him into the position of world's richest individual.[11] This came shortly after publicizing a relief fund the public can donate to for his contract employees working during the pandemic.[12] This was also against a background of controversy about treatment of workers. Strikes and walkouts were organized in protest at lack of worker protections, leading to at least one dismissal and other alleged retaliations.[13]

The only logical conclusion is that responsible business is the best option – and soon the only option – for a profitable business. Unhappy consumers can now quickly make their views known far and wide, punishing companies that have disappointed them. This is a considerable threat: an effective consumer boycott can cause much more damage than any class action suit and is much easier to organize.

Kellogg's

Reputation   Brand

The food manufacturing giant Kellogg's was threatened when GMO-Free USA called for a consumer boycott over the company's use of GMOs. In 2015, the organization claimed to have tested two Kellogg's cereal products and found both to contain GMOs and glyphosate, the active chemical ingredient in Monsanto's Roundup herbicide.[14] According to GMO-Free USA: "Kellogg's actively fought against food transparency and contributed nearly $2 million to propaganda campaigns to defeat citizens' ballot initiatives for mandatory GMO labeling in California, Washington, Oregon and Colorado." The campaign claimed that Kellogg's spent over $3.6 million lobbying the U.S. government in 2013 and 2014 to fight mandatory

> GMO labeling, something that it says is supported by over 90% of Americans. It said that the pesticides and herbicides that the company used "deplete the soil, harm earthworms and other beneficial non-target organisms, and put the Monarch butterfly, bees and other species in jeopardy." The campaign also chose to target Kellogg's due to that fact that it "heavily markets to children." As a result of this and other campaigns, Kellogg's was forced to review their policies and increased their transparency, launching the "Open for Breakfast" platform which allows dialogue with their customers about company policies and the products' ingredients.

Today, thanks largely to the smartphones in our hands, we live in a world of transparency. With just the touch of a finger, actions performed on one side of the world can be documented and forwarded to the other side. Manufacturers can no longer hide the conditions in their factories from public scrutiny. This global transparency has made a big change. We see fewer chemical companies exposing their workers to hazardous conditions. We meet fewer electronics companies using metals mined by children or forced labor. We also see more textile companies following a Fair Trade supply chain.

Life expectancy has dramatically increased in developed (and developing) countries. As a consequence, there is a greater focus among citizens globally (and therefore consumers) on improving quality of life rather than just an extension of life. This means an increased emphasis on the source and quality of our food and all aspects of food production. Companies favored under this new wave of consumer awareness and action are those that avoid dangerous and polluting pesticides, offer organic food, and avoid chemical preservatives. An increasing number of consumers are choosing food with a low carbon footprint and/or produced under high animal welfare standards.

Bulletproof your reputation

In every respect (including legally), a company's or brand's reputation is a valuable asset. In many cases (Facebook or Coca-Cola, for example), corporate reputation and brand equity are worth far more than the company's tangible assets such as factories, offices, machinery, and equipment. Sometimes, a company has no assets apart from its reputation, but it can still demand a sale price for the right to its name. Reputation has a critical impact on consumer purchase decisions. It drives supply and demand: a company with a higher brand value can demand a higher price for its products or services. Consumers confronted with two similar products are likely to choose the one offered by the company with the better reputation.

Reputation, of course, is not good/bad binary. A company can have a reputation for being "reliable", "youthful," "innovative," or "service-oriented." It can also have a reputation for being "predatory" and "environmentally unfriendly," or maybe "involved in the community," "a good employer," and "concerned about the future."

The research and advisory firm Reputation Institute has found a direct link between the following seven rational dimensions and positive corporate reputation:

- The company offers high-quality products and services (accounting for 18% of the company's reputation).
- A responsibly run company: ethical and transparent (15%).
- An innovative company (14%).
- Good corporate citizenship (14%).
- It treats its employees well (13%).
- It is managed effectively through strong leadership (13%).
- It delivers good financial results (13%).

It is plain to see that no less than 42% of a company's reputation is directly related to corporate responsibility (responsibly run, good corporate citizenship, treats its employees well)! This is an astonishing figure which demonstrates the close relationship between corporate responsibility and reputation. So one of the key benefits of advanced corporate responsibility is organizational reputation. A socially responsible company will have a more positive consumer response and face less negative feedback.

According to studies conducted at the University of Michigan,[15] an investment in corporate responsibility has greater impact than an investment in customer service in safeguarding companies from a negative reputation. This is especially true for those companies who are less customer-facing. Furthermore, companies identified as having a high level of corporate responsibility are more capable of managing a crisis or negative event.

Corporate responsibility improves reputation from within, precisely because of a concern with the organizational "how" (values, norms) rather than the "what" (products, services). Products can change, services can vary in quality, but if the values and norms of the company are positive – and properly communicated – they have a tremendous impact on corporate reputation, and therefore ultimately on the bottom line.

Take responsibility for innovation and learning

In today's world, a competitive advantage can disappear within a year. Companies will therefore be prepared to spend months on long-term strategic planning based solely on one competitive advantage. In order to establish their dominance, they must constantly launch new cycles of transient strategic initiatives. Strategic planning must be adaptable, fluid, customer-focused, and not industry-bound.

Companies must abandon the notion of competitive stability. It should not even be considered an operative goal. A company's strategies should promote change; it should adopt methodologies that encourage the creation of a portfolio of numerous advantages that will enable the company to thrive over time.

The fundamentals of strategic planning have not changed, however: it is still necessary to make the tough choices between "what to do" and "what not to do." But in this changing world, an expansion of the decision-making processes is a prerequisite since strategic planning no longer happens in stable environments. In light of this, the importance of strategic planning grows as complexities increase, but this planning must be conducted in more dynamic, innovative ways that bring about changes in paradigms while maintaining and leveraging existing strategic assets.[16] Strategic planning of this nature is based on eight fundamental principles.

1 The focus should be the arena – not the industry.
2 Central themes should be set and new approaches to solving problems should be explored.
3 Adopt metrics that support entrepreneurship (rather than financial metrics).
4 Focus on providing solutions to customer problems.
5 Build relationships and networks with customers and suppliers.
6 Brutal restructuring should be avoided and disengagement policies be set.
7 Establish clear and systematic rules for the assessment and support of intra-organizational entrepreneurship.
8 Re-examine existing methods and experiment with new ones.

An organization searching for social- and environmental-related solutions will find new and creative ways to do so. It will develop communication channels with other organizations and stakeholders which may lead to surprising collaborations. Moreover, the entrepreneurial and innovative processes that often accompany such solutions will carry over to other areas of the organization and leave a very positive impact. For example, the city of São Paulo – one of the largest in the world – has sought to bring together the main stakeholders related to green and sustainable technology on an online platform designed by Grant Thornton Brazil. "Green Sampa" advances solutions that will be prototyped in São Paulo to make the city smarter and more sustainable.

Stay ahead of regulation

Recall the first group of companies mentioned earlier in this chapter? They were the ones who anticipated markets by remaining ahead of the game. There is an additional bonus of being ahead of the curve as regards corporate responsibility, and that relates to regulation. The regulatory landscape is changing across the world in favor of tighter restrictions on corporate environmental and social behavior. It is important not to be one of the companies that finds itself having to react in firefighting mode to such new directives.

A striking example of the anticipated sea change is a U.S. federal act proposed in February 2019 by Senator Elizabeth Warren that aims to encourage socially favorable corporate behavior, middle-class growth, and regulation of U.S. corporations. The six provisions of the Accountable Capitalism Act (ACA) are:

- Corporations with over $1 billion in revenue need a federal charter.
- Company managers and directors must consider the interests of all stakeholders beyond shareholders.
- Employees are to comprise 40% of corporate boards.
- Directors and officers are to be denied the right for a duration of five years to sell shares received as compensation.
- Corporations are to be blocked from making political contributions without 75% approval from their directors and shareholders.
- The federal government can revoke the charters of corporations who engage in illegal activities.

As any act that aims to regulate corporations in the United States, the ACA proposal has met with resistance from the corporate sector, but it is a clear indication of which way the wind is blowing.

★ ★ ★

We will leave this chapter reinforcing the important message it carries. For long-term growth, you need long-term planning, a policy of "do no harm" and benefiting all of your stakeholders. As simple as it sounds, the only way to do well is by doing good.

Notes

1 Milton Friedman, "The social responsibility of business is to increase its profits." *New York Times*, September 13, 1970. https://graphics8.nytimes.com/packages/pdf/business/miltonfriedman1970.pdf.
2 https://www.coso.org/Pages/erm-integratedframework.aspx.
3 "Global risks report 2020." *Oliver Wyman*. https://www.oliverwyman.com/our-expertise/insights/2020/jan/globalrisks2020.html?utm_source=exacttarget&utm_medium=email&utm_campaign=risk-report.
4 Graham Hiscott and Alex Clarke, "Amazon pays just £62 million UK corporation tax in 20 years – after £7 billion revenue." *The Mirror*, January 31, 2019. https://www.mirror.co.uk/news/uk-news/amazon-storm-over-tax-bill-13936012.
5 "Amazon ordered to repay €250m by EU over 'illegal tax advantages'." *The Guardian*, October 4, 2017. https://www.theguardian.com/technology/2017/oct/04/amazon-eu-tax-irish-government-apple.
6 Alison Flood, "Amazon Christmas boycott campaign gathers weight." *The Guardian*, December 1, 2014. https://www.theguardian.com/books/2014/dec/01/amazon-christmas-boycott-campaign-amazon-anonymous.
7 Stephie Grob, "Here's why some activists and shoppers are calling for Amazon prime day boycotts." *Vox*, July 16, 2019. https://www.vox.com/the-goods/2019/7/16/20696392/amazon-prime-day-2019-boycott-strikes.
8 Jana Kasperkevic, "Amazon faces boycott ahead of holidays as public discontent grows." *The Guardian*, December 17, 2018. https://www.theguardian.com/technology/2018/dec/17/amazon-boycott-customers-holiday-shopping.
9 Americus Reed, "Social media boycotts succeed when they reflect a movement." *New York Times*, February 7, 2017. https://www.nytimes.com/roomfordebate/2017/02/07/when-do-consumer-boycotts-work.
10 Stefan Stern, "Why doesn't Jeff Bezos pay more tax instead of launching a $10bn green fund?" *The Guardian*, February 18, 2020. https://www.theguardian.com/commentisfree/2020/feb/18/jeff-bezos-amazon-10bn-more-taxes.
11 Daniel Wolfe, "Coronavirus has secured Jeff Bezos as the world's richest person." *Quartz*, April 19, 2020. https://qz.com/1841031/coronavirus-secures-amazons-jeff-bezos-as-worlds-richest-person/.
12 Danielle Zoellner, "Coronavirus: Jeff Bezos, world's richest man, asks public to donate to Amazon relief fund." *The Independent*, March 24, 2020. https://www.independent.co.uk/news/world/americas/coronavirus-amazon-jeff-bezos-relief-fund-covid-19-billionaire-net-worth-a9422236.html.
13 Kenya Evelyn, "Amazon CEO Jeff Bezos grows fortune by $24bn amid coronavirus pandemic." *The Guardian*, April 15, 2020. https://www.theguardian.com/technology/2020/apr/15/amazon-jeff-bezos-gains-24bn-coronavirus-pandemic.

14 "GMO free USA finds GMOs and weedkiller in Kellogg's Froot Loops." *CSR News*, January 29, 2015. https://www.csrwire.com/press_releases/37644-GMO-Free-USA-Finds-GMOs-and-Weedkiller-in-Kellogg-s-Froot-Loops.
15 Yeosun Yoon, Zeynep Gürhan-Canli, and Norbert Schwarz, "The effect of corporate social responsibility (CSR) activities on companies with bad reputations." *Journal of Consumer Psychology*, 16(4): 377–390. https://deepblue.lib.umich.edu/bitstream/handle/2027.42/141315/jcpy377.pdf?sequence=1.
16 Based on Rita McGrath, *The End of Competitive Advantage: How to Keep Your Strategy Moving as Fast as Your Business*. Boston, MA: Harvard Business School Press, 2013.

9 Whose responsibility is it?

Corporate responsibility is personal

The brightest people in the world are not usually to be found behind a ministerial desk in a government department. Look instead inside research laboratories, in front of computers running design software and around the conference tables of large corporations. This is, in fact, to be expected. To be elected, one has to be likeable and able to forge the right connections. But in order to be at the top of the game in a competitive business arena, you must be exceptional.

Fortunately, many such bright individuals in the private sector are beginning to recognize that they must take responsibility for the world around them – our world. The COVID-19 pandemic foregrounded this willingness to take responsibility and act, as we saw when companies reacted quickly in facilitating the logistics of donations and even changing production lines to make masks or handwash. The keen minds in the research labs, especially those engaged in planning, are currently undergoing an accelerated process of taking responsibility and accountability on board, as we can see from the tech examples already discussed. This is especially the case where the responsibility of business leaders is concerned. Leaders are coming to the realization – although this is still an ongoing process – that corporate responsibility is a personal matter. Organizations that promote sustainability are those that have their children and grandchildren in mind. Factories that take concerted action to reduce pollution are run by managers who do not want to see their children – or any children – inhaling dangerous particles or playing on tar-contaminated ground. Corporations that contribute to the society in which they operate are run by people who do not want to see the next generations afflicted by poverty and crime-infested neighborhoods.

Unilever

Leadership   New paradigms

Unilever is an oft-cited example of what can be achieved by a leader with a forward-looking vision for change. Paul Polman was its famous CEO from 2009 to 2019. Unilever doesn't have a corporate social responsibility department – that place to which most companies relegate their do-gooding activities. Instead the consumer goods giant integrated its approach to solving social issues – from food waste to climate change to poverty – into every part of its business. Polman's vision was to double Unilever's revenue while cutting its environmental footprint in half. Examples of Unilever's activities include a global handwashing campaign and an ambitious plan to improve the nutritional profile of its products. Speaking to *Forbes*, Polman said:

> Business needs to be part of the solution, not the problem. We cannot be bystanders. We need to be a giver, not a taker in a society that gives us life in the first place. It is – after all – not possible to have a strong, functioning business in a world of increasing inequality, poverty and climate change.[1]

> Following Polman's retirement, after a decade of leading and promoting corporate responsibility at the company's core, it will be interesting to see whether the sustainability revolution he initiated will be preserved by his successors. According to Professor Rebecca Henderson of Harvard Business School, Polman was able to commit Unilever only to sustainability at scale because the firm was full of people who were already trying to make a difference. But this does not detract from my argument that we need leadership to make the difference.

Corporate governance: the journey starts from the top

The board of directors is the highest organ in every organization. Its two main duties are: strategy setting; and steering and monitoring the executive management. The board is primarily concerned with the long term – and long-term success can happen only if the long-term interests of all stakeholders are taken into account.

To me, it is abundantly clear that the only way to adopt corporate responsibility strategically is to start from the board. It is up to the board to shape the strategy and lead the company's sustainability agenda by setting priorities among the different sustainability topics and by signaling their preference for the kind of organizational culture that will enable it.

The managerial area concerned with the framework of rules, practices, working models, and processes used to direct and control the company is called corporate governance. Corporate governance is sometimes addressed as part of the wider topic of corporate responsibility, but first it is important to determine where the differences lie between the two phenomena, and only then take a deeper look at the interfaces between them, and potential correlations. Fundamentally, whereas corporate responsibility in general is a matter of corporate policy, corporate governance derives from the law and internal procedures, making it a mandatory practice.

Corporate governance has evolved over the past two decades for several reasons:

1. Globalization alongside consumer maturation.
2. The growing impact of corporations, some of which have accrued such power that they have greater influence on society than governments.
3. GDP growth boosting longer-term savings, thereby strengthening the role of institutional investors as shareholders.
4. Corporate crises and major defaults such as Enron and the global financial crisis. The effects of COVID-19 on corporate governance are still to be seen.

The measure of good corporate governance is the ability of the board of directors to control compliance in the company, both bottom-up and top-down. Effective corporate governance is much like preventative medicine: aiming to forestall crises that might threaten the company's existence; or, if a crisis (operational, financial, local, or global) hits, to be prepared for the turbulence because the board asked the right questions. Corporate governance best practice means a well-organized board in an effective framework of procedures and self-regulation, ensuring that when an agenda is on the table, all relevant information is available and all questions are answered. Even if the vote is not unanimous, there must at least be consensus that all voices have been heard and the "business judgment rule" was applied.

The principal objective of good corporate governance – to oversee the work of one employee (the CEO) and to steer the company's strategy and policies – is, in fact, very ambitious. In a globalized world in which it is not unusual to see conglomerates running businesses, it is sometimes unrealistic to expect a board to exert effective control over a company's operations. But it is nonetheless feasible and desirable to impose a strong and steady framework as an infrastructure for the company.

A crucial difference between corporate governance and other components of social responsibility – community, environment, ethics, and human resources – is that the former is directly connected to resolutions taken by the top organ of the corporation, and under close scrutiny of stakeholders, even from a legal point of view in extreme cases of default. The latter have yet to become more central considerations in corporate decision-making. What all of these components of social responsibility have in common, however, is visibility: just as the corporate board must be seen to fully embrace the necessity of well-advised and organized decision-making, so must it nowadays be seen to consider environmental issues in transactions or other types of resolutions.

Interestingly, however, as much sense as corporate governance makes from a managerial perspective, it is worth bearing in mind that corporate leaders once needed considerable persuasion about its merits, much as they do with regard to corporate responsibility today.

The directors of the future

Boards of directors face extra responsibility year on year, partly as a result of increased compliance requirements and regulations but mainly because of the pace of change in the world: there is a year-on-year increase in the intensity, probability, and frequency of risks. With their role extending beyond the supervision of day-to-day management, the requirement of a having a good board of directors continues to increase in importance.

In fact, it is the board's job to prepare the company for the challenges of the upcoming decade. But what are these challenges? It is sufficient here to mention some recent mega-trends: increasing life expectancy, immigration, globalization and the growing competition between markets, urbanization and the development of mega-cities, climate change, concern over social and environmental issues, the cooperative economy, connectivity, networks, and cyber-crime.

Each of these trends has a unique impact on every sector, yet an organization's ability to stay ahead of these trends may determine whether it succeeds or fails. The previous organization I had headed, for example, faced a severe cyber-attack against which, it became evident, we were not properly prepared. This was a clear warning sign.

Directors of companies around the world have recently begun to formulate corporate governance codes and internal compliance programs. This is often as a response to regulatory pressure and the obligation to comply with new laws. However, in most cases the result merely satisfies present requirements and checks all the boxes in a technical and generic way. But a growing number of companies are in search of a more profound process, with much thought and examination going to create a tailored process suited to an organization's unique needs. In this respect, it is worth noting that a good board will insist on a self-evaluation process in order to improve its effectiveness.

We at Grant Thornton conducted a study[2] based on a survey of 2,500 CEOs, managing directors, and chairpersons across 36 different world economies on the subject of how boards of publicly listed (or public sector) companies are preparing for the challenges of the future. The study concluded with recommendations for boards who wish to survive and thrive, boiling it down to three key strategies: boost diversity, implement a cyber-strategy, and identify and nurture organizational talent. Let's examine this further: 88% of the survey's respondents recognized that their board needs to do more to encourage diversity, within the board itself and in the organization as a whole. A mosaic of people with different backgrounds and experiences can support an organization in facing future challenges. Regarding cyber-strategy, 60% of those surveyed saw cyber-security as a significant risk to their business, but just 46% believed that their organization is effectively mitigating that risk. Yet it is clear that advanced cyber and digital strategies can both exploit emerging opportunities and manage future risks. My previous organization, as mentioned previously, experienced this first-hand. The third point is that an effective board of directors needs to attract talent into the organization and then develop it. It is down to the board to ensure that career and personal development paths are outlined that will fully utilize potential talent within the organization.

The boards of the next decade need to develop an organizational culture that will make their company fit for the purpose of navigating future risks and challenges. This includes a long-term organizational strategy, an awareness of sustainability at the corporate core, and an implementation of advanced digital capabilities.

With regard to corporate responsibility and sustainability, boards should define what the company's purpose is and what does sustainability mean for the company and set targets for the management and oversight of its performance. The key issue is to develop the relevant organizational culture to support sustainability adoption by creating incentives that reward long-term performance, incorporating sustainability priorities and a clear message about recruiting, promoting, and compensation processes. Broadly, the aim is to integrate sustainability into all aspects of operations, including marketing, production, logistics, and even finance. Boards should also oversee the implementation by managers and the communication of sustainability performance to stakeholders. And, crucially, "walk the talk" and lead by example.

Many companies are already making use of designated board management software (such as diligence.com) which enhances data security and the decision-making effectiveness, providing clear and up-to-date information and monitoring the execution of board resolutions. Under its corporate responsibility commitments, a board must address the risks and opportunities of climate change, organizational ethics, employment diversity, and so forth.

Once the board's infrastructure is properly established, as a first priority it will reflect on the organization's resilience and ability to cope with challenges. A fit-for-purpose board will generate managerial and organizational synergies and will advance the organization without the need for additional resources.

> **SodaStream**
>
> Leadership
>
> Daniel Birnbaum is the former CEO of SodaStream, a manufacturing company specializing in home-carbonated sparkling water makers. He makes corporate responsibility a personal effort, on all fronts, and shares this effort with his customers and employees. Through its employment policy, in which it ensures it employs a diversified team of workers, SodaStream offers an example of Jewish–Arab co-existence in Israel, making its own contribution to promoting peace in the Middle East – in a move that is not without political ramifications and controversy.[3] From an environmental point of view, the SodaStream brand proposition is a positive one: it enables its customers to reduce global plastic bottle pollution by the simple expedient of using its product in favor of buying soft drinks in one-time-use plastic bottles. In 2018, PepsiCo acquired SodaStream for a substantial $3.2 billion, indicating a move toward a more environmentally friendly agenda from the drinks giant in the upcoming years.[4]

Let's take a bird's-eye view of the process.

Who is responsible for corporate responsibility?

Corporate responsibility is strategic, multidisciplinary, and multidimensional. In my experience, the matter should not be entrusted solely to a professional, internal or external, as this will exclude it from the critical path of core business activities. This is a broad subject, established over time, and therefore must be implemented as a continuous process or journey. As discussed earlier, corporate responsibility must come from the top and permeate the organization; therefore, ultimately, the bulk of the responsibility rests with the CEO or the chair of the board. They are required to make the difficult decisions, and they must do so while clearly and objectively assessing the realty of their business.

The CEO will, of course, delegate. As a rule, senior management must also be involved as they are essential for effectual implementation and for successful execution, and they must engage and connect all elements of the organization.

Chief sustainability officer

Leadership

As top firms seek to create and execute corporate sustainability strategies, CSR has entered into the C-suite in the role of chief sustainability officer. Mastercard, Nissan, Ralph Lauren, and Tyson Foods are just some of the companies that have created this new executive position in the last five years, indicating their shift toward a new integrated CSR approach.

Effective corporate responsibility is not measured by the success of a single project, but rather in the creation of systemic change. The way to effect such a change involves, among other things, harnessing the board to this journey – not just senior management. This way, it will be possible to integrate corporate responsibility within the management incentive structure.

Another route is via inter-sectoral and inter-organizational changes. For example, if we want to reduce the carbon footprint of seagoing cargo, environmentally friendly container ships alone will not be enough. It will need cooperation among inland transportation companies, the railway network, and various other players.

The individual appointed as director of corporate responsibility or corporate responsibility officer will play a significant, critical role. This person will be responsible for promoting the norms of responsible management and for adopting a strategic approach to corporate responsibility in all its dimensions – all this supported by the tailwind of the organization's leadership. The director will bring added value by relating the issues of sustainability to the workers, from the technical to the personal.

The appointee must be a senior manager or at least report directly to one. He or she must be well versed in a variety of disciplines, including business processes and business terms. He or she should be familiar with the organization, possess managerial experience, strategic vision, and understanding, and have a keen awareness of the sector's challenges. He or she must be able to lead processes, make decisions, ask questions, exhibit transparency, manage a team – and work as part of a team. Furthermore, he or she must bring a deep understanding of social issues and an openness to and awareness of the principles of diversity. This should be coupled with insight into various perspectives of corporate responsibility such as community involvement, ethics, sustainability, the work environment, and corporate governance.

It is important to place this position at a point where connections are easily made, where the scope of influence is significant, and where risks can be clearly identified. The officer's duties will include **establishing administrative infrastructures** up, down, and across the organization, among them a cultural infrastructure (a suitable organizational cultural climate), organizational visibility, knowledge and professional authority, partners and organizational alliances, a network of resources, and a regulatory and procedural infrastructure.

The officer will also **lead and manage** various processes, such as the company's investments in the community and the promotion of its societal presence. Other processes include supporting the integration of the ethical code and sustainability reporting (including the creation of quantifiable indices), and the communication of corporate responsibility both within the organization and externally.

Another task will be the creation of **inter- and intra-organizational partnerships**. This involves recognizing opportunities and initiating and supporting processes with the various organizational units. This might include developing opportunities for products or services with a social value, or working with human resources on employment diversity, work–life balance, or sexual harassment prevention. The role also involves establishing a discourse within the organization about ethical norms and ethical conduct, and promoting the right organizational culture at all levels of the organization (from establishing an ethical code to daily organizational conduct).

North Star Alliance

Society   Health

An example of a social venture cultivated within an existing organization is the North Star Alliance, established as a means to address the spread of HIV/AIDS among Africa's truck driver population. The project was initiated by the TNT global express shipping company, in cooperation with the United Nations World Food Program (WFP), with the aim of educating and protecting its thousands of truck drivers who have been hit particularly hard by the AIDS epidemic, creating a driver shortage across Africa.

Finally, the corporate responsibility officer will be entrusted with matters of sustainability and promote relevant initiatives in the professional units while integrating environmental considerations into organizational decision-making.

Notes

1 Dan Schawbel, "Unilever's Paul Polman: Why today's leaders need to commit to a purpose." *Forbes*, November 21, 2017. https://www.forbes.

com/sites/danschawbel/2017/11/21/paul-polman-why-todays-leaders-need-to-commit-to-a-purpose/#47d40ba61276.
2 *Grant Thornton*, "Boards of the future: Steering organisations to thrive. Grant Thornton corporate governance report 2016." https://www.grantthornton.global/globalassets/1.-member-firms/global/insights/article-pdfs/2016/grant-thornton-governance-report-2016-lr.pdf.
3 Cristina Maza, "Is economic opportunity a catalyst for peace at Israeli company SodaStream – or PR for Israel – or both?" *Newsweek*, June 25, 2019. https://www.newsweek.com/2019/07/05/economic-opportunity-catalyst-peace-israeli-company-sodastream-pr-israel-both-1445859.html.
4 Rachel Arthur, "PepsiCola completes SodaStream acquisition." *Beverage Daily*. https://www.beveragedaily.com/Article/2018/12/05/PepsiCo-completes-SodaStream-acquisition.

10 What does it involve?

Based on my many years of experience consulting for leading corporations, I can confidently say that, no matter its size, the industry in which it operates, or the starting point of the process, any organization can undertake a process of organizational responsibility. The real change, from which everything stems, is in the perception and attitude of the individuals who make up the organization: managers and employees. The functional change is nothing more complicated than a clear chain of organizational norms, decisions, and relatively simple practices. If the organization's leadership means for it to happen, it will.

Simon Zadek, a pioneer in the study of corporate responsibility and one of its leading scholars, defines the evolution of corporate responsibility in five developmental stages, forming a learning process.[1] This chain of events is likely to be observable in your organization, although some stages may be more prominent than others.

The first stage is **defensive**. Certain parties within the organization deny the company's responsibilities and mount some opposition to the new practices. Second comes the **compliance** stage, where the organization, for want of options, adopts a policy of compliance, simply aiming to do what is required. This is not an easy point to get to, but once completed, the hard part is already behind you.

The third stage of this evolutionary process occurs at the **managerial** level. The organization is now ready to accept the required changes and embed corporate responsibility in its management processes. But this is only in preparation for the fourth stage – **strategic** – where corporate responsibility is integrated into the organization's core business strategies. The road now leads to the fifth stage – **civil** – as the organization promotes broad sector or industry participation in corporate responsibility.

Giles Gibbons, my friend and CEO of Good Business, describes a slightly different evolutionary process.[2] He believes the starting point is corporate philanthropy, followed by social responsibility, from which point the organization can reach corporate responsibility. The last stage is value-led business.

Certainly, no organizational change is ever straightforward, and initiatives in pursuit of it will inevitably be met by opposition and delay tactics from those who are unwilling to leave their comfort zone or who simply fear failure. This is why change must come from the top, with management setting a personal example through their actions and public commitments.

A study by the management consulting firm Bain[3] concluded that only 2% of corporate sustainability programs achieved their goals. As a response, Jenny Davis-Peccoud, who leads Bain's sustainability and corporate responsibility practice, formulated a series of steps companies can take to improve their chances of success. They are: clear and public corporate commitment; personal involvement by management; introducing small and quick changes in order to create trust in the process; and, finally, integrating sustainability targets into the business plan and through the core organizational objectives.

How to integrate the organizational vision?

The organizational vision is the moral compass that is essential to any large entity. It describes nothing less than the purpose of the organization and its values. Therefore, as corporate responsibility is part of the corporate strategy, it must be synchronized with or incorporated into the organizational vision. Real and mature corporate responsibility is integrated into the organization's core business (Zadek's fourth stage).

The roadmap to corporate responsibility

On a practical level, five key steps are involved in the successful navigation of the path to corporate responsibility.

1 *Decision-making*. It must begin with a conscious and proactive decision at the highest echelon of the company. This will initiate the chain of events detailed in the following.
2 *Gap analysis*. Appoint a team or committee to define the goals of corporate responsibility in the organization, make a comparison with existing organizational practices – and identify the gap. This gap analysis will be conducted with reference to an external local or international index (such as GRI, Integrated Report, ISO 26000, Bloomberg, ESG, or a relevant sector index), benchmarked against competitors, measured against stakeholders' expectations, or against any other agreed-upon index.
3 *Corporate responsibility strategy*. Based on the gap analysis results and in concert with management and other relevant partners, objectives are set for the medium and long term (two to five years). Focus and priorities are defined within the corporate responsibility realm with reference to company values, capabilities, and needs.
4 *Work plan*. Implement a work plan, along with a recommendation to consult with the company's stakeholders. This should be done while defining work processes and areas of responsibility, such as staffing, training, and so on. As part of the work plan, an internal and external communication

plan should be designed and tasks, objectives, and indices defined.
5. *Assessment, evaluation, accountability, validation, and reporting.* These are critical to an organization's corporate responsibility ambitions. It is essential that a company regularly monitors its activity against its objectives.

Recreational Equipment Inc.

Community   Employees   Environment   Supply chain

Recreational Equipment Inc. (REI) is an American outdoor recreation company organized as a co-op. REI is committed to providing product sustainability, fostering an ethical community, and maintaining accessible outdoor lands. As a company, it gives over 70% of its profits to the outdoor community and invests around $8.8 billion in more than 400 nonprofit groups who fight to conserve public lands. As an employer, it has been voted as one of *Fortune* magazine's "100 Best Companies to Work For" for 20 years now, it promotes equality and diversity in hiring, and employees are given two paid days off to spend outdoors. The physical stores, headquarters, and distribution centers are "green" buildings, which use 100% renewable energy and have LEED-certified features. There are also plans to track, report, and reduce greenhouse gas emissions: REI has a goal to be climate-neutral by 2020.

The most notable aspect of the company is its commitment to minimizing each of its product's environmental footprints. It seeks out certifications such as Fair Trade, organically grown, and recycled materials. REI also works with certification groups, such as the Leather Working Group and the Responsible Wool Standard, to promote

> animal welfare in production, the Forest Stewardship Council to promote sustainable forestry, and BLUESIGN for certified chemical and textile safety. REI is pushing for its brands to fit within these certification principles, with the goal of all of its brands obeying all of the minimum brand standards by 2020. The belief is that if customers demand sustainability, business practices across the product industry will transform to meet the needs and desires of the consumer.

Setting timetables

How long should the process of embedding corporate responsibility take?

The answer is double: (1) CR is a journey and not a destination and (2) it depends – on the size of the organization, on the starting point of the process, and on management's commitment to it. It is a delicate process in which previous experience is a significant factor in its success and itself, in which case the process might take from three to five years. But it can easily take longer to transform the DNA of an entire organization.

We now have the benefit of some years' experience of this process, and the transition can be facilitated by the sizeable amount of expert knowledge that has been accumulated in the field. We now know the importance of the proper formulation of organizational processes involving numerous departments, and the importance of changing perceptions and attitudes.

The process in greater detail

The concepts discussed in this chapter represent merely a glimpse into the potential positive effects of corporate responsibility. In the next chapters we will examine additional benefits resulting from more specific actions in a step-by-step guide through eight key areas. Not all actions have an immediate effect on the interim bottom line – yet they can have a significant impact in the long term.

Notes

1 Simon Zadek, "The path to corporate responsibility." *Harvard Business Review*, December 2004. https://hbr.org/2004/12/the-path-to-corporate-responsibility.
2 Good Business workshop, Tel Aviv, 2010.
3 Jenny Davis-Peccoud, Paul Stone, and Clare Tovey, "Achieving breakthrough results in sustainability: CEOs who are passionate about change need to support the front line." *Bain & Company*, November 17, 2016. https://www.bain.com/insights/achieving-breakthrough-results-in-sustainability/.

Part 3
The good process
Step by step

There are two ways of starting the journey toward sustainability: top-down and bottom-up. But either way, in order to achieve sustainable organizational change, one has to aspire to a system-level approach, not a project-level one.

As discussed previously, the first stage is to get management commitment. Management also needs to understand the paradigm and the risks and opportunities involved: a company that sees this undertaking only at the level of technical implementation will never accrue the benefits that sustainability can offer, especially in the marketplace.

The second stage is to map a sustainability vision and working plan based on internal and external diagnostics and analysis. A governance plan should establish the main pillars. A sustainability officer must be appointed who will subsequently work with other officers such as HR, procurement, and marketing and will be backed by an inter-departmental working team to assist in the planning, execution, and evaluation of the roadmap for sustainability. The sustainability officer is usually essentially an integrator, with most of the organizational transformation to be executed by the departments themselves.

Naturally, as with all organizational change, not everyone in the organization will feel comfortable with the journey. One should not ignore such difficulties but rather manage the change wisely by enhancing communication and collaboration between departments.

11 Define your values

Capitalism is the system under which the world is now organized. It has become dominant to the extent that most people are unaware of alternatives. It has been largely responsible for the breathtaking advance of human civilization, particularly as regards its technology. Until very recently, especially in the optimistic years of the Western twentieth century, corporations went about their business largely unchallenged: they were generating wealth and enhancing society by delivering – a buzzword of the era – "progress." Maximization of shareholder wealth was the engine that drove them, and most of us were willing passengers.

However, a relentless pursuit of profit with no regard for the consequences is no longer given a free pass: opposition to "vulture" capitalism is now louder than ever and a force to be reckoned with. But unethical capitalism also carries with it the seeds of its own destruction: witness the demise of Enron and the financial and speculative bubbles of recent years. Unrestricted growth and profit-seeking will destroy – and is destroying – the very planetary resources on which the corporations and the society in which they operate depend. We have clearly moved on from Milton Friedman's doctrine of 1970 that "the social responsibility of business is to increase its profits": business can no longer operate in an ethical vacuum – it won't survive, for a start, and secondly, no one can any longer legitimately challenge the reality of human-made climate change or any of the other negative side effects of our industrial practices.

Corporations have now begun to realize that their policies must evolve – become more ethical, more conscious, more responsible. Indeed, in recent years we have seen a growing number of companies adopt and implement an organizational code of ethics. Ethics are the moral foundations on which corporate responsibility will be built in the next stages.

The journey toward corporate responsibility will usually begin by setting or updating the vision and the purpose organization. It will be followed by an ethical code that will transfer the high-level statements into more measurable behaviors and practices. In this chapter, we will have a closer look at that process.

It is no coincidence that the concept of corporate responsibility is closely linked to that same ethical code. After an era in which profit was often considered the highest – and often the only – measure of success, corporate responsibility is now introducing new benchmarks: helping businesses base their activities on fairness, trust, and ethics. Moreover, with data flowing rapidly in every direction, corporations can no longer conceal questionable business practices over time. Transparency has become essential not just for creating trust, but for business survival.

Thus, the first step in transitioning an organization to corporate responsibility is formulating an ethical code and composing a new set of organizational values.

What is an organizational code of ethics?

Business ethics consist of, according to Wikipedia, the practices that any individual or group exhibits within an organization that can negatively or positively affect the business's core values. It applies to all aspects of business conduct and is relevant to the conduct of individuals and entire organizations. A code of ethics is simply a formal and systematic document that presents and defines organizational values and norms. It describes the ethical business practices expected from the organization's employees. A code of ethics has several key benefits: reputation management, strengthening of corporate identity, risk and opportunity management, employee motivation, and learning and innovation. A code of ethics serves as an organization's support, reference, and ethical compass. When properly formulated and implemented, it can be a tool to support and reinforce an organization's overall strategy.

However, important as the code is, it should always be remembered that it is ultimately only a managerial tool.

Formulating a code of ethics

Without a doubt, the greatest challenge is to address the gap between, on the one hand, universal norms and values and, on the other, the organization's business and cultural environment. A code that fails to include aspects unique to the sector, and to the organization itself, will be too vague and academic. The code must reflect the uniqueness of the organization and express its needs and particular nuances. Such a code will be perceived as more concrete and reliable, and thus more easily implemented.

A successful code of ethics, in my opinion, will include more "do's" than "don'ts." In other words, it will more usefully direct organizational behavior toward the standards of proper conduct rather than discourage inappropriate conduct. As this field develops, greater expertise is called for, and an understanding that the statements contained within are much more than mere slogans.

A code of ethics can follow one of three basic structures. No single one has an advantage over the others, and each organization can choose the structure that best suits its needs. We shall review them in brief.

1 Organized by stakeholder

This type of structure divides a code of ethics according to the organization's various stakeholders: employees, customers, suppliers, regulators, the environment, and so on.

This code is organized into sections relating to various stakeholders, offering a profound consideration of their true role in the organization. For instance, with regard to customers, one can find a commitment to personal discretion and flexibility, as well as a recommendation for frequent training programs to promote high standards of service. This will later be transformed into measurable steps as a working plan.

2 Organized by values

In the El Al Airlines' code of ethics that we structured for them, for example, each section refers to one of the carrier's values: "Leadership," "Fairness and transparency," "Excellence and creativity," "Professionalism," and so on.

3 Organized by organizational function

Today, organizations are increasingly formulating a code of ethics for each department – marketing, sales, production, logistics, human resources, and so on – based on the organization's structure. This level of specificity means the resolution of a greater number of ethical dilemmas and greater relevance to everyday issues.

Writing the code

The first consideration is the time and budget available for the process. These must be defined before work begins.

Formulation and writing can take the form of either a closed or open process. In a closed process, the code writing is assigned to a specific group of employees within the organization. An external consultant is often hired to assist. An open process involves both internal stakeholders (employees and managers) and external stakeholders (customers, suppliers, etc.). Methods used are one-on-one interviews, focus groups, and workshops involving several employees at a time. An external consultant can be useful in reassuring interviewees of the confidentiality of the interviews and can also provide an objective voice if conflicts arise.

The first process benefits from simplicity and speed. The second offers greater accuracy and authenticity, along with the opportunity to share and engage – something that can kickstart the implementation of the code. At Good Vision, we identify three stages for either model.

1 Diagnosis and analysis

A code of ethics cannot be "off the peg": it must reflect the organizational culture and objectives. The first stage, therefore, is to read, analyze, and draw relevant conclusions from various sources. Start with the organization's own internal material (organizational vision, business strategy plan, brand values) and then broaden to include external resources, such as codes of ethics of similar companies along with relevant standards and indices (e.g. the GRI[1] and Global Compact[2] standards, or various sectoral indices).

2 Interviews

Taking this out of the boardroom is crucial: boardroom reality does not always reflect that of suppliers or customers, for example. As such, the second stage consists of interviews with a variety of stakeholders: customers, suppliers, partners, regulators, civil representatives, and so on. These interviews can help the organization gain valuable insight into its conduct and properly adjust its values to meet its aspired targets. Moreover, a code of ethics formulated in cooperation with the company's stakeholders has enhanced validity both at a functional level and at a public relations level.

> **Formulating a code of ethics: sample stakeholder interview questions**
>
> Ethics
>
> 1 What is your role and function in the organization?
> 2 What are your expectations from the organization in its dealings with you?
> 3 What do you recommend that the organization continues to uphold?
> 4 What do you recommend that the organization strives to improve?
> 5 Have you encountered ethical or other dilemmas in your relationship with the organization?
> 6 What does the organization mean to you?
> 7 How does the organization compare to others in the same industry?

In this stage, ethical dilemmas should be explored – in other words, those complex situations where two or more values are at odds. Examples are: assisting a colleague versus adhering to company regulations, and professionalism versus profitability. Gathering examples of such dilemmas during the code-writing stage will help in understanding the complex ethical realities facing the organization's employees during the implementation stage.

3 Formulating and writing

Having completed the research stages, conduct a calculated synthesis of the values, conclusions, vision, and reality as they emerged. A code of ethics should encompass the following four elements:

1 General clauses regarding the implementation of the code. For example:

- Purpose and applicability of the code.
- A comment/complaints box in case of an ethical violation or ethical dilemma.
- Who is the organization's ethics officer?

2. Self-analysis tests for determining ethical behavior. For example:

   - The mirror test: how will you feel about this behavior when you look in the mirror? The morning-after test: how will you feel about this behavior tomorrow morning? The front-page test: how would you like to see this behavior on the front page of your local newspaper?
   - Code violation consequences: what happens when an ethical code is broken?

3. Regulatory and administrative clauses. For example:

   - Employees may not offer or accept gifts.
   - Employees may not misuse their position in the company in order to receive personal or financial gain.
   - All employees are responsible for the protection and preservation of company assets.
   - Employees must maintain company loyalty.
   - Employees must uphold health and safety regulations.
   - A commitment to preventing bribery and corruption.
   - Procedures for avoiding conflicts of interest.

4. Founding values and expected behavioral norms.

The fourth and last point is the essence of the code and its most significant section. These values can be identified collectively at the beginning, during the course of the code, and/or integrated throughout its various sections. At least one value from each of the following value sets should be expressed:

- Universal moral values such as integrity, honesty, and transparency.
- Business values such as professionalism, responsiveness, leadership, and innovation.

- Interpersonal values such as dignity and well-being, empathy, and cooperation. This should also include principles regarding sexual harassment and workplace bullying (see Chapter 13).

Gaumnitz and Lere[3] analyzed corporate codes of ethics in various organizations in the U.S. and identified the following ethical themes:

- Honesty and integrity.
- Confidentiality and trust.
- Obligations to the profession.
- Obligation not to aid unethical behavior.
- Compliance with laws and regulations.
- Preventing discrimination and promoting equality.
- Social and environmental responsibility.

Now add some special ingredients

Supplementary chapters can be added to enhance the code and differentiate it from those of other companies. Here, creativity is not only possible but recommended. The following are various examples of "extras" that we at Good Vision helped our clients to incorporate:

- Real-life cases to demonstrate ethical conduct and give the code added relevance.
- Quotes from employees.
- A short glossary of potentially unfamiliar concepts, such as "stakeholders," "corporate responsibility," and "sustainable development."
- Management commitment. Some companies choose to place special emphasis on the importance of management's commitment to the codes of ethics in general, and the value of personal example in particular. Adding a chapter of this nature has its advantages and drawbacks, and should be considered based on the organizational culture of each company.

A customized code of ethics?

As per the third type of code structure outlined earlier, it is worth considering formulating a unique code of ethics tailored to the specific needs of selected units in the organization. This might be for a company division, its subsidiaries, or departments such as finance or procurement where ethical dilemmas may be different and risk may be high. It could even be – as the Israel Electric Corporation asked us to do – for its board of directors. This particular code was intended to "encourage a culture of integrity and responsibility, help directors understand and resolve ethical issues and provide means for reporting inappropriate conduct." Among other things, the code referred to professionalism in the workplace, conflicts of interest and incorruptibility, and appropriate use of data and assets.

How do you word a code of ethics?

At Good Vision, we believe that a code of ethics should be simply and clearly worded in a way that motivates and inspires. We recommend using the first-person plural ("we") in order to engage employees – while avoiding intimidating statements such as "All company employees are obliged to . . ." Remember: you want your employees to identify with the code, and to cherish it.

Write the code in either the present ("Company employees maintain data confidentiality . . .") or future tense ("Company employees shall maintain data confidentiality . . ."). The advantage of the present tense is that it implies currency and accuracy, whereas the future tense has the effect of bridging gaps between practice and goals, positioning the code as a guiding compass.

Code approval and launch

Since a code of ethics is a formal document binding all company entities, it is recommended that it be approved prior to launch by the CEO, management, and the board of directors. The

Sarbanes–Oxley Act ("SOX") in the United States requires that such documents also be approved by the CFO.

Following approval comes the launch. This stage serves as an introduction to the code and its contents for those employees who have not yet been part of the process. This is a significant corporate event, and should be treated as such. The code should not just be emailed to all employees or left on their desks, as is sometimes the case in intra-organizational campaigns. The CEO needs to communicate the importance of – and top management's commitment to – an ethical program in the organization before the launch event.

It is perfectly acceptable to take advantage of an existing company event as a launch platform – as long as it has the necessary gravitas. Alternatively, departmental managers could distribute the code to their teams accompanied by a presentation highlighting the values and norms enshrined within it. Many companies more recently have created a smartphone app to deliver a version of the code.

It is always recommended, in the name of transparency, to share the code of ethics on the company's website and/or outline it in the company's financial reports.

Walk the talk

Implementation is undoubtedly the most significant and challenging phase of the corporate ethics process. In many cases, an ethical code becomes merely a poster on the wall with no meaningful impact on the organizational culture, whereas the key aim is the integration of the ethical code into all company decisions, procedures, and actions. Time and effort must be devoted to the implementation phase, following as it usually does a peak period of interest during the writing and launch stages. This involves the following recommended steps:

- Build employee awareness of and familiarity with the code of ethics – its contents, its objectives, and its uses.
- Develop tools to help company employees and management resolve ethical dilemmas.

- Make sure all employees have access to the code through various intra-organizational channels.
- Acquire commitment by management to ethical workshops and training on promotion of everyday ethical work behavior.
- Monitor how the values of the code are being integrated throughout the organization, especially with regard to main working processes such as procurement, finance, and recruiting.

The Good Vision implementation model consists of five main axes. Let's review each of them briefly

1 Training and workshops axis

This axis is where knowledge and skills are imparted to address ethics and the ethical code. This is done through courses, workshops, and online training for managers and employees (with an emphasis on new employees), and is brought into focus in various professional forums. This stage is about reinforcing the values using interactive exercises and simulations that make them relatable to daily operations.

We developed such a program at Migdal Insurance Company, then an affiliate of the Italian insurance company Assicurazioni Generali. The program was entitled Dilemma Café, and we began by defining its objectives:

- Effectiveness. A brief and focused activity with defined and quantifiable goals.
- Identifying ethical risks. Employees and managers raise various ethical issues and dilemmas, determine where risks lie, and either eliminate the source or mitigate the risk while updating the ethical code as needed.
- Empowering managers. Management addresses professional and executive issues and discusses aspects of ethical employee conduct in an unmediated manner.
- A positive experience. A meaningful process creating an organizational "buzz" based on the code of ethics principles. A pleasant, stress-free atmosphere that allows an open

discussion of problems and issues and encourages employees to report and consult.

The Dilemma Café method promotes an open dialogue regarding ethical issues and dilemmas in a pleasant atmosphere that encourages communication and listening. The participants gather in groups of eight to ten and discuss a scenario-based ethical dilemma chosen from a "menu" of dilemmas. They examine the dilemma and the various alternatives for its resolution, considering the ethical implications of each alternative.

During the planning stage more than 100 ethical dilemmas common to everyday organizational activity were identified, and dozens of additional dilemmas were raised during the process. More recently, with Liat Cohen we developed an ethical "escape room," which met with success.

2 Ethical institutions axis

On this axis, ethical institutions within the organization are shaped and established. These can include a dedicated ethics officer, an ethics committee, and an ethics hotline or other anonymized methods for reporting unethical conduct. In fact, an array of communication channels for queries/complaints regarding ethical dilemmas or suspected ethical violations is a powerful way of anchoring ethical standards within the organization. Such channels could take the form of telephone, company website, email, ombudsman, and so on. The key to the success of this axis is ensuring the safety of those who come forward, either by guaranteeing anonymity or by providing protection. Organizations sometimes outsource hotline or email operation to a third party in order to emphasize the objectivity and anonymity of these channels.

3 Intra-organizational communication axis

This is where the company uses its portal, email, phone app, or other means to communicate aspects of the ethics program and dilemmas that arise.

4 Workflow axis

This is the most challenging axis. On this axis, examined for ethical risk are workflow processes such as procurement and supplier relations, customers and regulators, recruitment processes (employment and promotion), decision-making processes, and evaluation and mentoring processes. The challenge these days is to integrate the desired values into technological management systems and software, such as SAP ERP, etc. The aim with such processes is to forestall ethical dilemmas before they arise.

5 Control and measurement axis

On this axis, the process is evaluated and measured by use of periodic "pulse" surveys and other means, keeping in mind the timeless axiom of management consulting expert Peter Drucker, "What gets measured gets managed." It is recommended to measure the ethical culture and perceptions in the organization before, during the process, and at a given time after its implementation to acquire constructive feedback, both for organizational needs and in order to validate the process itself. There are several methods for assessing organizational ethical culture:

- Opinion surveys based on existing organizational systems.
- In-depth interviews with stakeholders.
- Review of the complaints and queries submitted to the ethics officer, the anonymous hotline, or the ethics committee.

A continuous process of renewal

Once every few years the code of ethics must be refreshed in a continuous process of honing and validation. Feedback from the field or significant organizational changes such as a merger or new management can serve as an opportunity for an update. Another possible reason for reviewing a code is change within the industry or in the relevant ecosystem, such as the rise in significance of social networking: perhaps the code was written without reference to the important issue of behavior on social networks such as Facebook or Instagram.

Updating the code can be either a short and subtle process or a collaborative, in-depth one, as deemed necessary. It is recommended that any updating process includes the following steps:

- A review of the dilemmas and challenges facing the company and sector.
- An appointment of a diverse steering committee.
- A review of code-related feedback received from internal and external stakeholders.

Notes

1 https://www.globalreporting.org/standards.
2 https://www.unglobalcompact.org/.
3 https://link.springer.com/article/10.1023/B:BUSI.0000021053.73525.23.

12 Start a dialogue

The notion that a company exists solely to serve its shareholders is a relic of the past. Like any other organization, a modern corporation serves the interests and expectations of all its various stakeholders.

Cooperation with various stakeholders is nothing new. But a real and ongoing dialogue with stakeholders is essential in embracing corporate responsibility. As you do so, you will understand the material issues the company is facing, you will understand the needs and expectations of your stakeholders, and you will expand the relationship with your stakeholders beyond minimum requirements and short-term commitment. There is now a 360° perspective of responsibility and attention toward stakeholders – as a leading and structured principle. This is a symbolic, ethics-oriented approach, yet it is also practical and feasible, especially today with such technological platforms as Insights available (see the Insights Box). This 360° perspective improves a company's perceptions and insights: often, significant issues are overlooked simply because no one thought to ask the right people – most stakeholders have not yet been invited to sit around the corporate conference table.

Insights

Technology   Dialogue

An innovative platform for stakeholder dialogue was developed by the software company Insights, headed by my friend

Dr. Gal Alon. Insights' web-based platform uses technology to tap the wisdom of crowds and enable companies to perform inclusive decision-making by consulting with different target audiences. It thereby helps organizations get quality advice from their stakeholders, leveraging AI to collect, analyze, and respond to feedback, cutting the enormous amount of time spent on interviews and meetings. It is tailored to the needs of product managers, marketing professionals, city managers, and government executives. It claims it can minimize preventable mistakes by organizations by up to 82%.

There is so much to gain

Attention and dialogue are central tools in risk and reputation management. And inclusive dialogues with stakeholders bring different sectoral elements together as well, around day-to-day operations, perspectives, needs, goals, work practices, bureaucratic procedures, hierarchical structure, budget concerns, and so on. A multi-sectoral discourse is not usually a daily practice, however, and often it's entirely avoided, deliberately. However, the potential benefits for all participants should not be ignored. Such collaboration improves coordination, bringing in new ideas and innovation as well as improving agility in updating, while eliminating redundant practices and communication barriers – which commonly slow things down and lead to mistrust and lost revenue.

Enlight Renewable Energy

Stakeholder   Dialogue

Enlight Renewable Energy is an international company, founded in 2008. The company specializes in the initiation, development, financing, construction, management, and operation of solar and wind energy projects both locally and globally. Enlight has successfully executed over 150 projects in in Europe and the Middle east at a capacity exceeding 500 MW encompassing a total construction cost of over US$1 billion.

> Stakeholder dialogue is the main pillar of the company's management approach. The dialogue allows Enlight to reach win-win solutions and assimilate its projects into the environment and the community rather than to impose their projects upon them. The company has numerous examples of taking costly, beyond compliance actions to find the common ground with the stakeholders, following their needs and company's values.
>
> As one of the examples, Enlight received a lot of concerns from green NGOs, government bodies and communities regarding preserving rare Griffon vultures that are habitants of the Golan Heights, where the company is building a wind farm. The company entered a long and deep dialogue and reached an unprecedented agreement with the Israeli Nature reserves Authority. As an outcome of this dialogue Enlight installed major protection system, including two radars, that can spot the vulture on a 6km distance and hired birdwatchers that confirm the direction of birds and give a sign to stop the wind turbines. This project causes tens stops a year, but brought outstanding cooperation with the local government and communities, created additional jobs and prevented death of the endangered vultures.

A growing number of corporations worldwide are initiating inclusive dialogues with customers, social and environmental representatives, employees, suppliers, competing organizations, governments, and the civic sector. Initiation of dialogue is a sign of strength and communicates a genuine desire to acquire and share knowledge. An open dialogue with stakeholders is evidence of a belief in the notion that the whole is greater than the sum of its parts. Cooperation can lead to resource efficiency and to solutions that no individual sector could have arrived at alone. It fosters stability and growth, and furthermore strengthens the image and reputation of all who participate.

Tools for successful dialogue

This real, ongoing dialogue with stakeholders is a key element in corporate responsibility implementation and should be applied as a management tool in the organization. It is an ethical and managerial tool that supports decision-making, the development of innovative products and services, and the adoption of strategy.

A stakeholder dialogue begins with a discussion, sharing of opinions, and a mutual learning process identifying each other's needs on a particular subject. The shared objective is to make use of combined strength and leverage the comparative advantages of each sector in finding solutions and addressing common challenges. This two-way dialogue needs to take place using controlled mechanisms and should be performed in a responsible and structured way.

Roche Pharmaceuticals: "The Trusted Scarf"

Community Health Dialogue

Good Vision and Roche Pharmaceuticals Israel, headed by Avi Danziger, initiated a dialogue with stakeholders in the pharmaceutical industry. Government officials, social and business representatives, nonprofit organizations, academics, and media personnel were all invited to attend. The dialogue led to an open and challenging discussion about expectations of the company in particular, and of the pharmaceutical industry in general, with regard to social and environmental responsibility. This dialogue was later led by crowd wisdom expert Dr. Lior Zoref, under whom a familiar problem was brought to light: medicine often disregards the patient experience. A program was developed for the distribution of scarves for women undergoing cancer treatment – a simple and effective solution for protecting modesty and privacy as well as keeping patients warm in cold treatment rooms, which was conceived solely as the result of this dialogue process.

We have witnessed dialogues that were not conducted properly, attracting criticism for being no more than a "fig leaf" – i.e. initiated for the sake of appearances only. To avoid this, there are several important principles:

- Comprehensive identification and analysis of all organizational stakeholders – through a systematic process of identifying and mapping.
- Identifying stakeholders' expectations and understanding the key issues concerning them. An organization initiating a dialogue must examine any issue that arises and not impose its own agenda.
- Establishing response mechanisms. The organization must accept that it will be required to deal with issues raised by the various stakeholders, or at least examine ways to address these issues and report back on measures that have been taken.

Apply the AA1000 Standard

The AA1000 Stakeholder Engagement Standard (SES)[1] is a generally applicable, open-source framework for designing, implementing, assessing, communicating, and confirming the quality of stakeholder dialogue. We had the privilege of participating in the global proceedings that helped formulate and ratify the standard, mainly through dialogues with business, social, and academic organizations.

The AA1000SES can be implemented in a variety of dialogues, including functional dialogues (such as customer service), dialogues on specific issues (such as human rights), and organization-wide dialogues (such as reporting and approval policies). The standard is based on three principles:

- Materiality. This principle requires familiarity with stakeholders' and the organization's material concerns.
- Completeness. This principle requires an understanding of stakeholder concerns: that is, views, needs, and performance expectations as well as perceptions and beliefs associated with their material issues.

- Responsiveness. This principle requires consistent responsiveness and accountability to stakeholders and the organization's material concerns.

The standard is part of the AA1000 series of consulting and sustainability standards firm AccountAbility and is consistent with its Assurance Standard published in 2003. AccountAbility is a nonprofit international network established in 1995 to promote accountability that advances sustainable development. The network works with businesses, governments, and civil institutions in order to promote responsible business activity and to establish cooperation between the public and public institutions. As a leading international professional institute, AccountAbility provides effective assurance and accountability management tools through its set of standards. For over two decades, large and small organizations have applied AccountAbility's standards to identify, prioritize, and respond to sustainability challenges to improve their overall long-term performance. The latest edition of the SES, to which we were proud to contribute, was published in 2018 and has been adapted to meet the new challenges facing organizations.

Note

1 https://www.accountability.org/standards/.

13 Look after your people

Your responsibility to your employees

Many companies invest considerable effort in projecting an image of corporate responsibility externally, yet they overlook the importance of establishing these values within their organization. It is too early at the time of writing to report on the fallout experienced by companies who chose to abandon their employees at the first hurdle during the COVID-19 pandemic, but we can confidently predict that their reputations will have been dealt a damaging blow. Billionaire owners requiring their workers to take weeks of unpaid leave made for an immediate and emotive narrative which was shared round the world in minutes. In contrast, those companies that chose to "do the right thing" caught the mood of the prevailing times and will reap the benefits.

In her book *Just Good Business*, Kellie McElhaney outlines the two dimensions of corporate responsibility: internal and external.[1] External operations include supply chain management, environment, human rights, community involvement and investment, transparency, reporting, information privacy, and, of course, stakeholder engagement. Internal operations include corporate governance, values, ethics, diversity, employee privacy, work–life balance, personal and professional development, health and safety, and, finally, downsizing and layoffs. A company's goal, according to McElhaney, should be to turn its employees into ambassadors for their brand and for corporate responsibility. This occurs through a three-step process:

1 Integration of corporate responsibility into existing training programs (management courses, new employee orientations, professional development courses, etc.).
2 Including elements of corporate responsibility in employee performance appraisals.
3 Synchronization of intra-organizational messages with external marketing campaigns.

In communicating your corporate responsibility process to your employees, review the steps taken and explain their significance, celebrate achievements, and demonstrate how corporate responsibility contributes to organizational and financial performance.

Happy employees

The benefits of a positive, committed workforce cannot be underestimated. Employees who arrive at their workplace in the morning (or sign in remotely) knowing that they are pursuing environment goals or helping the community are happier employees and can more easily identify with organizational goals. Basically, people like to feel that they are making a positive difference and that they are working for an organization that does good. This is one of the main reasons for working at nonprofit organizations (NPOs) when the wages are lower than those from a profit-based organization.

A company showing that it is driven by considerations beyond pure economic gain communicates an important message of morality and ethics to its employees. There is also a direct link between environmental stewardship and employee health and safety. An organization with a high commitment to corporate responsibility is de facto one that strives to maintain the health and safety of its employees, along with more generally. Employees will recognize the organization's commitment to their well-being – and in return will show commitment to the organization.

Happy employees benefit the bottom line

Professor Dan Ariely, who was my high-school friend and classmate, is an international expert in behavioral economics. He has written several best-selling books examining how economic processes are influenced by human behavior. Having examined employee satisfaction in various U.S. companies, he built a virtual investment portfolio of the companies with the highest employee satisfaction rating, and examined the return against the S&P500. His virtual portfolio generated a 17% higher return, implying that employee motivation has a tremendous impact on a company's financial results.

Raising employee awareness of your corporate responsibility practices does more than boost work satisfaction. Employees are the best communicators about your brand, promoting the company by word of mouth and sharing their experiences from within the organization.

Zappos

Employees

A company that has recognized the significant economic value of employee satisfaction is Zappos. CEO Tony Hsieh said that the company hires for cultural fit. For example, one of Zappos's core values is to "create fun and a little weirdness."[2] Zappos managers ask potential employees, "On a scale of one to ten, how weird are you?" The number is not as important as how people react to it. Zappos looks for people who have fun, have passion and personality, and are

> committed to customer service. Committed to transparency, Zappos shares everything – the good and the bad – with employees, partners, and vendors. With the philosophy that genuine partners don't hide the truth from one another, Zappos goes the extra mile to demonstrate transparency. Daily briefings and call statistics are posted on a whiteboard for everyone – guests as well as employees – to see. Even its all-hands company meetings are publicly available. If you have three hours, you can be privy to everything discussed. It's all there.

Change the work environment for the better

The concept of corporate responsibility transforms an organization into a positive force in its environment, driven by ethics and having a positive impact on people's lives. Such a transformation must stem from within.

Employees are an organization's most precious and valuable resource, and it is important to treat them as such. Angry and disgruntled employees, spending long hours in an unconducive work environment, will not project positivity to the outside world. Moreover, we are now in an era in which the majority of the workforce consists of Generation X and Y employees, and the high-quality members of those generations can be retained only by companies offering an interesting and meaningful work environment alongside good working conditions.

We must take into account factors such as work–life balance, welfare and leisure activities, safety and job security, accessibility, diversity, lifelong learning, caregiver procedures and the opportunity to volunteer within the framework of the organization. All these factors contribute to employee satisfaction and an ability to identify with the organization, which consequently enhance productivity and organizational loyalty.

In her article "The 3 Things Employees Really Want,"[3] Lori Goler, Head of HR at Facebook, finds workers' priorities to be strikingly similar across all age groups and functions. Goler and her team identified three principal employee motivators: career, community, and cause.

- Career. Having a job that provides autonomy and promotes learning and development.
- Community. Feeling respected and recognized by others. Having a sense of connection and belonging.
- Cause. Having a purpose. Feeling that you make a meaningful impact, identifying with the organization's mission, and believing that it does some good in the world.

There is certainly no doubt that employees who are treated with respect and feel that their job serves a meaningful purpose will be more motivated, perform better, and contribute more to the company's success. Earlier in this chapter we mentioned Dan Ariely, who has drawn similar conclusions from experiments showing that financial rewards are not the key motivators for job performance.[4]

A responsible and ethical work environment is something that should encompass all stages of the employment cycle. Beginning at recruitment and placement, it continues through professional training, development, and advancement, all the way through to termination. Even this final stage can and should be handled in an ethical and responsible way, providing the relevant tools to those concluding their employment (preparing employees for retirement, for example), and assisting them in coping with their professional and personal future.

One of the clearest models for a proper and adequate work environment is the British Business in the Community (BITC) Wellbeing Workwell Model,[5] which is based on four levels:

1 Better health and well-being: prevention, promotion, and whole-person approach.
2 Better work: good work, job design, and psychological safety.

3 Better specialist support: early interventions, adjustments, and retaining staff.
4 Better management: skills, support, accountability.

Create workplace diversity

Employment diversity means equality and equal opportunities with regard to the employment, recruitment, and advancement of groups characterized by social isolation, difficulties in integration, or who are in a minority position of influence, power, and connections, or experience long periods of underemployment.

Challenges in achieving workplace diversity vary by country (and sometimes by region). For example, Europe is grappling with the challenge of absorbing refugees from the Middle East and Africa, and their employment is among the region's most pressing concerns. Lack of diversity is often the result of discrimination or lack of equal opportunities because of race, religion, gender, disability, or age.

Diversity in the workplace confers various benefits, not least a work environment with a potential for innovation and originality. Employees from diverse groups will have different approaches, enabling more creative problem-solving, collaborations, and an expansion of the target customer base and the business's overall potential – a culturally diverse work environment reflects a wider range of customers, enabling the development of new markets and products. With a variety of perspectives at hand, better decisions can be made. In addition, multiculturalism provides a basis for working in an international market and can serve as a bridge for business with new countries and new markets.

Previously, companies might have embraced workplace diversity purely as a social policy, but it has now become abundantly clear that it confers competitive advantage and is key to organizational growth. A 2018 McKinsey study, based on hundreds of organizations in the UK, the U.S., Latin America, and Canada,[6] examined the correlation between diversity (gender, ethnic, cultural) in the leadership of large companies and financial performance. The results showed a statistically significant link:

organizations with gender diversity on executive teams were 21% more likely to outperform the national industry median, while organizations with ethnic/cultural diversity on executive teams were 33% more likely to have industry-leading profitability. Conversely, companies with low workforce diversity were less likely to achieve above-average results. Despite evidence such as this, the progress of diversity has been slow. Companies remain uncertain as to how they can most effectively use inclusion and diversity to support their growth.

Becoming a more inclusive organization

Employees

In Grant Thornton Australia, there has been a strong emphasis on creating a more inclusive environment within the firm to reduce fear of discrimination or prejudice and to encourage diversity. In 2018, the PRISM network was launched to drive LGBTI+ awareness and develop initiatives for LGBTI+ people and their allies. Since inception, the network has gained more than 300 members across all offices, and in 2019, the firm was recognized as a Bronze Employer in the Australian Workplace Equality Index (AWEI).

In *Workplace Diversity*, Esty, Griffin, and Schorr write: "When we are not the same as the majority of other people in the workplace setting, we tend to notice our membership in the less numerous group."[7] Managers in general, and corporate responsibility and human resources managers in particular, would do well to heed this insight and allow themselves to see the organization through the eyes of a member of a minority, and thereby acquire some empathy for such members of their teams. But such an approach also has significant advantages for the organization itself. According to Esty, Griffin, and Schorr, these include:

- Increased productivity. Employees who feel included and respected cease to feel like outsiders and work more productively, showing greater loyalty to the organization.
- Fewer lawsuits based on discrimination.
- Image. In seeking partnerships with public institutions or other companies, an organization may well be required to demonstrate a clear commitment to workplace diversity.
- New markets. As discussed earlier in this section, a diverse team of employees can provide insights into marketing strategies to reach different market segments.
- Recruitment. The organization opens itself up to the largest possible pool of talent.
- Becoming an employer of choice. Workplace diversity will position the company as a good place for people to work, providing an advantage over those with a reputation for not supporting, for example, parents or women.
- Better morale. Employees whose workplace went from homogeneous to diverse reported a better and livelier ambience.
- Heightened creativity. Diverse teams foster creativity. Task forces are often diverse in nature, drawing their members from different levels and functions of the organization. This is why they are characterized by strong creativity, especially in providing solutions to long-standing problems.

Diversifying recruitment

A detailed job description should focus on the relevant requirements for the role but avoid ambiguous personal characteristics such as "dynamic nature" or "sense of humor," and of course anything discriminatory such as aspects of the candidate's appearance. Ensure that the requested skills are genuinely essential to the job. The position should be advertised to as many target populations as possible and through a variety of platforms in order to reach the widest possible range of candidates. If using a recruitment agency or headhunter, ensure they adhere to these principles.

Job interviews and screenings should be conducted by more than one person. The questions and tasks should be consistent across candidates, and there should be multicultural, nondiscriminatory screening exams, in the interviewee's first language whenever possible. Avoid questions that might be construed as discriminatory. At the screening stage, at least two interviewers should be present. And at least two people should be involved in making the selection, which should be made based on qualifications for the job, ignoring assumptions about the candidate. The candidate should be informed of the decision as soon as possible.

Disabilities

How does an organization with a sense of organizational responsibility view people with physical, sensory, or intellectual disabilities? Even taking into account that nowadays technology has helped people overcome many disabilities, in general, the percentage of people with disabilities that are integrated in the workforce is low. Most from these groups who are employed lack professional skills and training, and they often find themselves at jobs that do not require specialization, limiting their opportunities for professional or financial advancement. But, of course, those who are educated and possess a high capacity for learning will become demotivated in jobs unsuited to their skills. Unemployment rates among the mentally disabled are in the 75–90% range in the U.S. and 61–73% in the UK. Studies indicate many in this population want to become a viable part of the workforce. Yet social stigma and the absence of proper training programs deprive them of their basic right to employment.

In the early 1980s, supported employment models began to emerge in the U.S. These programs include placement and training for people with disabilities in local jobs that are not necessarily designated for a special-needs population. The objective was to ensure that disabled individuals can acquire the emotional, social, and intellectual skills necessary to independently live, learn, and work in a community. A socially responsible organization should adopt such a model.

Employing people with disabilities is an ethical, financial, and strategic step that provides a business with a competitive advantage through enhancing diversity and boosting employee satisfaction and motivation. This population is a source of dedicated and loyal employees whose disability should not pose a barrier to their integration in the workforce.

Invest in accessibility

If an organization is to employ people with disabilities, it must be equipped to receive them: in other words, an accessible work environment for all employees.

Outsourced workers

One of the challenges of corporate responsibility is extending the scope of ethical and responsible conduct up and down the supply chain (see Chapter 14). This applies also to outsourcing as well as to temp agencies, which tend to exploit the weaker job-seeking population. It is easy to turn a blind eye to the conditions of workers who are outsourced via agencies or subcontractors, but burying one's head in the sand will not make the problem disappear. The public gaze will always fall on the large, branded organization, not its subcontractors. An organization that exploits its workers – however far down the chain – will ultimately taint its brand.

Gender

Despite the fact that we are well into the twenty-first century, women almost everywhere are still experiencing gender discrimination. Even the strongest women in the most advanced companies are facing a struggle to balance a career with family commitments, as Sheryl Sandberg, VP of Facebook, shares in her book *Lean In*.[8]

Professions that have been traditionally majority female command lower wages; professions that are not obviously gendered generally pay women less than men. Gender discrimination is deeply embedded into societal norms, such as ideas that women are unsuited to leadership roles. It manifests in lack of social connections and intra-organizational barriers such as wage inequality and lack of work flexibility to account for family roles. Even today, at the beginning of the third decade of the twenty-first century, it is rare to see women in senior management roles – even in highly tech-based companies or sophisticated venture capitals.[9]

An organization striving for social responsibility cannot allow these norms to persist.

Sexual harassment

A socially responsible organization will have responsive and effective policies for dealing with bullying and other forms of abuse. For the purposes of this chapter we will focus on one aspect, sexual harassment, which is a topical and controversial subject and, sadly, the most ingrained form of workplace misconduct. It should be borne in mind that the strategies and practices to address sexual harassment are largely transferable to other kinds of workplace abuse.

Sexual harassment was treated as an unpleasant but marginal issue until very recently, being catapulted into the foreground thanks to the #MeToo campaign which swept the world in early 2018. The high-profile case of Harvey Weinstein is the most prominent but certainly not the only example. It is only right that this issue receives the attention it deserves. Preventing sexual harassment is an imperative for any organization, reflecting an organization's commitment to protecting an individual's dignity and freedom while adhering to the law and ensuring the personal safety of its employees. Moreover, the prevention of sexual harassment is important from an organizational-managerial perspective; prevention training should not be seen as a burden. Sexual harassment prevention creates an effective work environment free of distractions, contributing to a more focused and goal-oriented organization. When management is dedicated to establishing a pleasant work environment for *all* its employees, it communicates an important message: the aspiration to be a moral and ethical organization.

A responsible organization must take reasonable measures to prevent sexual harassment or provocation within the workplace. However, this is not a simple task. It begins with finding a working definition of sexual harassment. Every country has its own legal definition, and every organization must act in accordance with the law, but there are some fundamental principles. Sexual harassment is one-sided, violates one's dignity, triggers feelings of helplessness, is power-based, may include negative touching, is unwanted, invasive, and demeaning, and invokes negative self-esteem. Furthermore, it creates a hostile or offensive environment in the workplace. Sex-based harassment relates to the sex of the target but isn't necessarily sexual in nature.

Difficulties in implementing policies often come from a genuine lack of understanding about changing norms. Another reason is the gray area – between workplace friendships or romances and sexual harassment – that employees often claim to be confused by (sometimes genuinely and sometimes disingenuously: the word "consent" is important here). There is also the issue of a legal ruling on the matter, which is currently in its developmental stages. Finally, it should be remembered that those who have experienced harassment or bullying are often reluctant to report it to their supervisors. An employer must provide effective methods for filing complaints. Once a complaint is received, the employer's legal duty is to investigate and take appropriate action against the harassment and prevent it from recurring in the future.

An employer must also appoint a prevention officer who will be responsible for receiving complaints, investigating, advising, and providing information and guidance. Nonetheless, it must always be remembered that overall responsibility rests with the managers and the leaders of the company. Prevention officers should be qualified as per regulatory requirements, with the number of officers determined by the size and structure of the company. The employer must accept the conclusions of any inquiry and decide on how to proceed. It is the organization's responsibility to ensure all employees are aware of who the prevention officer is and ensure simple communication channels. Furthermore, the company must arrange regular training seminars and information sessions. An effective and proper response to complaints promotes trust and strengthens employees' confidence in their rights; it enhances company loyalty, improves organizational culture, and significantly supports risk management.

The following tools will assist in implementing a fair, safe, and supportive work environment:

- Sexual harassment prevention training.
- Integration of the subject into existing training programs (e.g. management training courses).
- Integration of the subject into new employee orientations (presentations, etc.).
- Use of the company's online portal to submit complaints or receive information (essential for companies with remote locations away from headquarters).
- An open-door policy.
- Publicizing of cases (anonymously) as an example and deterrence.
- Encouragement of complaints.

Training should be mandatory for all employees, regardless of gender, at all levels of the organization. Management should undertake additional training to aid them in implementing the policies in their departments. A comprehensive sexual harassment training session will address the relevant articles of the law and the applicable sections of the organizational code of ethics (see Chapter 11). It will be clear about what constitutes sexual harassment, emphasize the different power balances in co-worker relationships compared to relationships across hierarchical boundaries (here the case of McDonald's CEO Stephen Easterbrook serves as a useful reminder)[10] and review ways to oppose sexual harassment and to document it.

> **Cassiopeia**
>
> Technology Employees
>
> Cassiopeia is a service that seeks to reduce sexual harassment and bullying in the workplace, a technology that has arrived at a very opportune moment. In light of employees' reluctance to report harassment or bullying, Cassiopeia uses anonymous communication channels and machine learning to collect feedback and detect when employees are at risk of harassment. This service could have a drastic, positive effect on the social climate of many workplaces, providing companies with accurate information on levels of harassment and bullying in their workplaces. Only once they are aware of misconduct can companies take the necessary measures to address it. Since safety and well-being in the work environment is crucial to maintaining a socially responsible organization, Cassiopeia's technology could move many companies in the right direction.

Responsible organizations are expected to take a similar structured and zero-tolerance approach to workplace bullying.

Work–life balance

The COVID-19 pandemic has made homeworkers of millions who are new to the experience. Perspectives about differentiation between work and home life will never be the same again. Flexibility becomes the norm as employees suddenly have power over how they structure their work and balance it with family time.

Work–life balance, much like other elements of corporate responsibility, is a part of the global agenda. A growing number of workers devote too little time to their families, whether by working overtime or by working additional hours from home. Technology plays a dual role: it allows the flexibility of working from home or distance-working, but also keeps us 24/7 connected and accessible. This is an area for continued negotiation in the post-corona world.

Flexible working used to be the preserve of the liberal professions, but today it encompasses all areas of activity. The current discourse between workers and employers is not just about financial compensation; it might involve employees' identification and engagement with their workplace, for example.

The results are clearly demonstrated in companies such as Zappos, which we saw earlier, that create a very high level of engagement among employees (and customers). Further examples can be found in the outstanding book, *Delivering Happiness*.[11]

Retraining and upskilling

Tech skills matter: currently, 70% of UK technology employers, for example, are facing a skills shortage.[12] There is also an anticipated need worldwide for a renewal of "soft skills." As jobs become more cognitively challenging, there will be an increased need for creative and strategic career skills. And existing employees need to develop new skill sets in order to fill internal vacancies. Klaus Schwab, Founder and Executive Chairman of the World Economic Forum, has made strong recommendations[13] about the importance of investing in your workforce. He claims that "many employers' retraining and upskilling efforts remain focused on a narrow set of current highly-skilled, highly-valued employees," whereas "businesses will need to recognize human capital investment as an asset rather than a liability." Workforces need to be reskilled and upskilled to meet the demands of the changing technological landscape. Schwab identifies a "virtuous cycle between new technologies and upskilling" with an agile, future-proofed workforce able to take advantages of the new tech that will drive business growth. Conversely, companies with a deskilled workforce – and management – will lose out.

Jonathan Richards, CEO and co-founder of HR software vendor Breathe, agrees: "Enhancing the existing skills of your companies' workforce will not only increase productivity, but really demonstrates the company is welcoming of the tech-savvy influx of new minds."[14]

Future of work predictions

As discussed in some detail in the Introduction, the rise of Millennials will accelerate the tech revolution in the workplace. They grew up with tech. For example, face-to-face meetings will decline, to be replaced by video-conferencing. As the implications of the COVID-19 pandemic become embedded, the tech-savvy Millennials and Gen Zs, safely in their comfort zone with remote video technology, will surely emerge more empowered – "Generation Zoom." Immersed in social networking, they are collaborative by nature, so interaction and small-group teamwork will blossom.[15] And Millennials will step up their demands for a flexible working policy – "work from home" – all the more since COVID-19 intensified the moral dimension of reducing travel, so investment in chat technologies and video software is non-optional. Joel Farrow, MD for EMEA at HR tech company Hibob, claims that "Communicating constantly will be crucial and making sure agile collaboration guidelines are established from the outset is essential."[16] Companies will have to implement the appropriate technology as well as adapt to and embrace the change in flexible working policies in order to keep their employees productive and engaged.

As companies incorporate technology to accommodate remote work, there is an anticipated positive impact on diversity and inclusion in the workplace. This is another of Gartner's 2010 predictions (see the Introduction) that has come to fruition. According to new Glassdoor research, companies worldwide are becoming alert to the issue of diversity and inclusion and investing in senior-level talent to deliver on their programs.[17] With more employees who specialize in diversity and inclusion, companies will be better able to create lasting impacts.

One of Gartner's bolder predictions was the cultivation of employees who work alongside their artificially intelligent "colleagues." Just as computers and cellphones have been enhancing productivity for years, AI will serve as a tool to allow humans to focus on "the real value-add" while it deals with the mundane but necessary tasks. As tech-based, robotic, and AI solutions become the standard, employers will need to bear the burden of developing their employees' skills, as discussed in this chapter.

★ ★ ★

Employees will always be critical stakeholders: a company that wants to succeed needs happy and engaged people. Corporate responsibility alongside technological agility are the means by which you increase your employees' motivation and engagement, with implications for recruitment through to retirement.

Notes

1 Kellie A. McElhaney, *Just Good Business: The Strategic Guide to Aligning Corporate Responsibility and Brand*. San Francisco: Berrett-Koehler, 2008.
2 "Zappos 10 core values." https://www.zapposinsights.com/about/core-values.
3 Lori Goler, Janelle Gale, Brynn Harrington, and Adam Grant, "The 3 things employees really want: Career, community, cause." *Harvard Business Review*, February 20, 2018. https://hbr.org/2018/02/people-want-3-things-from-work-but-most-companies-are-built-around-only-one.
4 Dan Ariely, *Payoff: The Hidden Logic That Shapes Our Motivations*. New York: TED Books, 2016.
5 https://www.bitc.org.uk/the-wellbeing-workwell-model.
6 Vivian Hunt, Sara Prince, Sundiatu Dixon-Fyle, and Lareina Yee, *Delivering Through Diversity*. McKinsey & Co., January 2018. https://www.mckinsey.com/~/media/McKinsey/Business%20Functions/Organization/Our%20Insights/Delivering%20through%20diversity/Delivering-through-diversity_full-report.ashx.
7 Katharine Esty, Richard Griffin, and Marcie Schorr Hirsch, *Workplace Diversity: A Manager's Guide to Solving Problems and Turning Diversity into a Competitive Advantage*. Holbrook, MA: Adams Media Corporation, 1995.
8 Sheryl Sandberg, *Lean In: Women, Work, and the Will to Lead*. New York: Alfred A. Knopf, 2013.

9 See *Grant Thornton*, "Women in business: Building a blueprint for action." March 2019. https://www.grantthornton.global/globalassets/global-insights–do-not-edit/2019/women-in-business/gtil-wib-report_grant-thornton-spreads-low-res.pdf.
10 Alexia Fernández, "The firing of McDonald's CEO won't solve the chain's sexual harassment problem." *Vox*, November 4, 2019. https://www.vox.com/identities/2019/11/4/20947689/mcdonalds-ceo-steve-easterbrook-fired.
11 Tony Hsieh, *Delivering Happiness: A Path to Profits, Passion, and Purpose*. New York: Boston, 2010.
12 "70% of the tech industry experience skills shortages." *Robert Walters*. https://www.robertwalters.co.uk/solving-the-uk-skills-shortage/technology-research.html.
13 World Economic Forum/Centre for the New Economy and Society, *The Future of Jobs Report 2018*. Geneva: WEF, 2018. http://www3.weforum.org/docs/WEF_Future_of_Jobs_2018.pdf.
14 Charlotte Trueman, "Future of work predictions for 2020: From augmented collaboration to renewed diversity efforts, what trends can we expect to impact the workplace of 2020?" *Computerworld*, January 3, 2020. https://www.computerworld.com/article/3510637/future-of-work-predictions-for-2020.html.
15 Economy, *op.cit*.
16 Trueman, *op. cit*.
17 Daniel Zhao, "Increasing investment in diversity & inclusion: Evidence from the growing job market." *Glassdoor*, October 23, 2019. https://www.glassdoor.com/research/diversity-inclusion-jobs/.

14 Be responsible for your supply chain

In this globalized age, an organization's supply chain is a dominant source of competitive advantage. In fact, an efficient and precise supply chain is becoming indispensable. With materials and services being sourced from all over the world – and increasingly from the developing world in order to reduce costs – due diligence and quality assurance is complicated. The risks associated with a distant and complex supply chain are not merely economic ones: brand and image are vulnerable. Child labor practices discovered at Nike's suppliers' factories in the Far East is one example. Sweatshop conditions in factories owned by Apple's iPhone manufacturer is another. The damaging allegations were reflected in hits to the companies' share prices and to their revenues. A responsible supply chain not only helps a company to manage its risk but also adds value to its products and customers by increasing the positive impact of the company and its products. Transparency is key to building a responsible supply chain, and more and more companies are implementing it. An interesting manifestation of this is at L'Oréal's platform, which discloses the materials in its products: https://inside-our-products.loreal.com/.

Furthermore, climate change and demographic shifts are also affecting supply chains, with impacts on schedules and budgets. Technology, as elsewhere, has a major role to play in supply chains, primarily with regard to management and monitoring. The fashion industry, with its complex supply chains, is a case in point (see the Cotton Box).

> **Cotton**
>
> Technology   Society
>
> Demand for cotton in the world supply chain is higher than for any other natural fiber. But it is a controversial product on account of the pesticides, herbicides, fertilizers, and large amounts of water used in its production and the subsequent, substantial, negative environmental impact. Upstream, responsibility lies with the fashion industry to identify and monitor contentious points in the supply chain, and to improve them in cooperation with their suppliers, with increased transparency and traceability being key.[1] Here, blockchain has emerged as a transparency system that cotton producers are learning to use, an example being Grant Thornton India, headed by my friend Vishesh Chandiok, which has developed the Digital Smart Traceability tool that creates audit trails for assurance of organic credentials and companies' other quality and ethical requirements. Using blockchain as a traceability solution reduces counterfeiting and the blending of organic and nonorganic by value chain players. As government laws and regulations pertaining to transparency and traceability emerge, only those companies adept at implementing transparency systems will survive. In the process, the environment is protected, producers are spared negative publicity, and child labor, unacceptable working conditions, and water shortages are all mitigated.

Companies like to advertise their sponsorship of change-making programs, and rightly so. A good example is Lipton, Unilever's tea brand, with its "doing good" campaign, and even Nespresso is shifting away from its signature star-studded campaigns featuring George Clooney to a new ad campaign focused on farmers and communities in an effort to shed light on its sustainability efforts. This is a huge change in focus, in line with consumer demand and purchasing behavior.

Build a responsible supply chain

Supply chain management, in its broadest definition, encompasses various stages of the business process, from the procurement of raw materials to the distribution of the finished product to the customer. This will of course vary from sector to sector. Today, corporate responsibility is progressively being integrated across every stage of the supply chain: a responsible supply chain policy considers the environmental and social impact of a product and all factors involved, across all tiers of the supply chain, until its final destination. It consists of the following elements:

- Assessing risk (reputation, environment, quality, and human rights).
- Defining vision and procurement policies (compliance with the code of ethics and the company values both internally and externally).
- Defining requirements from suppliers (regarding ethics, environment, employees, and community).
- Establishing tools and procedures (dialogue, supplier evaluation, training, supply chain mapping, and implementation).
- Training employees (procurement, logistics, and others).
- Selecting and mapping of strategic suppliers for implementation.
- Implementing work processes (procedures and workflow processes).

Green, social, or sustainable procurement is an approach that takes economic, environmental, and social sustainability into account in all purchasing decisions. It aims to maximize value for money and to locate a product or service of optimal price, quality, and functionality. In addition, this approach considers a product's environmental and social impact over its entire lifecycle (from creation to disposal) and a service's social effects such as poverty, worker exploitation, human rights, etc. Green/sustainable procurement must follow the strategic aims of the business; otherwise, it cannot be considered as such.

Sustainable procurement is, in fact, smart procurement: it improves procurement efficiency while using the organization's purchasing power to bring about environmental and social changes and benefits locally and globally. Vast sums of money change hands in large-scale organizational procurement. In a world in climate crisis, the purchasing power of organizations is a tremendous tool to drive the market in a responsible and sustainable direction. Procurement departments not only can significantly affect the environmental and social impact of their own organization but can affect environmental and social patterns in the business sector, and hence the natural environment itself. For example, an across-the-board demand by business-sector procurement departments for energy-efficient electronic products can steer the market to phase out less efficient models (whole market impact). Furthermore, procurement departments can serve as a key driver for innovation and creativity by exerting pressure on suppliers to meet their requirements for sustainable products and services.

TerraCycle

Environment   Supply chain

TerraCycle, a private recycling company, is considered a social enterprise or "fourth sector" organization – one driven by both social/environmental purpose and market-based financial objectives. The company is unique in that it creates supply chains for hard-to-recycle materials, from snack bags and food packaging to pens, coffee capsules, and cigarette butts. TerraCycle partners with consumer product companies and retailers, tapping into their marketing budgets to fund costly recycling programs. The waste is collected through a unique business model which enables individuals, organizations, groups, or communities to register for free waste collection, and to send it, free of charge, to be recycled. Participants accrue redeemable "points" that can be used toward a donation to a nonprofit organization or school of their choice. This way, participants can both recycle the waste they generate and earn money for their favorite cause. The donations, as well as the cost of collecting and processing, are subsidized by the manufacturers of the various products. By sponsoring these programs, manufacturers take responsibility for the end-of-life of their products.

TerraCycle also operates innovative collection programs for complex waste, such as power tools, laboratory waste, protective gear, and even old toys. Through this model, which is not funded by manufacturers, the company invites organizations to purchase recycling services for the waste they generate. The company's "Zero Waste Boxes" are available for purchase where the products themselves are sold. For example, recycling boxes for office supplies or old binders can be ordered from Staples, an American office products retailer.

Every company makes many decisions and imposes multiple demands regarding quality, price, quantities, delivery time, and flexibility, and they can also impose sanctions on a supplier. This is a recipe for tension and even conflict as both sides strive for a fair, appropriate, and sustainable work environment. Any company aspiring toward a responsible supply chain must understand the significance of the demands it imposes on a supplier. Additionally, it needs to respect long-term relationships and transparent dialogue with its suppliers. In this respect, COVID-19 has acted as a litmus test for good buyer–supplier relationships.

Is green procurement more expensive?

Not necessarily. Green procurement considers the whole product lifecycle, including "hidden" costs such as procurement, use, maintenance (repair options), and disposal costs. In general, maintenance and disposal costs of green products are lower. Also, they have a longer shelf life and can sometimes be repaired, reused, or recycled. For example, an energy-saving light bulb is significantly more expensive than a conventional incandescent light bulb, but it lasts longer and uses a quarter of the energy of traditional bulbs. In this way, green procurement can produce a higher return on investment.

Green procurement in practice

A responsible supply chain begins with a properly planned procurement process, which should consist of five key steps:

- Step 1: favor energy-efficient machines and equipment.
- Step 2: buy raw materials in bulk to minimize costs and packaging.
- Step 3: favor suppliers with a strong environmental policy and/or commitment to sustainability and/or environmentally friendly alternatives.
- Step 4: favor local suppliers (see the Heineken Box) and products committed to "Fair Trade."
- Step 5: favor products that meet environmental standards set by regulatory agencies.

Heineken

Environment   Community

The Dutch brewing company Heineken aims to become an industry leader in corporate responsibility. This is reflected in various steps, from its "Enjoy Responsibly" social marketing campaign calling for moderate alcohol consumption, to measures encouraging Fair Trade and reducing

> environmental impacts. The company now aims for at least 50% locally sourced raw materials in 40 factories worldwide, reducing environmental impact while saving money and financially empowering local farmers and their communities.

From a social perspective, choose suppliers that ensure fair and legal employment for their workers. Here, too, supply is directly related to demand: as demand grows, so will the range of suppliers with robust social standards, alongside those offering green products and services.

In his book, *Let My People Go Surfing*,[2] Yvon Chouinard, CEO of the outdoor clothing company Patagonia, outlines his company's successful strategy of doing as much business as it can with as few suppliers as possible by establishing long-term relationships. In doing this, the company makes a considerable investment in the selection, screening, and training of suppliers:

> Obviously we put a lot of effort into choosing factories that have healthy relationships with their employees. We audit potential partners to determine how they manage workers, we interview workers to determine their perspective on the factory, and we engage civil society to verify that the factory has a positive employment record.

This is a clear example of a strategy that extends corporate responsibility down the entire supply chain.

Patagonia

Brand   Society

For over 30 years, Patagonia has donated 1% of its annual sales to environmental charities and grassroots organizations.

> The company views these contributions not as some arbitrary form of corporate philanthropy but as one of its basic costs of doing business – something that is as much a core element of Patagonia as selling shirts and jackets.
>
> Patagonia recycles its used and old products under the slogan "Never in the landfill,"[3] but perhaps its most high-profile initiative has been the advertising campaign insisting that consumers "Don't Buy Our Jackets." These slyly subversive ads were placed to coincide with the annual consumer frenzy that is Black Friday. This was not an impulse to commit commercial suicide on Patagonia's part; the anti-consumerist message was designed to persuade consumers not to buy more products than were absolutely necessary for their lifestyle. As such, it was a message echoing Patagonia's longstanding *overall* values, which in fact helped to "strengthen the bonds with existing customers and make for curious new ones."

Responsible sourcing: some pointers

In selecting a product there are several important considerations.

- First and foremost, is the purchase necessary at all? Frequently it isn't.
- What raw materials are used in the product? Are they hazardous? Are they nonrenewable?
- Under what conditions is the product made, and how is it assembled? Is the production process polluting the environment? To what extent are pollutants used in the production process?

There are additional underlying considerations surrounding the product. For example, is the product packaging necessary? Is it biodegradable? Can the product be reused, repurposed, or recycled? And, no less important, is it produced under acceptable working conditions?

It is important to remember that green product purchasing is not binary (green/not green): it is a direction of travel. Green products do not "fix" the environment; neither will they have zero impact. The point is that their environmental impacts are lower than those of competing products, and this direction of travel must continue to accelerate. Lifecycle assessment (LCA) professionals will show that product A is greener than product B if its LCA indicators are lower. And a product is called "green" when its LCA impacts are lower than those of the benchmark. Managers frequently label a product "green" when it scores high in just one of its attributes. Bio-based materials, products with recycled content, and hybrid cars may have the "green" label attached to them without genuine analysis. An alternative approach, called "net green," calculates the net impact on the environment, after accounting for all factors, including the impact that the product or service has on markets and consumer behavior.

It can be argued that packaging made from recycled plastic is green in comparison to identical packaging made from primary polymer. But, of course, no packaging at all is most likely greener still. Green products might grow market demand: perhaps the product's greenness, as advertised, led a consumer to purchase it as an alternative to buying nothing. Recycling itself, in recovering scrap material from discarded products and turning it into secondary material, has its own environmental impacts, although LCAs show that those impacts are generally much smaller than producing the material from primary resources. So, if increased production of recycled material were to generate an equal decrease in primary material production, total environmental impact would be reduced. But that is not necessarily how it works: recycling may not just reduce primary material production but also grow the overall size of the market. Good news for industry; bad news for the environment.

Fair trade

In the affluent West, it is easy to ignore the fact that, elsewhere, child labor is still widespread, men and women work long hours in sweatshops, and farmers are forced to sell their crops for less than what it costs to produce them. Billions endure hunger and poverty. By current estimates, around 10% of the world's population are still trying to survive on less than $2 a day.[4] Extreme poverty and harsh labor conditions, combined with free market forces, increasingly limit the employment opportunities of a weak population, making them vulnerable and easily exploited. In the absence of choice, millions of people, including children, are forced to live without the possibility of escaping the growing cycle of poverty.

The Fair Trade initiative was established to improve the lives of workers, tradespeople, farmers, and producers in developing nations by allowing them to earn their living with dignity and escape the cycle of extreme poverty. Fair Trade products generally come with a higher price for the consumer – a premium that is paid to the farmer or producer so that they can maintain a decent and dignified livelihood and develop a sustainable production process and community. Fair Trade mechanisms minimize the gap between production cost and retail price, and they ensure fair compensation to the workers at the bottom of the production chain. Experience shows that Fair Trade promotes sustainable development and helps to reduce poverty and improve working conditions in developing countries.

A rapidly growing trend

The Fair Trade market has been expanding in recent years: currently, the European Union is the largest market for Fair Trade products, with an estimated 60–70% of global sales, and growing at an average of 20% per year since 2000. These products can now be found not only in specialized shops but in retail supermarkets across Europe and the United States. An increasing number of companies are joining the Fair Trade movement, and with good reason: it confers a significant "public dividend," attracting positive public attention and being perceived as a valuable objective. Moreover, the price difference is frequently lower than consumers expect, and they find that the products themselves are better-tasting and higher-quality.

Fair Trade encourages consumers to recognize and consider the social, economic, and environmental impact of their purchases. It is a moral and conscious choice, which can be made on a daily basis. It enables consumers in developed countries to declare our support for social justice and sustainable development as part of our daily routine, while activating market forces in favor of a more equitable supply chain. It raises social and environmental awareness among those who might not engage in other ways. Furthermore, purchasing a Fair Trade product inspires a sense of positive action and meaningful contribution to the global or local community.

In your organization, choosing Fair Trade gifts for company employees and other stakeholders, or in production or work processes, can play a role in raising awareness of the issue, creating a positive sense of partnership when contributing to the community and serving as a standard for credibility and fairness in the eyes of the company's customers and other stakeholders.

Joining the trend

Joining the Fair Trade trend can be done in one of two ways. The easiest and most immediate approach is to integrate as many Fair Trade certified products and organizations into the supply chain as possible. However, the best approach will be to become one of those organizations.

The principles of Fair Trade vary from product to product and according to industry, but are based mainly on the conventions of the International Labour Organization (ILO) and on the human and children's rights charters provided by the United Nations. Fair Trade is an additional dimension of these principles. Products can achieve Fair Trade certification if they meet the required international standards. Organizations seeking Fair Trade certification must adhere to principles that include: mutual respect between buyer and producer; direct market access for local manufacturers; fair pricing, fair wages, and immediate payment; a social premium for community development or improving production, including environmentally friendly methods; a safe work environment;

178 *The good process*

capacity building and empowerment for producers; and consumer awareness-raising.

Fair Trade is a social contract, with buyers agreeing to do more than is expected by the conventional market. Producers, on their part, commit to use the benefits of Fair Trade to improve their social and economic conditions. In this way, Fair Trade is not charity but a partnership for change and development through trade.

EcoVadis

Risk   Data

EcoVadis has become the world's most trusted provider of business sustainability ratings, intelligence, and collaborative performance improvement tools for global supply chains. Its comprehensive CSR analysis system covers 21 criteria across four themes: environment; fair labor and human rights; ethics; and sustainable procurement. The criteria are based on the Global Reporting Initiative, the United Nations Global Compact, and ISO 26000, covering 190 spending categories and 150 countries. EcoVadis provides actionable sustainability records for more than 300 leading multinational organizations, 198 purchasing categories, 155 countries, and 55,000 businesses. Its overall mission is to enable businesses to reduce risk, drive performance, and improve environmental and social outcomes through results, account management, supplier onboarding, training, consulting, integration, and custom IT services and partners.

This chapter has zoned in on Fair Trade, but it is important to remember that there are a plethora of labels and certifications available, many of them industry-specific, such as those of the Rainforest Alliance, the FSC (Forest Stewardship Council) and the MSC (Marine Stewardship Council). Increasingly, companies and products without certain certifications are being seen as laggards.

Notes

1 *Fashion for Good*, "Tracing organic cotton from farm to consumer: Key findings from a pioneering pilot using on-product markers and blockchain solutions." November 2019. https://fashionforgood.com/wp-content/uploads/2019/12/Fashion-for-Good-Organic-Cotton-Traceability-Pilot-Report.pdf.
2 Yvon Chouinard, *Let My People Go Surfing: The Education of a Reluctant Businessman*. London: Penguin, 2005.
3 "Never in the landfill." *Patagonia*. https://eu.patagonia.com/se/en/reuse-recycle.html.
4 "Decline of global extreme poverty continues but has slowed." *World Bank*, September 19, 2018. https://www.worldbank.org/en/news/press-release/2018/09/19/decline-of-global-extreme-poverty-continues-but-has-slowed-world-bank.

15 Be responsible for your environment

Corporate environmental responsibility is driven by several factors: increased public awareness of sustainability issues; rising fuel, water, and electricity prices; and evolving local and global regulations and commitments, such as those of the OECD and the Kyoto Protocol. It has an ethical imperative but can also generate organizational and financial dividends. These include savings and efficiencies, employee engagement and loyalty, raising environmental awareness beyond your company boundaries, and differentiation through a brand image of leadership and innovation. COVID-19 has had a marked effect on our environmental impact simply by inhibiting our flying, driving, and shopping. It has thrown into sharp relief what proportion of these activities were truly ever necessary, and the long-term outcome must be a re-evaluation of our potential to change behavior in a more responsible direction. On the other hand, there is a risk that it may serve as an excuse during the recovery years to obstruct external or internal regulation in the name of increased and unfettered production.

Create an organizational environmental policy and set goals

An environmental policy establishes an organization's position and its commitment. If it is going to be genuinely effective, it must be an integral part of company strategy. Just like any statement of intentions or departmental policies, it is imperative that it accounts for all parts of the company's daily operations. It should be the cornerstone of a program to reduce the organization's adverse environmental impacts across the board, addressing carbon footprint, waste management and recycling, natural resource use, and so on.

Pukka

Environment Society

A small business that integrates sustainability into its DNA is Pukka Herbs. Founded by Tim Westwell and Sebastian Pole, the company strives to lower its environmental impact while providing a high-quality, Fair Trade product. Unique to the company is its recyclable tea envelopes, which took years of development. (Regular tea envelopes are not recyclable due to the thick plastic lamination used to keep the leaves fresh – meaning they are unsuitable for recycling with paper. In addition, the actual tea bag is compostable, made from natural fibers, with no staples.

Pukka is meticulous in tracking its carbon footprint, up and down the supply chain. "From crop to cup," Pukka tracks all aspects of production, distribution, and even consumer use, taking all such information into account in assessing its contribution. As nearly 50% of the company's carbon footprint derives from consumer kettle boiling, Pukka strives to engage with product users educating them to reduce boiling times. The company is now certified carbon-neutral.

Pukka is a member of "1% for the Planet,"[1] an international organization whose members contribute at least 1% of their annual sales to environmental causes. In 2017, Pukka donated 100% of its Black Friday sales to charity to

> help their local community of Bristol, UK. A business such as Pukka, with its embedded sustainable values, plays an exemplary role by proving to stakeholders that a business can be an engine for change and not an additional burden on planetary resources.

A comprehensive and effective environmental policy might include the following: a declaration of intent; a baseline with a clear statement of the reasons for undertaking this process; an outline of actual environmental impacts; and principles such as those pertaining to sustainability and efficient use of finite resources (with regard to regional and national issues [e.g. water scarcity] and at global level [e.g. climate change]). It will acknowledge legal, regulatory, and self-regulatory requirements along with risks, such as supply chain disruption and adverse reputation. Stakeholder dialogue and employee engagement are also critical and should be enshrined in the policy, as should management commitment. Finally, there should be an undertaking to review and update at regular intervals.

The next step is to publicize. Publicly announcing the policy as an official organizational document gives meaning to the process and improves stakeholder transparency.

> **Interface**
>
> Brand   New paradigms
>
> Interface, the carpet and floor tile company, is recognized as a global leader in sustainability. In 1994, it was one of the first companies to publicly commit to sustainability. With a policy called Mission Zero®, it pledged to achieve net-zero impact on the environment by 2020. The manufacturing

> facility in the Netherlands now runs on 100% renewable energy (both gas and electric), the company uses virtually no water in the manufacturing processes, and its European facilities send no waste to landfill.

Setting goals

Setting goals is the next step, and equally important. "Green goals" reflect the company's commitment to the environment, both externally and internally. It begins with calculating your baseline in categories such as water, energy, and waste, only after which can goals be set for each material issue. Goals should be quantifiable and subject to a specific time frame. There are methodologies around goal setting using science-based targets which provide companies with a clearly defined pathway to future-proof growth by specifying how much and how quickly they need to reduce their greenhouse gas emissions with reference to the SDG compass, which helps companies align their goals with the UN Sustainable Development Goals. However, the choice of methodology itself is less important than commitment and integration into a measurable working plan. This will not always come as good news to departmental managers, who may be concerned that an inability to meet them may be perceived as failure. It is therefore important to engage with them in this process, offering reassurance that this is not a "heads will roll" approach.

Carbon footprint

Accelerated and potentially catastrophic climate change – increased temperatures and rising sea levels – is caused by "greenhouse gases" (GHGs), specifically carbon dioxide (CO_2), methane (CH_4), and nitrous oxide (N_2O), which accumulate in the atmosphere and create the greenhouse effect. A carbon footprint is a measure that assesses the impact of human activity on climate change. The term refers to the amount of greenhouse gases emitted as a result of human activity (such as transportation, industry, and use of electricity), mainly through the burning of fossil fuels such as oil, coal, and gas. We can calculate the carbon footprint of any person or organization. A company's carbon footprint is calculated as the sum of all CO_2 and other GHG emissions produced directly or indirectly to support its operations within a certain time frame, usually one calendar year.

Reducing your organization's carbon footprint is the key goal in addressing climate change. It is undoubtedly a management challenge, and it requires a scientific approach.

The first stage is to implement a "carbon management" mechanism that defines required measurements, reduction, and control of CO_2 emissions generated by the company's operations. This process will, of course, involve bringing experts in, but it is important that you as managers understand its key points. For simple calculations – e.g. carbon footprint of your office, your vehicle – calculators are readily available online.

The Carbon Trust

Climate

The Carbon Trust offers "third party assurance of carbon measurement, reduction and neutrality claims" and awards the Carbon Trust Footprint Label[2] to brands or products that meet its criteria. A product bearing this label informs the consumer that the manufacturer is committed to reducing its resource footprint. The label confers significant marketing value, being public-facing and differentiating the brand.

In carbon footprint reporting, it is important to adhere to a number of principles to ensure reliable and unbiased results that present a true picture of the organization's environmental impact.

This is a formal (and sometimes harsh) analysis of reality that will likely not compliment the organization. Therefore, the process must maintain **transparency** (a clear and comprehensible assessment of the company's carbon footprint), **relevance**, **accuracy** (emission levels should be accurate, uncertainties must be clearly stated), **consistency**, and **completeness** (reporting all emission sources within the defined boundary of the organization).

CDP

Environment Data

CDP is a nonprofit organization dedicated to providing investors, companies, cities, and countries with environmental impact management solutions. CDP's network of investors, representing over $100 trillion, along with policymakers around the globe, use the organization's data and insights to make better-informed decisions. Through its offices and partners in 50 countries, CDP has generated unprecedented levels of environmental disclosure.

The GHG (Greenhouse Gas) Protocol

The Good Vision model for measuring and reporting carbon footprint is based on the GHG (Greenhouse Gas) Protocol, which defines, among other things, organizational and operational boundaries of emissions sources, direct and indirect emissions, and how to identify and verify them. The GHG Protocol publishes the world's most widely used greenhouse gas accounting standards, which often form the basis for accounting resources designed by organizations or consultancies, such as sector-specific guidance, calculation tools, and reporting programs. The "Built on GHG Protocol" mark is a way for the GHG Protocol to recognize products that have been developed in conformance with a GHG Protocol standard. Those that acquire the mark will benefit from the GHG Protocol's reputation as the gold standard for greenhouse gas accounting.

For the purpose of GHG accounting and reporting, the first step is to choose a base year for which verifiable emissions data are available. The boundaries of the organization should then be set and three "scopes" of emissions should be defined:

1 Direct emissions. Emissions from sources that are owned or controlled by the organization: for example, generation of electricity, heat, or steam; fossil fuel combustion (generators, company cars, etc.); chemical or physical processing (cement, aluminum, fertilizer, etc.).
2 Indirect emissions from energy consumption. Emissions from the generation of purchased electricity, steam, hot water, etc., consumed by the organization.
3 Other indirect emissions. Emissions from water consumption, emissions of greenhouse gases from waste processing and landfills, emissions from paper use, business air travel, and outsourcing activities.

The results of this report will enable the organization to draw the necessary conclusions and establish a plan of action that will reduce the organizational carbon footprint in the most efficient manner.

Sustainable transportation

Vehicle traffic accounts for a high percentage of global carbon monoxide emissions, as well as a significant portion of emissions of other gases. In addition, road and highway infrastructure depletes green spaces and damages the ecological integrity of our cities. This alone creates an imperative for a shift to sustainable transportation, but a key factor for forward-looking companies is decoupling from the fossil fuel economy. Oil is a finite resource; data on reserves are uncertain and fluctuate, not least because feasibility of mining them is based on sale price. The price is volatile and subject to political developments. The case for reducing or even eliminating fossil fuel dependency is clear when considering long-term scenarios.

As this book was being written, the COVID-19 pandemic broke. With flights being cancelled, airlines across the world are facing bankruptcy and petitioning governments to bail them out.[3] This raises enormous implications for a possible post-coronavirus world. Will the airline industry remain intact to deliver the same volume of flights? And, in any case, will a new "normal" have established itself in which nonessential flights are deemed unacceptable expenses, both financially and environmentally? And, how will the concept of "essential" be renegotiated? The UK's *Guardian* declared in March 2020, "Business travel that has been postponed for health fears may end up looking like an unaffordable expense for many firms, should coronavirus lead to recession."[4]

The profile of international travel may therefore be entering a new phase. Will a new consciousness emerge for land travel, and commuting in particular, now that so many employees have adjusted to homeworking? For the first time in living memory, the global population has had the opportunity to witness the environmental effects – blue skies, clean air, birdsong – of a massive drop in fossil-fuel-based activity. But a deeper message is that it takes a massive coronavirus-induced global economic downturn to effect a lowering of CO_2 emissions somewhere around a predicted 0.5%: "That it requires a global pandemic with thousands of deaths, rapidly increasing unemployment, and huge amounts of economic dislocation to reduce emissions by a relatively small amount, should instead be one more wake-up call to the scale of the climate challenge and the complexity of solving it."[5] The imperative for corporate responsibility around this area, therefore, will only increase, with fossil fuel use being the prime target.

The first thing to consider is how to still meet personal and organizational needs while reducing fossil fuel use. Single-car use is the low-hanging target here, so the question is how it can be replaced with walking, cycling, public transport, or carpooling.

From a tech solutions perspective, alternative technologies should be explored. There are those related to vehicle propulsion systems, i.e. hybrid and electric cars. It is recommended that medium-term strategies at least are investigated here, as legislation around fossil-fuel engines is being implemented right now, with targets being set for their abolition (see the UK legislation Box). Intelligent navigation systems, such as Waze, reduce travel time and distance. Advanced driver assistance systems, such as Mobileye, prevent accidents and increase fuel efficiency by improving braking behavior. Services such as Uber offer potential environmental improvements compared to traditional taxis by limiting the amount of time drivers spend searching for customers. Ride-sharing apps can also facilitate carpooling.

UK legislation

Climate

The UK government plans to move its ban on the sale of new petrol, diesel, or hybrid cars forward to from 2040 to 2035 as part of UK efforts to become carbon-neutral by 2050. The policy would enforce the sale and purchase of only electric and hydrogen vehicles. The new date aims to ensure petroleum-based vehicles are off the roads by 2050. Prime Minister Boris Johnson announced the policy in November 2019 at COP26, an annual UN-led gathering set up to assess progress on tackling climate change. The government's goal of removing petrol and diesel cars from the roads will require legislation, not just industry cooperation and investment.[6]

Beyond the bottom-line advantages of reducing fuel costs, the "soft" benefits of sustainable transportation are a level of environmental consciousness in employees' daily lives and improvement in organizational image among employees and other stakeholders.

Citi Bike

Sustainable   Transportation

Citi Bike is a bike-share program, with 12,000 bikes and 750 stations across Manhattan, Brooklyn, Queens, and Jersey City in the U.S. It was designed for quick trips with convenience in mind, and it encourages people away from fuel vehicles, improving carbon footprint and health simultaneously.

The good news: it is relatively simple to implement a sustainable transportation policy in an organization. It can be done in just five steps.

Step 1: a survey of practices and routines

As any manager knows, it is important to establish the baseline, so review the current transportation routines, requirements, and the existing means of transportation in the company.

Step 2: employee engagement

Engaging employees in the process is a complex but necessary undertaking. Begin with awareness training on the concept. This can be introduced as part of routine employee training, orientations, or driver safety instructions. Use these sessions to advocate public transportation and communicate such opportunities through the company's portal or website.

At the same time, promote awareness of safe and cost-effective driving by sharing tips through the company's employee portal. Our experience has shown us it is worthwhile announcing a departmental or individual competition for fuel saving, and incentivizing employees by awarding environmentally friendly prizes (e.g. an electric scooter or top-of-the-range bike).

A carbon footprint calculator can be used to estimate an individual's impact on the environment, which can then be visibly reduced by the use of greener means of transportation. It is important to provide employees with feedback and report environmental performance data in such areas as the reduction of energy and paper and fuel consumption, as an incentive to continue conservation efforts, raise awareness, and maintain buy-in.

Step 3: implementation of procedures

In the third stage there is a deeper implementation, change is more substantial, and improvement takes place over time. At this stage, leasing or purchasing company vehicles is based on emissions standards, incentives are offered to employees who relinquish their parking space, carpools are encouraged with reserved parking (the Waze app offers a carpooling option to connect people traveling similar routes), and the company shifts to hiring cars by the hour.

Other steps include arranging shuttles from the local train station, facilitating bicycle commuting by providing showers and lockers (popular with mega-corporations such as Google and Apple), and establishing carpool procedures for events (or using company passenger vehicles). You could reward departments based on their cumulative fuel savings (against the baseline), subsidize the use of hybrid vehicles, public transportation, or bicycles, and minimize business travel by tech solutions such as video-conferencing whenever possible. The COVID-19 pandemic forced many across the world into an immediate dependency on such technology, and at the time of writing it remains to be seen the extent to which these patterns of behavior become permanently established.

Step 4: implementation at core business level

This step is a sector-specific one and therefore relevant only to certain companies where sustainable transportation is the company business. Here we are concerned with, for example, the production and promotion of products and services that encourage the use of shared vehicles and alternative transportation.

Step 5: reduce fuel dependence and demand

By this stage, you are switching to low-emissions vehicles with smaller and/or more fuel-efficient engines, or hybrid engines. Incentives can be offered to drivers who record and report their fuel efficiency (miles per gallon), which not only encourages fuel consumption reduction but also enables the company to monitor and adjust its sustainability program.

The success of these steps depends on the extent of management's commitment to the issue and the personal example set by senior executives who lead the process. Publicize the policy launch with a special event in order to engage employees and other stakeholders.

At the 4th international Maala conference in December 2019,[7] I participated in the green transportation panel alongside representatives from Intel, Waze, Western Digital, and Applied Materials. Discussing the challenges, I made the point that we are facing a paradox: on one hand, new technology seems to emerge almost daily – carpool applications, sharing modes of driving such as via Waze Carpool and Moovit – yet, on the other hand, even while traffic jams are getting worse, especially in big cities, we are not seeing any major change in commuting habits. Behavioral and attitude change is the real challenge. So, to reiterate the points made earlier, a company that manages to engage and educate its employees has a major opportunity to make a difference and lead by example.

Go green for corporate events

Events – whether for the general public, employees, customers, or franchise operators – serve as an organization's calling card to a wide range of stakeholders. An environmentally responsible policy in this area will provide significant added value to a company's image and help differentiate it. Events often require a broad logistical infrastructure, consume extensive resources, and produce significant amounts of waste, so responsible event planning can make a difference to a company's environmental impact.

As part of the growing global trend for green event planning, we were asked to advise the city of Tel Aviv about how to make the 2019 Eurovision Song Contest a sustainable event. The city partnered with the C40 City Solutions Platform in a workshop looking to achieve zero waste and sustainable food solutions. We consulted with experts from all over the world including Eurovision sustainability advisors from Malmö, Sweden, and learned lessons from previous similar events held in Vienna and Lisbon. The TLV municipality global events team headed by Eitan Shvartz and chief environmental officer Eitan BenAmi guided hotel and restaurant representatives along with other local stakeholders to operate in a more sustainable manner. We selected suppliers favoring those with green proposals, participated in production planning meetings, and led the project setting green standards for the event. After the event we submitted a sustainability report detailing the efforts and actions taken as part of the ISO 20101 framework. (See Chapter 18.)

How do you turn an event green?

In the course of my work I often find myself lecturing at event planning workshops trying to challenge the participants to adopt an environmental mind-set. My advice is to follow three guiding principles.

Principle 1. Adopt an environmental and social outlook at the planning stage. In other words, the environmental and social impact of the event is not an afterthought but rather a strategic guideline from the outset. This allows you to consider alternative solutions within your budget with a view to minimizing environmental impact.

Principle 2. Environmental and social management should be implemented across every tier of the supply chain – from light bulbs, tableware, and flowers, to food, sound systems, and electricity. In general, suppliers committed to ecological sustainability in their daily operations – and fair and legal employment practices – should be favored.

Principle 3. Promotion, publicity, and public relations. Publicizing the event as socially responsible and sustainable will position the company favorably as an environmentally and socially conscious leader among its customers, competitors, and the general public. In addition, it will raise public awareness and advance the importance of environmental issues in the corporate sector and/or in a particular industry, encouraging other companies to follow suit. Post informative displays throughout the event and incorporate information on the subject in all promotional material, before and after the event.

There are other layers of corporate responsibility that can be considered: transparency, for example, is always a good thing. Maintain inclusive dialogue with stakeholders. Define your objectives and communicate your expectations to your suppliers. Coordinate with those who may be affected by the event such as neighboring businesses or residents (see the Eurovision case study in Chapter 15).

Turn the green office concept into a green business model

A growing environmental awareness is reflected in many areas: investment and economics, planning and architecture, energy and water. However, most people are not aware of the extent of their individual impact on the environment, and of the difference that relatively small changes in the daily routine can make. Responsible activity at a personal level means basic things like turning off office lights and equipment when not in use, double-sided printing, thinking twice about traveling when video is feasible – something the COVID-19 pandemic brought into sharp focus – and choosing sustainable forms of waste disposal. All these actions, of course, are win–win as they save costs at the same time. And the cumulative benefits over time can be huge.

We also know that among many Millennials, there is a passion about environmental issues, and the easiest way to engage employees in this demographic is through the "green office" concept, which evolved into the "green business" model, supporting organizations in bringing environmental awareness into their daily operations. The focus is on energy efficiency and the concept of the "green building," whether it is either built for purpose or retrofitted. It also integrates office activities with environmental significance, such as waste, water, paper, food, and travel. There are seven key areas in the green business model: energy consumption (the company's carbon footprint), waste (reduce, reuse, recycle), water conservation, paper use, printing (reduce, recycled paper, ecoprint), food and office lunches (avoid single-use items), and business travel and commuting (minimizing, greener vehicles, video-conferencing).

Changing patterns

Employee motivation can be hampered by a perfectly understandable inability to see the bigger picture: "How can my small actions as an individual make a difference?" In a large, thriving organization, instructions to print double-sided might seem like a petty cost-saving initiative. But the rationale is not about saving a few cents. Developed countries produce over 1,300 lbs of waste per capita annually. As we saw earlier, the cumulative effects are appalling, and it is only increasing.

If we are to address the global waste problem, we all need to change our consumption habits. There does not have to be a trade-off in effectiveness of everyday operations; and there are organizational cost savings as a bonus. To turn consumption habits around, you simply follow the five Rs (refuse, reduce, recycle, repair, refill). Improved employee awareness can feed upwards as well. An engaged and informed workforce is more likely to resist bad company policy if it goes against their principles: they can exert positive pressure for change.

Improving energy efficiency

The ultimate solution where energy is concerned is to use as high a proportion as possible from renewable sources: solar, wind, hydro, etc. This is not always an easy option – especially for SMEs – so improving energy efficiency is both an ethical and a prudent way forward, reducing carbon footprint and cutting costs. It is quite simply using less energy to produce the same product or service at the same quality.

The first step is simply to change consumption habits. The next step is to transition to advanced technologies or streamlined processes. Like any other development, this is implemented in stages.

Step 1: control and measurement

Itemize all office devices. Check electricity meter readings at the beginning and end of each work day, and also check power consumption outside office hours (lighting, devices in sleep mode or still drawing charge). Now use one of the calculators available online to calculate the carbon footprint of your electricity consumption (see the "Carbon footprint" section earlier in this chapter).

Step 2: reduce consumption and become more energy-conscious

There are numerous ways of reducing energy consumption, and countless guides on the subject. We will explore several options here.

1. Cut down on travel by coordinating meetings and errands in time- and distance-efficient ways. The COVID-19 pandemic will likely change the landscape of business travel, initially from a logistical perspective – travel restrictions followed by the

as-yet-unknown international air travel market post-pandemic – and from an ethical one. As discussed in the Introduction and in Chapter 13, the rise of video-conferencing as a default option is one outcome.

2   Train employees in energy management and encourage energy-efficient use of equipment. Again, this is not about saving a few cents: this is about collective responsibility for the welfare of the planet. For example: make it policy to shut down unused devices rather than leave them in standby mode (which continues to consume energy). This is significant: a computer monitor working eight hours a day can produce up to 1,300 lbs of greenhouse gases per year. This can be facilitated by installing timers that automatically shut devices off when not in use. In fact, ensure that devices are switched off at the power source: this way, electricity consumption is reduced to zero. Use energy-efficient light bulbs (in both fixed and portable lighting), and LED lights instead of incandescent bulbs; even better, make use of natural light sources where possible. Install motion or room occupancy sensors in areas where there are sustained periods of inactivity.

3   Continue monitoring energy consumption levels at all stages of the process in order to ensure that the changes implemented are reflected in energy usage and costs.

Step 3: energy-efficient devices

A shift to energy-efficient devices is vital. Although they may cost more than their conventional counterparts, over their operational lifetime they save energy costs and reduce the company's carbon footprint, offsetting the initial investment.

The energy rating of an electrical device will be listed in its technical specification, represented by a scale of A to G, where A1 is the most energy-efficient rating and G the least. When comparing costs, consider not just the purchase price but ongoing running costs as well. Choices should be made based on a lifecycle assessment (LCA). Many countries have adopted the "Energy Star" label issued by the U.S. Environmental

Protection Agency and the U.S. Department of Energy, which enables consumers to easily identify energy-efficient products in the market.

The five Rs of sustainable consumption

1. Reduce. This is the simplest principle because it does not require any action. Buy what you really need, and bear in mind that the product's packaging usually ends in the trash.
2. Reuse. After a product has fulfilled its primary function, it may still be reused. It is surprising how useful empty containers can be. If you no longer have a use for something, consider donating it: from clothing to computer equipment, there are always organizations, charities, and individuals who will gladly accept them.
3. Recycle. Products that cannot be reused can be recycled – but not always, so always favor products with a "recyclable" label or similar indication. Waste separation by the consumer improves recycling efficiency.
4. Repair/recover. Purchase high-quality items that will last or can be repaired. Furniture, for example, can often be easily repaired, worthwhile even if the repair cost comes close to the price of a new one. Many of today's appliances are so cheap that they make repair seem pointless, but a high-quality, higher-price product will return its investment over the long term.
5. Refuse. It is not easy to say no to a new product. We have become accustomed to constant updates and improvements. Deals such as "buy one, get one free" encourage us to purchase greater quantity than we need. Make a shopping list and try not to stray from it. When buying an item, stop for a moment and consider whether you really need it – often the answer is no.

Integrate these concepts within employee training and development: form a green volunteer team and internally communicate the scope of these initiatives to your employees.

The plastic war

The repercussions of our reliance on plastic as a raw material and the accumulation of plastic waste in the biosphere have been documented in Chapter 5. One of the most significant pressures that we can bring to bear at an individual level is to halt the tide of single-use plastic in our culture. But it is a confusing area, so at Good Vision we are developing a service to help clients reduce or eliminate single-use plastic consumption in the workplace, with workshops and strategies based on current research.

There are numerous variables to be considered in making purchasing decisions around plastics: it is often difficult to ascertain which is the better product. First of all, the lifecycle impact has to be assessed: the production process, how it is used, and the impact of its disposal. There are different types of environmental impacts to be considered: alongside energy, emissions, biodiversity, and natural resources, value and social values must also be taken into account, which are difficult to quantify, but their contribution is significant.

Substitutions

Look for plastic substitutes from natural materials: corn starch, paper, wood, or bamboo, for example. Again, lifecycle costs must be considered: agricultural land and water is required to produce them, and maybe pesticides and fertilizers. Biodegradable plastic is a good option but only if properly disposed of: throwing it away with the rest of the waste just adds to the plastic waste problem and actually increases GHG emissions; it must be separated in the office and transported to a composting facility for recycling.

Disposable versus reusable. Single use versus multi-use

The production process of multi-use cups is more complex and has a higher environmental impact, but this is more than offset by multiple use. The goal is to use each cup as many times as possible. Instead of ending up in landfill – or, worse, the sea – some longer-life cups can be recycled, or, if made of glass or ceramic, are relatively benign in landfill.

The greatest barrier to change is cultural and behavioral. According to Dr. Beverly Goodman Chernow of the School of Marine Sciences at the University of Haifa, "We've gotten so used to the comfort of the disposable that we use it without thinking twice. It has become standard, even in places where multifaceted use should be taken for granted like the office or home."

Today, in many cases the initiative arises from the bottom up from committed employees, and in order to leverage such motivation into something more systematic, Good Vision has developed a 360° program for companies to move beyond the single-use culture:

- Public statement on the organization's strategy.
- Explanation, explanation, explanation. Multi-use items can be perceived by employees as being at the expense of their convenience and as a disruption, so the rationale and the goals must be shared clearly and simply.
- Engage employees throughout the process. Methods include a dedicated phone line, team participation to lead the movement, a suggestion box, brainstorming, and so on. Make it an educational experience for them.
- Supportive action. If the policy is to have credibility, it must be part of a wider environmental campaign to include, for example, reducing paper use, recycled paper use, or encouraging electricity savings.
- Personal example. Management can set a scalable example, which will be a significant driver in the process.
- Set up a volunteer day. This could be litter-picking on beaches, for example. These often turn out to be enjoyable, team-building experiences.
- Inform. Send tips to staff, via email, for example, on how to reduce plastic use at home. Screen a film on the topic or host a lecture. Ensure functional solutions for specific populations.

Benefits

Many benefits can accrue from being a leader in the war against unsustainable use of plastic:

- Reduction of environmental footprint.
- Long-term financial savings, including waste expenditure.
- Differentiation by being an industry leader and strengthening your reputation. Set an example for value and environmental behavior, in line with global trends.
- Preparation for the future: first-mover advantage in a period of emerging new regulations.
- Potential for growth: customers and investors with similar values will identify with the company's values.
- Strengthening employees' sense of loyalty and identification with the organization's values. Employee awareness creates a discourse and a virtuous circle of engagement.

Conserve water

We have already stressed the importance of water conservation in this book. Technology is constantly developing to assist us in this; however, much of it focuses on large-scale operations, e.g. monitoring leaks (watersign.co.il) or precise measurement of water requirements in agriculture or industry. Having said that, there are practices that can be adopted in the home or office.

NetBeat™ by Netafim

Technology   Environment

Netafim is a global company that provides creative technology solutions for growing food with less resource input. "Adoption of advanced agricultural technologies, including

> innovative digital solutions, is becoming increasingly necessary for addressing the needs of feeding a growing population while ensuring more efficient use of natural resources," says Gaby Miodownik, Netafim's CEO and President. NetBeat™ is a digital irrigation and fertigation management system providing farmers with a better way to manage their work and optimize their yields. It delivers real-time smart recommendations based on data about plant, soil, and weather conditions throughout all stages of the crop lifecycle. The data is analyzed in the cloud, using the proprietary Dynamic Crop Models system, which is a product of Netafim's 50 years of experience and research in agronomy and hydraulics.

Mechanical measures to reduce use

One quick and simple step forward, requiring just an easy management decision, is installation of mechanical water-saving devices. In a relatively effortless move, water use can be reduced by installing faucet aerators, low-flow showerheads (if relevant), low- or dual-flush toilets, or (at home) a water-efficient dishwasher.

Water leaks are important to identify but often go overlooked. At home, they tend to receive immediate attention, but in office buildings, they can remain undetected for months. As a precaution, consider shutting off the main water supply for areas that are not in use.

Change wasteful habits

Bad habits are hard to break – but that doesn't mean we shouldn't try. Raising awareness through posters, signs, and other guidance can have a slow but ultimately significant effect. For example, post signs in the office kitchen and bathrooms to remind employees to conserve water, such as "An average flush uses 3.6 gallons of water. One person uses 18.8 gallons per day. When possible, use the half-flush button."

Adopt a conservation culture

Once wasteful habits have been targeted, move on to a comprehensive conservation culture. For example, water-efficient landscaping is achieved by low-water-use plants watered with air conditioner condensation (that same water, incidentally, can also be used for office cleaning). Maintenance and cleaning crews can be under instructions to report any leaks they detect and perform regular inspections of water valves. Contact details of the maintenance person can be posted in kitchens and bathrooms for use by any personnel in case of leaks or malfunctions. Make comparisons of water bills before and after the new policy and present this information to employees. Employee engagement in the company's water conservation plan confers a sense of pride, not for the financial savings, but for their environmental contribution.

Green construction

Most organizations rely on physical structures or buildings, whether for production, logistics, or administration, and maybe all three. As regards the environmental impact of this, the numbers are quite astounding. Building construction consumes 50% of global materials production and 40% of global energy production, accounts for 17% of global freshwater consumption, and uses 25% of the annual global wood harvest. Construction also accounts for 55% of the world's waste and approximately 30–50% of global greenhouse gas emissions. Just imagine the impact that green construction could have.

What is a green building?

A green, or sustainable, building is designed to use energy, water, land, and materials efficiently and cost-effectively. Green construction is based on architecture and design features that provide a higher quality of life for residents while conserving natural resources and prioritizing environmental considerations. This is achieved through green technologies and a multidisciplinary integration of construction elements. In fact, one of the key principles of green construction is the integrated operation of all design and construction factors from the earliest stages of planning: only through such an integrated approach can an efficient and sustainable system be created. A wide range of environmental issues are considered, such as water and energy consumption, surface runoff handling, use of ecological and nontoxic materials, open and undeveloped areas, air quality, access to natural light, and landscaping.

There are three main international green building certification systems in use today: the American Leadership in Energy and Environmental Design (LEED) system, the British Building Research Establishment Environmental Assessment Method (BREEAM), and the Australian Green Star standard.

The benefits

These include water and energy efficiency, waste management, reduced maintenance and operating costs, reduced resource use, and less air pollution and greenhouse gas emissions. A green building positively impacts those who occupy it, with natural lighting, for example, preferred over artificial light and indoor air quality being equally important. The financial value of such benefits is reflected in higher employee productivity, fewer sick days, and overall workplace satisfaction.

Do green buildings cost more?

Until recently, it was believed to be so. Perhaps because it was a new and innovative approach, green construction was commonly perceived to be significantly more expensive than conventional construction, thereby providing less economic value. However, those companies and organizations that have gone down this route have demonstrated that this is not the case. A U.S. study[8] comparing the costs of green with those of conventional construction showed an average premium for green buildings of slightly less than 2% – perhaps not negligible, but definitely worth the extra cost. Interestingly, the majority of that premium was attributable to the extra architectural and engineering time, along with time integrating sustainable building practices into the projects. Essentially, the earlier green building features are incorporated into the design process, the lower the cost. Also, the cost of green construction steadily declines as the number of green buildings rises: a combination of experience and growing market demand.

Green construction in practice

1 Indoor environmental quality. Air quality, lighting, landscape, and acoustics all have a significant impact on the health and quality of life of the occupants. Green building design should be climate-sensitive, optimizing sunlight angles to allow natural light into the building while decreasing the need for artificial light, which, when used, should be focused and cost-effective to reduce energy consumption. Natural light allows employees to sense time and enjoy the scenery outside, and it reduces eye strain. Clean air, free from contaminants such as building materials or outdoor pollution, improves employee health and productivity. Air conditioning systems should be kept clean and away from polluting elements. Also maintain air quality by reducing or avoiding substances that emit toxic fumes: paint, furnishings, adhesives, surfaces, etc., favoring natural materials.
2 Thermal insulation. A green building delays and reduces the impact of outdoor temperature changes on conditioned indoor environments, minimizing the need for artificial cooling in summer and heating in winter. Taking into consideration parameters such as wind direction and area topography improves air circulation and reduces the need for air conditioning, thereby helping to dissipate condensation and toxic gases.
3 Renewable energy. Green design uses solar energy to heat water and generate electricity using photovoltaic solar panels, or wind turbines to produce electricity on a local scale.

4 Water use. Technical measures for water conservation include making use of gray water.
5 A green roof. Rooftop gardens keep buildings cooler, help to reduce "heat islands" in cities, and keep stormwater runoff from putting pressure on the city's drainage system. The growing vegetation absorbs toxic gases, produces oxygen, and attracts insects and birds. Additional benefits include thermal and acoustic insulation and better flashing for sealing the building's roof.
6 Location. This includes the land the building is constructed on and its impact on its immediate neighborhood. A good location is one near an already developed area, protecting land resources and parkland when possible. Such a location also capitalizes on existing infrastructure, reducing costs and minimizing environmental impact. In the planning process, incorporate the building into the existing environment. The use of local plants in the landscaping design will be in visual harmony with the local setting, minimize water consumption, and create accessible habitats for local birds and insects. Consider rehabilitating degraded land (an area once contaminated by a factory, for example). Note that renovating a building is more sustainable than demolishing one. Added benefits accrue from a mixed-use approach for the building or its surrounding area, such as residential alongside commercial or office buildings with retail facilities on the ground floor. Mixed-use development focuses primarily on the welfare of residents and businesses; it provides a dynamic community that encourages walking and enhances quality of life. A green building is accessible with minimum energy costs: it should be near public transport or bicycle routes, allowing employees to leave their cars at home.
7 Green materials. Use recycled, recyclable, nontoxic material produced in a low-emission process or used in a controlled manner that allows renewal. Select materials with a longer lifespan. Also choose locally sourced products, which reduce transportation costs and promote the local economy.

8 Construction waste. This can be reduced through better planning, error-free project management, off-site production, and the establishment of on-site collecting, sorting, and renewal of construction material. This will provide immediate economic incentives to contractors by enabling them to sell on any remaining construction material and eliminate the costs of hauling waste to landfill.
9 Waste in use phase. Office or factory waste can be significantly reduced by a design that encourages waste separation and reuse of materials.
10 Supervision. From the planning stage through construction and operation, proper supervision will help control the use of resources and minimize environmental impact. Supervision includes integrative planning, incorporating all aspects of green construction and defining common goals. It concerns electrical systems, water, air conditioning, elevators, waste disposal, and safety features based on energy-saving occupancy sensors.

Green construction innovation

What role does technology have to play in greening the construction industry? In short, a lot. Innovative technologies can streamline processes, shorten construction time, and minimize the environmental impact of needing to correct problems. Resources can be managed more efficiently through coordination, synchronized operation, smart site management, safety, and proper waste management. Quality, environmentally friendly construction that reduces costs and increases productivity relies on innovative advances, such as robotics, sensors, three-dimensional printing, material development, automation, and digitization. All of these technologies, even without it being the expressed intention of using them, are helping to reduce the environmental footprint of the construction process.

However, innovation in the construction industry is not just technological. It begins with a conceptual shift to better construction, leading to innovation in thought, process, organization, and technology, creating a culture that encourages field testing, analysis, improvement, and perception of a structure as a product to be measured over a long period.[9] Often, planning and building costs seem trivial in comparison with the costs of maintenance, renovation, and energy consumption. Actual building performance should be measured, so an infrastructure and a database of innovations and improvements need to be established. Sadly, construction companies are mostly channeling an insufficient amount into innovative projects and ideas, and many countries have not seen their construction industries change much in recent decades. This is unfortunate: such investment would have enormous profit potential for the construction industry globally.

Green teams and committees

Until quite recently, the common perception was that practical environmental issues were handled by the maintenance department or the building supervisor. We now understand that a company seeking to create a real and profound cultural change must rely on employee commitment across the organization, going beyond mere compliance with company policies. One of the best ways to achieve this is to establish a volunteer green team. This engages employees in working toward a common goal – one of being part of an environmentally conscious organization, working to reduce the impact of its activity on the environment and contributing to its protection.

A green team consists of employee-volunteers led by the corporate responsibility officer or the company's environmental officer. The team members serve as environmental ambassadors or mentors and can inspire other organizations' employees. The team meets regularly to raise ideas and promote sustainable behavior in daily operations.

Often, the initiative to create such a team comes from the field, driven by employees. If the decision comes from executive level, efforts should be made to engage team members and keep them interested in giving up their free time. It should be noted that voluntary rather than obligatory activity will be more meaningful for the organization and more likely to succeed.

Organizational profit, employee profit

A green team is a contributing factor for any organization that wishes to promote environmental values, protect the environment, and be a role model for other companies in the sector, differentiating the organization from its competitors, positioning it as an environmental leader, and conferring competitive advantage. It also strengthens employees' commitment to the company and encourages initiatives and creativity. Members enjoy the sense of belonging to a small and prestigious team, working together toward meaningful goals. The sense of pride spreads across the organization: the team strengthens employee commitment to the company by giving them genuine influence on issues that matter to them. A green team contributes to improved operational efficiency and risk management, and generates cost savings by reducing consumption and minimizing waste. It promotes a culture of innovation, initiative, and inter-departmental cooperation.

Green team tips

It is important that the volunteers find a balance between their daily tasks and their green team efforts. Start small, and make sure not to promise unattainable results. As with any business operation, it is important to establish applicable indices for success and monitor activity. Conduct a "lessons learned" session after each activity.

Integrate the company's policy in general, and its corporate responsibility policy in particular, with the green team's objectives. The operations department and those involved in intra-organizational communication are vital. Including members of the business development department and division managers for whom the team is forming its recommendations will make it more likely that the recommendations are accepted. Use a variety of formal and informal platforms: engage suppliers, customers, and other stakeholders in the process, extending the green team's circle of influence within and outside the company.

Often, recommendations involve changing employee behavior (waste separation, for example). Green corporate events – green parties, exhibitions, incentives, and publicizing annual results – are effective tools for raising employee awareness and promoting behavioral change. Incentives can be offered to team members and other employees: group activities, environmental fun days and celebrations, competitions, and awards.

Inform employees about environmental issues via lectures, training, and excursions, etc. Give green team members additional data to enrich their knowledge base and reward them for their work. They are doing this out of a personal commitment to the program and the company, and thus it is important to value their efforts and express the company's appreciation in a variety of ways.

Environmental management system

An environmental management system (EMS) is a framework for developing and implementing an organization's environmental policy and objectives. It assists an organization in achieving its environmental footprint targets by: a comprehensive review of the organization's overall impact on the environment; a clear division of roles in the organization; setting goals and objectives; establishing work and operational procedures; instilling documentation procedures; measurement and control; and more.

An EMS can be internal or external. Organizations wishing to conform to an internationally accepted standard have the ISO 14001 standard at their disposal. Another recognized tool is the European Union's EMAS (Eco-Management and Audit Scheme).

An effective and comprehensive EMS incorporates, first of all, an identification of environmental impacts, and of legal implications. An environmental officer will be appointed and division of responsibility will be defined to foster inter-departmental cooperation. Financial and logistical implications will be identified and objectives and targets determined. Training sessions to raise employee awareness will be established, and the benefits of the organization's targets will be communicated. A stakeholder dialogue system will be set up. Documentation (management of records) and due diligence are key, with reporting to the organization's stakeholders the ultimate aim, e.g. as part of the corporate responsibility report. Have an independent third-party auditor validate documents and reports. To this end, operational controls and monitoring (for example, of power and fuel consumption) are critical. Finally, environmental procedures will be implemented that include operational controls regarding every environmental aspect relevant to the organization, and emergency procedures will be established.

Notes

1 https://www.onepercentfortheplanet.org/.
2 https://www.carbontrust.com/what-we-do/assurance-and-certification/product-footprint-certification.
3 Tom Burridge, "Coronavirus: Airlines 'entering danger zone.'" *BBC News*, March 29, 2020. https://www.bbc.co.uk/news/business-52083523.
4 "Coronavirus has emptied flights. It could end up changing flying forever." *The Guardian*, March 15, 2020. https://www.theguardian.com/business/2020/mar/15/coronavirus-airlines-emptied-flights-changing-flying.
5 Jennifer T. Gordon, "The implications of the coronavirus crisis on the global energy sector and the environment." *New Atlanticist*, March 24, 2020. https://www.atlanticcouncil.org/blogs/new-atlanticist/the-implications-of-the-coronavirus-crisis-on-the-global-energy-sector-and-the-environment/.
6 "Petrol and diesel car sales ban brought forward to 2035." *The Guardian*, February 4, 2020. https://www.bbc.co.uk/news/science-environment-51366123.
7 http://www.maala-en.org.il/maala-international-conference-2019/.
8 Nora Knox, "Green building costs and savings." *U.S. Green Business Council*, March 25, 2015. https://www.usgbc.org/articles/green-building-costs-and-savings.
9 "How companies can adapt to climate change." *McKinsey & Co.*, July 2015. https://www.mckinsey.com/business-functions/sustainability-and-resource-productivity/our-insights/how-companies-can-adapt-to-climate-change; IHS Global insight.

16 Plant roots in your community

"Businesses cannot succeed in societies that fail" is a simple and inescapable truth articulated by the World Business Council for Sustainable Development (WBCSD). Henry Ford believed that his employees should be his best customers and made sure they could afford to buy one of his Model Ts. The ethic with which he ran his business was: what is good for the community is good for the company.

COVID-19 soon revealed the leaders in this area. Hundreds of companies in the corporate sector, even while facing uncertainty, showed commitment by finding creative ways to help the community: from babysitting services for medical staff to quickly changing production lines to manufacture ventilators.

Put simply, the community is one of the organization's most important stakeholders. So it is important to establish and maintain a close connection with it. An organization depends on the community from which it draws its customers, employees, suppliers, and neighbors. And investing in the community helps confer an organization's social license to operate. Businesses have long since found ways of contributing to the community in which they operate, whether through financial contribution, in-kind donation, or organizational or personal volunteering, but only recently, however, have efforts been made to formally and systematically manage corporate community outreach programs. Although a financial contribution is still the most common community engagement practice, there are many ways in which an organization can give back to its community. In *Corporate Social Responsibility*, Philip Kotler and Nancy Lee[1] define six options for corporate social initiatives. It will be illuminating to look at these and determine which ones happen in your organization.

1. Cause promotions. Providing funds or in-kind contributions to increase awareness of a social cause.
2. Cause-related marketing. Donating a percentage of revenues or profits to a specific social cause. Often this initiative is announced for a specific product and for a specified charity.
3. Corporate social marketing. A corporate marketing campaign in support of a social cause.
4. Corporate philanthropy. A direct financial contribution to a charity or cause.
5. Community volunteering. Employee volunteer activities organized by the corporation and often during work hours.
6. Socially responsible business practices. Integrating social and environmental matters within the organization's core business, similar to the Shared Value model. This initiative is clearly the most challenging and interesting option. It can be reflected in social and environmental considerations across the supply and procurement chain, or through corporate recruitment and employment policies. Another option is employee training on social issues or developing unique products that meet specific social needs.

Technology serves a critical role here – and will increasingly do so in the future – in planning and monitoring. Crucially, it allows an awareness of how resources are being utilized; if there is a communication gap here between the company and its NGO partners, there is a strong possibility that the program will fail to have an impact. Tech-based program management platforms allow companies to get regular reports from their NGO partners and help in drawing up clear value statements for the board-level executives. If a project is complex with multiple tiers of implementation, a streamlined project management approach is required. This can be achieved by adopting innovative technological solutions, such as blockchain, the "internet of things" (IoT), and artificial intelligence (AI) – disruptive technologies that offer a wide array of solutions.[2]

One example is Round-Up International, a nonprofit organization that allows credit card users to automatically round up each of their payments to the nearest round figure with the difference being directed to a charity of choice. The many small donations of several cents each accumulate to make a significant social contribution. Small change makes a big difference. Many companies today, especially after the COVID-19 outbreak, are using video-conferencing technology for their social engagement, which I will discuss next.

Community engagement/community relations strategy

As with many areas, there is a well-trodden route from sporadic initiatives to formalized agendas. First, a well-meaning organization will donate to various charities that are unrelated to the organization's activity and to each other. The charities likely received a one-off contribution and had to repeatedly return for more. A strategically planned social policy, however, shifts the responsibility for charitable contributions to the organization, which can then review alternatives and choose the most suitable option for itself and for the community's best interests.

A proper community engagement strategy provides real benefits. It positions the organization as a leader in corporate responsibility, enhances its reputation, and boosts employee satisfaction. But this is just the tip of the iceberg. A well-structured community strategy can bolster stakeholder relationships, build trust and respect, create brand loyalty and differentiation, and even reach a new target audience (minorities or other under-represented communities).

214 *The good process*

> **Google Foundation**
>
> Tech giants   Community
>
> In 2005, Google created the Google Foundation, otherwise known as Google.org. The foundation works to link non-profit innovators with funding, tools, and Google volunteers to create tangible impact at scale. Funding and support are concentrated on the following main areas to accelerate their reach and development: creating economic impact, developing education, promoting inclusion, responding to crises, and enhancing communities.[3] Google volunteers notoriously spend 200,000 hours of time annually collaborating with nonprofits and offering their engineering skills and innovative abilities as a path to swift growth. Google.org's goal is to contribute 1 million volunteer-hours to nonprofits over the course of the next five years. As a tangent to its volunteer work, Google.org commits billions of dollars annually to nonprofits that support the development of online family privacy, trust, and safety across Sub-Saharan Africa.[4] Its combination of funding and volunteering makes for an innovative way to tackle global challenges.

Issues and dilemmas

Social contribution as a strategic management tool is often prone to biases that can draw criticism with regard to a business's priorities or external influence. Be aware of the pitfalls from the outset.

- *A tendency to donate to large, well-known charities* that are supposedly good for the business's image yet might divert aid from smaller "under the radar" charities that require more assistance.
- *A tendency to favor more "attractive" social causes* such as children in preference to, for example, the elderly.

- *A tendency to favor major city centers* because most large firms are located there and choose charities in close proximity rather than those based in the suburbs, for example.
- *Avoidance of non-consensus social issues* such as promotion of social change or equality, in case such support is viewed as a political statement.
- *Governmental withdrawal from responsibility*. Corporate contributions to the community can give governments an excuse to retreat from their own commitments. This criticism is often voiced from both a moral and an operational (e.g. budget redundancies).

Give careful consideration to the following areas, both from an operational and a reputational perspective:

- *Anonymous donation versus social marketing*. Do you choose low-profile or even anonymous contributions, or a high-profile campaign with a strong media presence? Most companies usually take a middle road with some donations and volunteer work being publicized and others conducted away from the limelight.
- *Charity in the digital age*. The information revolution has created new opportunities for social contribution. Crowdfunding is an obvious example, and campaigns can now be easily conducted within and between corporations. Management can actively connect employees with charities and allow them to participate in decision-making.

JGive

Technology   Platforms   Society

The nonprofit sector lags behind its for-profit counterparts in its use of technology. Much of the fundraising is still done through costly phone campaigns and professionally produced campaigns. When charities do move online, they're faced with enormous costs to reach potential donors and to maintain websites and security for donors' financial information. Existing platforms for nonprofits charge exorbitant fees usually exceeding 10% of donations. Ultimately, more money goes into overhead and less into helping society. JGive allows direct donations to hundreds of Israeli organizations, linking nonprofits with donors. Unlike other nonprofit platforms, charities can use JGive for free, and all money, other than a small credit card service fee, is transferred directly to the charity. In exchange, the charities provide full disclosure on how the money will be used. An advanced digital platform such as this makes donating secure, transparent, and easy.

There is no reason within a corporate responsibility policy not to publicize an organization's contribution provided that it upholds the privacy and rights of the recipient. But community engagement in general and volunteer work in particular should be integrated as part of organizational objectives and work plans.

360Giving

Technology   Platforms

360Giving is a platform that supports British organizations in publishing and sharing their grants data, e.g. sector, location, and organization type and size. The ability to compare information about charities and charitable funders reduces duplicated efforts and leverages contributions.

Flagship community projects

A leading trend in recent years is one of focused and leveraged contributions over a relatively long period of time as a replacement for one-off separate contributions. In corporate responsibility terms, this is a "flagship community project." As part of organizational social policy, such a project is an initiative to develop and implement a program for community engagement which addresses a clear and quantifiable social need while leveraging and differentiating the organization's values and motivating employees.

A flagship community project must first address the needs of the organization. In doing this, it will maximize its effectiveness both for the organization and for the cause. This is not a marginal decision; it is a strategic and significant one, and in order for it to fulfill its purpose, it must be well planned.

Strategic planning

1 Define the project's goals and objectives across both business and social aspects.
2 Conduct a social and business needs survey to help identify the best alternatives, identifying social needs that also serve a business need (social cause, geographic area, budget, etc.).
3 Interview company managers, employees, and relevant external parties to raise ideas and determine real needs from the field. These interviews can serve as an introduction to engagement in the next stage of community action.
4 Set benchmarks for project measurement. For example, examine existing projects in similar sectors around the world.

Choosing a flagship project

The most effective project will offer a win–win situation for the organization and the community. Important characteristics include originality and authenticity, fit to the company (size, context, ability to assist, etc.), relevance to a real social need, and the potential for support and commitment across as much of the company as possible. Many corporations find it hard to choose between community or environmental activities. On the one hand, social activity may be perceived as more meaningful and immediate, but on the other hand, environmental sustainability is of fundamental importance to the organization and there will always be a common desire to devote resources to this matter. In any event, any organization launching a flagship project must reach the understanding that it is an integral part of the community in which it operates. One of the projects that I am particularly proud of is called Spreading Seeds of Science which I helped build for Adama, a global crop protection company (www.Adama.com). It is based on agricultural and scientific training and empowerment of children in various communities.

Measurement and evaluation

As with any project, a flagship project needs to be measured and evaluated. Numerous parameters must be considered, including time and budget constraints, and effective use of connections and influence. Measurements can be performed at three different levels:

1 Social change level (the public/social impact). A measure of the extent of social change achieved in the field.
2 Branding and positioning level (the brand). A measure of brand awareness and the positioning of the corporation as contributor to the project. This assesses whether the project corresponds to the promotional message and company and brand values.
3 Intra-organizational level (the firm). An evaluation of employee and volunteer satisfaction, level of exposure within the company, percentage of active volunteers, etc.

Engagement termination

Since this is a strategic partnership rather than a one-time donation, carefully plan an exit strategy that will benefit all parties. There are four options:

1 Gradual conclusion. Define a time frame through which the corporation's involvement is gradually decreased.

2 Passing the baton. Introduce a new contributing partner and conduct an organized transfer of responsibilities.
3 Managing expectations. Clearly define the engagement time frame during the initial stages of involvement.
4 A countdown of successes and achievements.

Employee volunteering and engagement

In the relationship between the business sector and the community, employee volunteer work is becoming an important topic. Although volunteer work has been a prevailing aspect of CSR since the 1900s, today corporate volunteering is no longer just a PR tool but an effective means of furthering society and a strategic human resources tool.[5] Meaningful employee engagement is a necessary part of a firm's commitment to making community involvement strategic, alongside engaging them in the overall mission for sustainability and corporate responsibility.

Friends for Health

Technology   Circular economy   Health

An example of a volunteer initiative that links technology and the circular economy – and one that Good Vision assisted with in its early stages – is the Friends for Health project. Recognizing that unused medicines worth millions of dollars are thrown away every year, this initiative collects unused medication and then distributes it for free to those who need it most. The Friends for Health initiative involves both professionals and hundreds of volunteers in pharmacies and distribution centers and relies on a GPS-based app. With this reclaimed medication, the project has succeeded in treating thousands of cancer and chronically ill patients each month.[6]

There are many ways of volunteering, especially with today's technology. In fact, online volunteering was key in helping to bridge the social distancing problem during COVID-19.

There are reasons for establishing a volunteering program that go beyond corporate image. First and foremost, it touches the lives of people in the community in a way that simply donating money does not, and, most importantly, brings real, sustainable change in the community. Crucially, volunteering can have far-reaching positive effects on your workforce:

- Retain and attract a quality workforce, earning a reputation among existing and potential employees as an ethical workplace.
- Increase employees' identification with the organizational vision and values.
- Foster team building, motivation, and organizational spirit.
- Facilitate informal interaction between employees outside the workplace.
- Bring out creative energies that do not always find an outlet at work. A low-level IT employee may find she has excellent training and organizational skills, for example.
- Allow a refreshing break in the routine along with a sense of meaning and accomplishment.
- Facilitate inter-departmental social connections, potentially improving intra-organizational collaboration.
- Empower employees with a sense of responsibility and confidence: the temporary hierarchical structure allows employees with previous volunteering experience or skills to guide their managers and colleagues.
- Create an additional parameter for employee evaluation, or even a platform for fostering leadership.

Of course, there are organizational implications. The volunteering process costs money and time: maintaining and retaining volunteers, administration, adding flexibility into the organizational timetables. But it is worth heeding a popular maxim from the UK business community: $CR - HR = PR$. In other words, if employees are not engaged, corporate social responsibility is merely an exercise in public relations. Even so, employee time is an organization's most precious resource and therefore not easily reallocated to community projects. But, for all the reasons stated earlier, it is worth the effort.

As a first move, conduct a survey or review of employees' preferences and capabilities. The more options you make available, the more likely employees' needs and capabilities will be catered to. Prepare a framework for several projects and allow employees to choose. Concurrently, ask the community, nonprofit organization, or charity to map its needs so as to minimize cultural or procedural obstacles and manage expectations on both sides.

Employee training and orientation

If volunteering in the community is a simple and intuitive process, why does it require training? When a company's employees volunteer their time, they represent the organization, so risk management must be part of the process. A strategic initiative such as this cannot be allowed to fail, so training and orientation is required to reduce uncertainties and knowledge gaps before work begins. This is especially important when volunteering with special populations such as troubled youth or senior citizens.

Leading by example

We recommend limited involvement of senior managers in the operation itself. The usual bureaucratic hierarchy carries less weight in a volunteering situation in any case. Instead, the personal example set by a direct supervisor is key.

Employee compensation

Some volunteer work is done within regular work hours at the company's expense; some is done outside of work hours. The most common option is a combination of the two, in which case there is a joint commitment by both the company and the employee. An organization's funding of volunteer hours conveys to employees the importance it attaches to the project.

Non-financial rewards are important. Demonstrate appreciation by publicizing volunteer work throughout the organization (company website, newsletter, conferences, events, etc.) and honoring all volunteers in general and outstanding volunteers in particular. When communicating volunteer work internally, encourage healthy competition among departments and their managers in meeting volunteering as well as sustainability objectives.

Lessons learned: a volunteer database

Share learning to engage employees further while improving the effectiveness of the work. This is an opportunity to increase employee participation, which leads to higher satisfaction and identification with company values. Create a database of accumulated knowledge as a basis for an ongoing program of volunteer work, progressively improving and consistently appropriate to the organization.

Volunteerability

There are three components that must coincide to create "volunteerability," i.e. the likelihood that an individual will volunteer:

1 *Willingness* to help others, to promote a social goal; to escape the workday routine; to become involved; etc.
2 Emotional and physical *availability*.
3 Personal *capability* to join the activity.

Is volunteering for all companies?

Before embarking on this journey, consider the business's lifecycle stage. A startup currently recruiting investors and fighting for its financial stability will likely struggle to maintain an intensive employee volunteer program, whereas a mature or growing company can easily launch a program that will grow and improve along with the company: a volunteer program demonstrates a company's stability manifested by its willingness to devote its energy and resources to ethical matters. Companies undergoing mergers or acquisitions are advised to tailor the volunteer program (or launch a new one) to integrate the organizational and volunteer cultures of all merged companies.

Cross-sectoral steering committee

Cross-sectoral steering committee meetings are advised across the life of the project. All parties involved should be represented: for example, the local council in charge of the cause (e.g. youth council), the relevant government department (e.g. an inspector from the Department of Education), the charity's CEO or chair, community representatives, alongside company representatives (e.g. corporate responsibility officer, social relations manager). The steering committee facilitates implementation and delivers the most for – and gets the best out of – the parties involved. This is where a complex logistical task, for example, gets assigned to the right player. If there is a significant obstacle that only a corporate financial contribution will solve – such as arranging transportation – this is where the decision is made.

DonorsChoose

Technology Society

DonorsChoose helps you make a donation of any size for school supplies assisting teachers in high-need communities. Choose a project, and once it receives enough funding, DonorsChoose buys and ships the materials to the teacher. Within a few days, you can connect with who you helped.

Online volunteering

Volunteer projects don't have to be physically demanding or logistically challenging. There are groundbreaking platforms to connect the digital world to the needs of the "real" world. Lessons, courses (and even psychological counseling) are all available online, and significant sums of money are raised through crowdfunding. There is an increasing array of mobile apps to facilitate such purposes. During COVID-19, the advantages of online volunteering were brought into focus. Useful projects included addressing loneliness among the elderly who were isolated at home; an interesting application in this respect is 2gether. fun which aims to help elderly people with memory issues by interacting through music.

GiveGab

Technology   Society

GiveGab is about making volunteering a fun, social experience. The app connects you with over 400,000 nonprofits based on your interests and profile. It also lets you log your volunteer hours and post pictures, which other volunteers can see on the app's newsfeed, "The Gab."

The internet and social media in particular has become a critical tool for charities and NPOs to promote their activities, advertise, engage, drive donations, and even enable actual volunteer work. If you have employees who can't leave the office, you can always find a charity that offers online volunteering opportunities. Here are some practical examples of how employees can offer assistance in various creative ways by giving up, for example, one hour per week: research, data collection and analysis, content writing, translation and editing, advising, tasks such as website design, social media promotion – or assistance in any field accessible to the organization and serving the charity's needs. Such assistance can provide real benefits by drawing on an organization's professional resources, such as technical infrastructure (hardware, networks, software) and employee expertise and experience.

> **VolunteerMatch**
>
> Technology   Society
>
> As corporate volunteering opportunities have developed into a critical aspect of talent management and resource allocation, efficient tech solutions like VolunteerMatch in the U.S. have emerged. Since 1998, Volunteer Match has been connecting millions of corporate, government, and academic agencies such as AT&T, Groupon, Humana, JetBlue, Johnson & Johnson, L'Oréal, Morgan Stanley, Nationwide, NBC Universal, Sony Pictures Entertainment, and Starbucks with national nonprofit partners such as Partners American Red Cross, California State Library, Easter Seals, Girl Scouts of the USA, National CASA, and National MS Society Select. As the web's largest volunteering engagement network, it has provided over 103,000 active volunteering opportunities to over 150 network partners.

The third sector

In democratic societies, social and nonprofit civic organizations serving social and/or environmental objectives are collectively referred to as the "third sector," with the first sector being the public sector – government and its institutions and ministries – and the second sector the private sector, consisting of businesses and corporations. Included in the third sector are formal, institutionalized, long-standing organizations, nonprofits, charities, voluntary organizations, and cooperatives. It is the civic arena for activity that combines concern for public welfare (related to public sector policies) with free, nonbinding voluntary action.

Cross-sectoral alliances and collaborations

Collaborations between businesses and nonprofit organizations are increasingly prevalent – the concept of cross-sectoral alliances is one of the fundamental principles of corporate responsibility. Genuine partnerships must be forged between businesses, nonprofits, and sometimes even governments in order to further the social agenda. Partners come from different backgrounds, with different sets of cultural norms and terms, yet with the right approach the relative advantages of each sector can be harnessed. Remember: diversity is an asset, not a liability. Needless to say that these practices are not meant just for huge companies; for example, one of my clients Tahini El Arz, a small company, has decided to support the LGBT community in the Arab sector of Israel. The brave move has not only helped the cause but also gained him a lot of support and brand recognition.

It is important to understand how to initiate such a partnership, maintain it over time, and maximize its efficiency for both parties, so that it is not undertaken for appearances' sake only.

The third sector faces a constant challenge in finding resources for various reasons, including redundancies and lack of real influence on social and economic policy. For that reason, the third sector is an excellent partner for private sector social responsibility initiatives looking for a win–win scenario for the firm and the cause, with businesses offering their capacity, skills, and resources to improve nonprofits' operations. As such, it is advisable to focus a company's efforts on just one or two causes.

Businesses will usually want to differentiate and become leaders in their field of activity, selecting the right partner to maintain consistency with corporate strategy while providing an effective contribution.

> **Stella Artois**
>
> Society
>
> Since 2015, Stella Artois has been a partner of Water.org, thereby helping bring safe water and sanitation to more than 1.7 million people in developing countries. From donations attached to each sale of a Stella Artois or limited-edition chalice under its #POURITFORWARD campaign, the company has contributed over $21 million. The aim is to increase its reach to 3.5 million by 2020.

What is an effective contribution?

Corporate culture is predicated on information-based decision-making: measurement and evaluation of market share, customer satisfaction, sales targets, and so on. However, such quantitative measures are less common within civil society, so instilling a measurement culture is something to offer your third-sector partner. With regard to the effectiveness of community contribution, the importance of measuring has been increasingly acknowledged of late, and of speaking in terms of output or outcome rather than just input. For example: "20 of our program participants earned their teaching degrees and began working as teachers themselves," rather than "we donated $150,000 to a program promoting education excellence in developing areas." However, such improvements should be encouraged rather than coerced (e.g. by threatening to discontinue donations); for example, by funding assessment measures or requesting information and success statistics. Adapt your quantitative indicators to the social sphere in a manner that will not be construed as condescending or the forcing of business practices on the community.

The road toward a culture of measurement and evaluation is a long one, all the same. Many donors avoid contributing to the development of organizational frameworks, preferring a direct contribution (to a child at risk, for example). After all, an unmediated donation to children or the elderly is more poignant and offers a greater sense of satisfaction. It also creates greater media impact. However, in the long run, fishing rods are better than fish. With a mature organizational outlook, and a sophisticated approach to maximizing the effectiveness of a contribution, you will most likely have greater impact channeling your donations toward a system for measurement and evaluation rather than handing cash to a program for a hundred more children at risk.

Notes

1 Nancy Lee and Philip Kotler, *Corporate Social Responsibility: Doing the Most Good for Your Company and Your Cause*. Hoboken, NJ: John Wiley, 2005.
2 Namita Vikas, "Group President & Global Head, Climate Strategy & Responsible Banking, YES Bank: Technology: An enabler for corporate social responsibility." *The CSR Journal*, May 5, 2018. https://thecsrjournal.in/technology-enabler-corporate-social-responsibility.
3 *Google.org*, "Our work." https://www.google.org/our-work/.
4 Chinaka Okoro, "Google launches $1m grant for children." *The Nation*, February 17, 2020. https://thenationonlineng.net/google-launches-1m-grant-for-children/.
5 "Corporate volunteering: Underestimated opportunities in aging societies?" *The Conversation*, December 20, 2017. https://theconversation.com/corporate-volunteering-underestimated-opportunities-in-aging-societies-87892.
6 See https://www.haverim.org.il.

17 Revolutionize your marketing and service

Treat customers as the real shareholders of the organization

The service/marketing notion that "the customer is always right" is greatly influenced by, and has an influence on, the world of corporate responsibility. Indeed, according to this adage, customers are the driving force behind the private sector. As such, the strength of the business sector is defined primarily by its customers, their needs, and their insights.

In fact, a brand becomes a brand (with its image and reputation) only when it is recognized as such in the hearts and minds of consumers. A company's reputation, shaped also by aspects of its corporate responsibility, is defined by its customers and the public. Similarly, a service can be considered effective only after it has been provided to its users and has received their feedback.

A strong brand is a fully integrated part of the entire organization aligned around multiple touch points. Sustainability – both internally and externally – is one such meaningful touch point. The potential connections between sustainability and branding are clear. The rationale is even clearer these days because customers are increasingly looking for a brand or product with a positive social or environmental profile.

Customers are among a company's primary and dominant stakeholders. For this reason, a corporation's activities in all spheres of corporate responsibility (environmental, social, ethical, etc.) are also directed at them. They demand special consideration, and certain elements of corporate responsibility are purely about customers. It begins with quality and standards of products and services, and it continues with credibility and fairness in advertising. From there attention should be paid to avoiding offending certain groups in marketing and advertising campaigns, and to upholding adequate and transparent handling of consumer complaints. Much more is required, of course. It is important to avoid the exploitation of extreme market conditions such as monopolies, discourage price fixing, and refrain from manipulating weak and vulnerable customers.

These points should be discussed in an open dialogue conducted between the organization and its customers. If customers are not already part of the dialogue, they should be added. The British organization Business in the Community (BITC) has laid out a set of principles of corporate responsibility in the marketplace:[1]

- Respect your customers.
- Support vulnerable customers.
- Seek potential customers within excluded groups.
- Manage the impact of product or service.
- Discourage product misuse.
- Ensure a responsible supply chain.
- Treat suppliers as partners.
- Work with the rule makers.
- Keep consistent standards.

In an era in which the battle for consumers' hearts and minds – and dollars – is becoming increasingly dynamic and complex, products and services are becoming more indistinguishable. Now that conventional options for product differentiation are proving harder to find, such competitive advantage can be more easily attained by raising and communicating the company's social and environmental profile. Corporate sustainability is therefore both a potential tool for differentiation and a base for segmentation. Consumer awareness of companies' impacts is steadily increasing, and such messages rise above the general media noise to a consumer base that is more attuned than ever to receiving them. A 2017 U.S. Cone Communications survey found that:

- 63% want businesses to take the lead in driving social and environmental change.
- 78% want companies to address social justice issues.
- 87% will purchase a product because a company advocated for an issue they cared about.
- 76% will avoid a company's products or services if it supported an issue contrary to their beliefs.[2]

And remember: alongside this "pull" from the consumer side, you will be experiencing a "push" from your various stakeholders to improve your environmental and social profile.

From the technological point of view, customers can compare and evaluate services and products much more easily these days. Social networks allow customers to report and share on quality, reliability, and service issues within seconds. Because of this, brands and reputations are much more vulnerable.

So what role does your marketing function play? The first and most obvious point is that your marketing does not "go green" without being a component of a concerted program of corporate social and environmental responsibility. Many companies have attempted "green" as a mere branding or PR strategy and come unstuck (see the "Greenwashing" section later in this chapter). Companies that are serious about associating their brands with social and environmental benefits according to their customers' expectations should be prepared to invest in working processes before launching the marketing stage.

COVID-19 implications

As thrown into sharp relief by the COVID-19 crisis, for the sake of your company reputation, brand, and indeed actual long-term survival, a considered, well-communicated approach with the good of the wider community as a priority is required – essentially, corporate responsibility. As brand consultant and former marketing professor Mark Ritson said in March 2020,

> It might seem superficially mercantile to discuss brands, pricing and customer behavior as we stare down the barrel of a pandemic. But the practical reality of global economic trade means that we need to market now for the good of all mankind.[3]

Renowned marketer Neil Patel warned other marketers to be bold, to see long-term opportunities, and not to cynically exploit the situation.[4] Even in the early stages of the crisis, we saw leaders responding quickly and appropriately and getting that message across: Walmart, Starbucks, and Home Depot, for example. Essential services such as food retail were not just visible in paid ads; they were news, so COVID-19 response policy quickly became common knowledge. Marketing and comms played a pivotal role (see also the "Digital marketing," section later in this chapter).

The strategy

Done right, socially responsible marketing (or green marketing) is the development of environmentally and socially friendly products and/or services and advertising and selling them in a manner that will also enable consumers to make a better-informed choice with regard to the environmental or societal impact of products while identifying with the brand's values. A product might also help promote an environmental cause. Products that can be marketed as environmentally or socially friendly include those that:

- Are sourced from sustainable raw materials such as organic food, recycled paper, or eco-fleece clothing.
- Help conserve natural resources, such as hybrid cars or energy-efficient light bulbs.
- Have an energy-efficient or sustainable production process (minimum emissions and conservation of resources).

- Are made or sold by individuals with special needs, or by companies who devote a portion of their profits to promote social or environmental causes.
- Have qualified for an environmental or social certification or label – the Marine Stewardship Council label, for example (such accreditation is available at organizational level as well, such as ISO 14001 and EMAS).
- (During the pandemic) are those can be ordered and delivered minimizing unnecessary social contact.

Numerous companies trade on brand differentiation based on these kinds of messages and values, among them the Timberland shoe company, Whole Foods supermarkets, and the floor tile company Interface.

---

sweetgreen

Community   Environment

Founded in 2007 by student friends in the U.S., sweetgreen is a fast-casual food outlet that serves healthy, locally sourced, organic food. It aims to make eating healthy "easy, fun, and approachable" and has built up a network of local suppliers and partners, supporting communities and creating meaningful relationships. The sweetgreen team regularly visits public schools to educate children about healthy food supply chains. They also organize block parties and festivals, with community engagement being one of their core values. "We exist to create experiences where passion and purpose come together," they claim, and aim to "connect with people through food."[5]

An effective green marketing strategy is emphatically not a PR exercise and is not something that can be achieved by the marketing department in isolation. It must be predicated on the company's genuine commitment to products and services that deliver environmental and/or social benefits or else markedly reduce impacts relative to the competition. Marketing therefore necessarily follows operational change or adaptation, although it may also be used to communicate that a process of change is under way. A good example of a company with sustainability as part of its brand is sweetgreen (see the sweetgreen Box).

P&G

Society

Procter & Gamble (P&G), one of Unilever's competitors, is making progress with its corporate responsibility, defining it as one of its global business strategies. As an example, 20% of P&G's advertising budget in some countries (under the banner of its Pantene brand) is earmarked for campaigns that promote hair donations to make wigs for women and girls undergoing cancer treatment.[6] These campaigns have led to a growing awareness of the issue, and hair donations have flooded in. The donations are a source of pride for those girls who donate, allowing them a sense of purpose and to demonstrate their compassion. From the perspective of the company's bottom line, there was a marked increase in Pantene sales during these campaigns.

Greenwashing

Greenwashing is the practice of disseminating marketing or PR to promote a company or brand's socially or environmentally friendly credentials when the claims either cannot be fully substantiated or when they attempt to misdirect away from a company's less acceptable practices. In the information age, this practice will eventually and inevitably be exposed for what it is, discrediting the organization and damaging its relationship with its customers and the public at large. Abusing the public's trust is counter to all the values of corporate responsibility we have described in this book; the resulting crisis will be expensive, and it will take a long time before trust is restored.

Greenwashing tactics include:

- Ambiguous terminology.
- A green campaign from a known polluter.
- According green benefits to a non-sustainable product.
- "Green" imagery and visuals, implying even if not stating (unsubstantiated) benefits.
- Organizational positioning when the benchmark is low, e.g. claiming to be the "greenest" among a group of polluting companies.
- Unsupported scientific explanations.
- Quotes from "experts" with no recognized affiliations.

Similarly, organizations can also falsely sell themselves as conferring social benefits – even going as far as referring to themselves as "social enterprises." Such practices when exposed are referred to as "social-washing." With companies eager to espouse the socially aware values of Millennials and Gen Zs, a new term has also entered the lexicon: "woke-washing" (see the Pepsi Box).[7]

Pepsi

Reputation   Brand

In 2017 Pepsi launched an ad in which reality TV star Kendall Jenner is seen interrupting a protest to offer a policeman a can of the fizzy drink. It was immediately criticized by both public and media for cynically capitalizing on, and trivializing, genuine protests for social justice, particular the recent Black Lives Matter campaigns. Also, crucially, according to marketing expert Mike Jackson, Pepsi had no previous history of championing social causes.[8] In the face of a storm of backlash, the ad was withdrawn in less than 24 hours. "It's a unique skill to have #boycottpepsi trending among both the right and the left. It managed to alienate both sides of an increasingly polarized consumer universe," said Nicola Kemp, trends editor at advertising trade magazine *Campaign*.[9]

In practice

The strategy will require a holistic approach and comes from an understanding that every product or service has social, economic, and environmental implications. Green marketing gives equal prominence to a product's environmental or social benefits along with, for example, performance, aesthetics, or reliability. It also sells the company at the same time, communicating its commitment in order to establish the brand's credibility – and it does so with substantiated evidence, not empty slogans.

Here are some key guidelines:

1 *Differentiate.* For example, be the first company in your sector to calculate its carbon footprint.
2 *Understand your target audience.* Choose actions that can be easily explained: reducing environmental impact by taking vehicles off the road, for example. And *use clear language*, avoiding ambiguity or technical terms.
3 *"Pass it forward."* Invite consumers to participate, for example, in sustainability initiatives. Foster customer *empathy and engagement*, using personal stories as well as statistics.
4 *Communicate the real benefits only.* Avoid making unsubstantiated or superficial claims.

5 *Give yourself feedback.* As well as congratulating yourself for your achievements, review issues that need improvement and conduct a self-assessment. This is the one that organizations often find difficult, but public and stakeholder scrutiny is inevitable. Voluntary and honest self-appraisal will only serve to increase the brand's credibility.

TOMS

Society

One for-profit company promoting change while providing a positive user experience for its customers is TOMS.[10] The shoe company donates a pair of shoes to those in need in developing countries for every pair purchased in its stores. More recently, it has extended its social impact work to include eyewear and safe drinking water.

The green consumer and social marketing

Green marketing must be seen in the context of a time in which transparency is of increased importance to consumers and indeed all stakeholders. Your marketing efforts are part of a genuine dialogue with the public in order to establish a trusting relationship. This is a public that more than ever will demand its right to know and to be involved. Socially and environmentally conscious consumers are fast becoming the norm.

In seeking your target market, it is worth noting that there is a paradox at play. It would seem that there has never been a better time to launch a sustainable offering, with consumers – particularly Millennials – increasingly demanding brands that embrace purpose and sustainability However, we need to look at the data on how many consumers who report positive attitudes toward eco-friendly products and services follow through with their wallets.

In one recent survey, 65% said they want to buy purpose-driven brands that advocate sustainability but only about 26% actually did so. Narrowing this "intention–action gap" is therefore possibly the marketing function's key challenge. In an age in which advertising and marketing is viewed with increased skepticism, this area can in fact deliver true real-world benefits – in driving consumers toward more responsible behavior and buying habits (see the Goodvertising Box). Consumer goods giant Unilever has estimated that almost 70% of its lifecycle GHG footprint is dependent on consumer behavior: i.e. which products their customers buy and how they use and dispose of them.[11] Recently, we have seen many prominent brands coming forward and making their presence felt during COVID-19 to support medical teams and people in need.

Goodvertising

Reputation

Goodvertising,[12] a concept created by Thomas Kolster, helps brands earn their audiences' trust, based on the ten fundamentals of transparency, connection, simplicity, collaboration, passion, creativity, contagiousness, generosity, insight, and full commitment. Kolster sees a growing correlation between the triple bottom line and a brand's image. In an accompanying book,[13] Kolster demonstrates how Goodvertising can help develop the values of truth, trust, and responsibility in the context of organizations as diverse as governmental agencies, advertising firms, branding and media agencies, corporations, foundations, and nonprofits. Nike, Amnesty International, WWF, Fiat, and Bank of Aland have all caught wind of this idea and successfully leveraged it to improve both their internal operations and external image.

Social marketing

The power of brands can be a force for good and can help to create social value, as articulated by Giles Gibbons, writing in *The Economist*'s *Brands and Branding*.[14] There are two routes to achieve this. The first is to harness the cultural power of brands for positive social change. The second is to apply brand power to the urgent task of spreading the benefits of globalization; a good example of this is the Dove soap "Campaign for Real Beauty," which used a diverse range of models to challenge the conventional advertising stereotypes that can be detrimental to self-esteem. And we now see an increasing number of brands getting behind important social issues such as #MeToo or LGBTQ+ equality.

Digital marketing

In the COVID-19 crisis, an immediate reversal was in evidence. Instead of asking, "Do I need to do this online?" we were forced to ask, "Is there any reason why I need to do this in person?"[15] Digital communication between companies and their customers was in many cases the only thing that kept the former in business (see also the "COVID-19 implications" section earlier in this chapter).

Many digital marketing assets are at your disposal, such as your website, video content, images including branded assets such as logos, written content, online products or tools, reviews, and social media pages. Similarly, there are a myriad of strategies or combinations depending on your business and your target market.[16] Today, 69% of adult internet users are on at least one social media platform; 95% of Americans aged 18–29 own a smartphone; and there are countries where you are more likely to own a smartphone than have running water. Marketers have to keep up with constantly evolving digital trends: technology is persistently disruptive, and the rules keep changing. Here are some current insights:[17]

- Our traditional ideas about marketing were formed in an era of limited media: now the media market is infinite.

- Brands are all-important – customers want experience.
- There is no longer such a thing as an impulse buy: thanks to technology, all purchases can be informed and therefore considered.
- AI is now simply how you reach your consumers: it's not optional.
- Four times as many consumers would rather watch a video about a product than read about it.
- The vast majority of customers are now confident in using the internet and feel they can keep up with the constant flow of information.
- They demand high-quality content.
- You need a mobile strategy: 60% of internet activity takes place on mobile devices.

A major challenge is differentiating yourself among this tsunami of information, as well as dealing with the level of data you can recoup. You need to know which metrics are important and have the staff on board with the analytical skills to process it. Your relationship with your public is changing. Intimacy is the new catchword, especially when targeting younger generations: 85% of users are more likely to buy a product if the message is personalized and supported by social. Innovation will play a key role for many: some established companies are achieving this by collaborating with the disruptors, HSBC and JP Morgan being examples from the financial sector.[18]

There are huge implications around corporate responsibility where online marketing is concerned. First of all is data privacy, an issue that has blighted Facebook's reputation with the collection of personally identifiable information of millions of users by the political consulting and strategic communication firm Cambridge Analytica. Data protection in itself is potentially a new form of corporate social responsibility, with sound corporate policy allowing data processing in a responsible and sustainable way.[19] The very nature of digital marketing, with its direct and targeted content, means that transparency is key. Customers want to know about the companies they interact with and purchase from,[20] so the company needs to transmit its personality and its ethos. As well as accurate labeling, transparency extends to other aspects such as how the company treats its employees and what it does for the community. An intelligent digital strategy will therefore keep customers informed even when the message is less positive. Such openness is rewarded with loyalty: 94% of consumers will stay loyal to a company that is being transparent, and 73% will pay more for a product that offers transparency.[21] A case in point is food retailing: customers increasingly want to know what is in what they eat. With the term "fake news" on everyone's lips, recent years have seen manipulation of information increase dramatically, from the U.S. presidential elections to commercial campaigns – and the public is now alert to it.

As with any crisis, it is the agile and adaptable that have the best chance of survival. Even in the first couple of weeks of isolation enforced by the COVID-19 pandemic, there was inspiring evidence of how to adapt your service and your marketing channels and to communicate it to your customers. And those who are adept at online marketing have an immediate advantage. Customers of the interiors company The Schaefer House can FaceTime employees and text or Facebook-message the business for design advice. Summersalt, a swimwear startup, is repurposing its regular customer service channels to provide emotional support to consumers. In fact, traditional marketing channels were predicted to take a hit, with the possible exception of TV advertising. Online marketing is set to increase massively, with a "huge increase in digital ad spend" anticipated. In a Dentsu Aegis Network survey, 14% of clients said they were moving budget online away from offline media. Social media use is up (not least because we are looking at our phones more frequently to check the news), with consumer-led brands harnessing the power of social media to engage their audiences.[22]

Other target audiences

In communicating the process it is undertaking, each organization has its own various target audiences, not just consumers, and they all need to be addressed. A good place to start is the general business community, a relevant audience for any organization, and one that can be reached via numerous media outlets. Then there is the professional community within the organization's field of activity, as well as the specific professional community associated with corporate responsibility. Remember to include your community of stakeholders: charities, foundations, organizations, neighbors, customers, suppliers, and so on, all of whom can be reached through the relevant media channels. Important members of your stakeholder audience will likely be specific individuals, sometimes no more than 20 or 30, holding key positions in relevant government ministries, NGOs, etc., who can be reached via more direct means such as phone, email, or meetings.

Finally, as explained in greater detail in Chapter 13, an organization must also communicate its commitment to its employees, to ensure company-wide buy-in to the process, while improving employee satisfaction at the same time. In addition, employees are the best communicators of any brand, promoting the company by word of mouth and sharing their experiences from within the organization. As any good marketer knows, word-of-mouth is one of the most powerful forms of advertising: it has been reported that 92% of consumers trust their friends over traditional media.[23]

Notes

1 Business in the Community, *The Marketplace Responsibility Principles.* http://svb.ua/sites/default/files/Marketplace_Responsibility_Princi ples_PDF.pdf.
2 *2017 Cone Communications CSR Study.* https://www.conecomm.com/research-blog/2017-csr-study.
3 Mark Ritson, "Marketing in the time of Covid-19." *MarketingWeek*, March 17, 2020. https://www.marketingweek.com/mark-ritson-market ing-covid-19.
4 Neil Patel, "What the coronavirus (COVID-19) means for marketers." *Neil Patel Blog.* https://neilpatel.com/blog/coronavirus/.
5 "The sweetgreen story." *YouTube.* https://www.youtube.com/watch?time_continue=2&v=o2MNNPX_x1I&feature=emb_logo.

6 Loic Tassel, "Being a force for good and a force for growth: P&G and Pantene in Israel." *LinkedIn*, June 7, 2019. https://www.linkedin.com/pulse/being-forceforgood-forceforgrowth-loic-tassel.
7 Arwa Mahdawi, "Woke-washing brands cash in on social justice. It's lazy and hypocritical." *The Guardian*, August 10, 2018. https://www.theguardian.com/commentisfree/2018/aug/10/fellow-kids-woke-washing-cynical-alignment-worthy-causes.
8 Mack Hogan, "Kendall Jenner ad uproar 'shows how far Pepsi has fallen,' marketing exec says." *CNBC*, April 5, 2017. https://www.cnbc.com/2017/04/05/kendall-jenner-ad-uproar-shows-how-far-pepsi-has-fallen-marketer.html.
9 Rebecca Nicholson, "From Coke's flower power to Kendall Jenner's Pepsi ad – how ads co-opt protest." *The Guardian*, April 5, 2017. https://www.theguardian.com/business/2017/apr/05/from-cokes-flower-power-to-kendall-jenners-pepsi-ad-how-ads-co-opt-protest.
10 *TOMS*. https://www.toms.com.
11 Katherine White, David J. Hardisty, and Rishad Habib, "The elusive green consumer." *Harvard Business Review*, July–August 2019. https://hbr.org/2019/07/the-elusive-green-consumer.
12 https://goodvertising.site.
13 Thomas Kolster, *Goodvertising: Creative Advertising That Cares*. London: Thames & Hudson, 2012.
14 Giles Gibbons, "The social value of brands." In Rita Clifton, *Brands and Branding*, pp. 45–60. London: The Economist/Profile Books, 2009.
15 Deborah Tannen, "The personal becomes dangerous," in "Coronavirus will change the world permanently. Here's how." *Politico*, March 19, 2020. https://www.politico.com/news/magazine/2020/03/19/coronavirus-effect-economy-life-society-analysis-covid-135579.
16 Aden Andrus, "What is digital marketing and how do I get started?" *Disruptive Advertising*, April 22, 2018. https://www.disruptiveadvertising.com/marketing/digital-marketing/.
17 "The future of marketing is about customer experience, not tools." *American Marketing Association*, August 6, 2019. https://www.ama.org/2019/08/06/the-future-of-marketing-is-about-customer-experience-not-tools; Mark Yeager, "4 telling trends that predict the future of content marketing." *Convince & Convert*. https://www.convinceandconvert.com/content-marketing/4-telling-trends-that-predict-the-future-of-content-marketing; John B. Horrigan, "Information overload." *Pew Research Centre*, December 7, 2016. https://www.pewresearch.org/internet/2016/12/07/information-overload; "The U.S. mobile app report." *Comscore Whitepaper*, August 21, 2014. https://www.comscore.com/Insights/Presentations-and-Whitepapers/2014/The-US-Mobile-App-Report?cs_edgescape_cc=US.

18 *DMI Daily Digest*, "9 ways digital has changed business forever." https://digitalmarketinginstitute.com/en-us/blog/9-ways-digital-has-changed-business-forever.
19 *Paolo Balboni*, "Data protection as a corporate social responsibility." May 21, 2018. https://www.paolobalboni.eu/index.php/2018/05/21/data-protection-as-a-corporate-social-responsibility/.
20 *DMI Daily Digest, op. cit.*
21 "Drive long-term trust and loyalty through transparency." *Label Insight Transparency ROI Study*. https://www.labelinsight.com/Transparency-ROI-Study.
22 Ben Jeffries, "Coronavirus and the marketing industry: What happens next?" *The Drum*, March 20, 2020. https://www.thedrum.com/opinion/2020/03/20/coronavirus-and-the-marketing-industry-what-happens-next.
23 Will Kenton, "Word-of-mouth marketing (WOM Marketing)." *Investopedia*, March 29, 2020. https://www.investopedia.com/terms/w/word-of-mouth-marketing.asp.

18 Be transparent

The information revolution and the ubiquity of social media have made organizational transparency critical. As a result, a growing number of corporations and public organizations now embrace transparency as a core management value and as a foundation for establishing stakeholder trust. In a word: reporting.

Why report?

Sound and well-established business strategy revolves around a four-point continuous cycle of "plan – execute – measure – report." We are all familiar with the father of modern management Peter Drucker's argument that "What gets measured gets improved." Once we report transparently on our sustainability performance in a measurable manner, it increases the company's commitment to sustainability and invites feedback, which then improves performance.

Social and environmental reporting promotes corporate responsibility within the organization and increases transparency and dialogue with stakeholders. It is a means rather than a goal and follows, not leads, an integrated corporate responsibility strategy. Having said that, it is not necessary to wait for perfection before beginning the process: the report also serves as a management tool for identifying gaps, weaknesses, and risks. Good-quality corporate responsibility reporting is not a trivial task, however. It is an integral part of an organizational strategy, especially if it is carried out voluntarily.

In fact, regular reporting, in accordance with international guidelines can be:

- A tool to attract ESG investors.
- An effective means of both external and internal communication.
- A means of comparison among organizations.
- A means of establishing a reputation as a responsible, green, and transparent organization to all stakeholders (investors, employees, customers, media, authorities, etc.).
- A tool for communicating leadership and differentiation to stakeholders (investors, employees, customers, suppliers).
- A means of fostering employee satisfaction and organizational pride.
- A practical tool for risk management in the company and across the supply chain.

A common reporting format goes by the name of either the Corporate Social Report, the Environmental Responsibility Report, or the Sustainability Report. In *Valuing Corporate Responsibility*,[1] Professor Rory Sullivan describes the value of corporate responsibility reports, noting that, first of all, they demonstrate that corporate responsibility is part of the organizational agenda, which is in itself a key message even without delving into the details. Within its pages are details on organizational boundaries, management of subsidiary activities, and governance of international operations. The report's methodology can also indicate the level of attention paid to different issues: for example, was the process carried out in cooperation with external and internal stakeholders? And, of course, a review of how corporate responsibility is managed and the position of the relevant functions in the organizational hierarchy reveals much about the importance of this field in the corporation. Also, those issues that are omitted can speak volumes by their absence.

Mandatory reporting and assurance

There are indications that corporate responsibility reports will ultimately be required by law. Already in Europe, an EU directive on nonfinancial disclosure has come into force requiring every large public interest company with more than 500 employees to disclose information on the way they manage social and environmental challenges. This covers approximately 6,000 large companies and groups across the EU, including listed companies, banks, insurance companies, and others that were defined as public interest entities by national authorities.[2]

In a financial context, companies are usually required to publish annual reports that contain audited financial statements, helping shareholders and other interested parties to hold directors accountable. Recently, the same concerns have arisen regarding the reliability of nonfinancial information with the rise of corporate reporting on sustainability, employment practices, and governance issues. While the aforementioned directive does not currently mandate assurance, in some countries such as Italy, France, and Germany, assurance of the nonfinancial information statement in the annual reports is already mandatory.[3]

As a response to the changing demands of the market, an increasing demand can be observed for audit and assurance of nonfinancial information and sustainability reports.[4] Two main assurance standards are used to assure sustainability reports: AA1000AS and ISAE 3000.

The AA1000 AccountAbility Assurance Standard (2008) (as this is written, a revised version is being prepared for launch in 2020) is part of the AccountAbility series of standards that set the four main principles of an accountable organization: inclusivity, materiality, responsiveness, and impact.[5] The AA1000AS requirements for conducting assurance include evaluation of whether an organization:

- Is responsible and transparent about the impact that it creates.
- Is engaging with and being responsive to its stakeholders.

The ISAE 3000 standard is published by the International Auditing and Assurance Standards Board (IAASB). Just as with its "big brothers" – the board's financial audit standards – ISAE 3000 focuses on processes for assessing the reliability of information revealed in a report or, in the language of the standard itself: building confidence that there are no material misstatements in a report.[6]

The World Business Council for Sustainable Development (WBCSD), together with the Institute of Chartered Accountants in England and Wales (ICAEW), published a "Buyer's Guide to Assurance on Non-financial Information" which demystifies common misconceptions about assurance and helps users procure fit-for-purpose assurance services. This is a useful document for anyone who needs to delve more deeply into what assurance is, how the process works, and what organizations need to consider when seeking to procure assurance services.[7]

Investors

As mentioned in Chapter 7, investors are increasingly looking at nonfinancial disclosures as presented in sustainability reports. This is true not only for the so-called "impact investors" who seek to generate beneficial social or environmental impact alongside financial rewards, but also for the mainstream investors that are incorporating ESG (environment, social, and governance) factors into their analysis. They are looking for valuable data regarding the quality of management, management of nonfinancial risks, and the company's ability to create value in the long term. The importance of sustainability reports is therefore higher than ever.

To attain a global reach and ensure a professional assessment of companies' sustainability disclosures and/or performance, investors are increasingly turning to the databases and reports of the ESG ranking agencies. These are, to name just a few: Sustainalytics, Bloomberg (which launched the Bloomberg ESG Disclosure Score), ISS-ESG, Vigeo Eiris, MSCI, Arabesque

ESG, and RobecoSAM. These agencies review thousands of sustainability reports and apply their internally developed methodologies to calculate an ESG score/ranking for the companies concerned.

The assessment process and the score might focus on quite different criteria, with each investor choosing the one that suits their purposes. The agencies might assess whether certain information is being disclosed (for example, level of customer complaints or information breaches), or they might assess a company's performance (for example, GHG emission reduction). They also show a keen interest in the management approach to sustainability, by assessing, for example, whether a certain material topic is mentioned in the corporate sustainability policy, or whether a manager is in place who bears responsibility for a certain issue; or they might be looking at tracking and accountability regarding the goals published in previous reports.

If a company wants to attract more investors, a properly planned and prepared sustainability report is one of the ultimate tools. Therefore, it is of crucial importance to start thinking about investors' specific ESG information requirements at the very beginning of the reporting process.

The good practice of planning, implementing, and reporting on your sustainability efforts can improve your relationships with investors in general and ESG investors in particular, as in the case of ICL (see the Box).

ICL ESG reporting

Technology   Investment

"Our innovative and highly elaborated Corporate Responsibility web-report is critical in meeting investors requirements and expectations. Our company is dually

> listed in the New York and the Tel Aviv Stock Exchanges. We receive hundreds of investor queries and data requests each year which either include or focus solely on sustainable practices, including environmental protection, climate change, health and safety, fair and diverse employment, ethics, corporate governance, responsible procurement, community engagement and other topics. We are also ranked on an ever-growing number of sustainability and ESG rankings, which have become a common tool for investors to structurally include sustainability in investment decisions. Having a public, highly detailed and easily accessible CSR report website (with a designated URL to each topic and sub-topic), greatly helps to cost-effectively answer these numerous data requests. Most ESG analysts rely heavily on these reports, and demand all analyzed data, policies and management practices to be public. The more accessible and easily found the data is the higher the chances the analysts will take it into consideration, raising companies scores. Our commitment to advanced reporting and to structured improvement based on the requirements arising from these reporting frameworks rankings, allowed ICL to receive very high and industry leading scores in several indexes. This greatly helps us to meet stakeholder expectations, raising the investment appeal of our organization."
>
> Roy Weidberg ICL ESG officer

In practice

Standards and frameworks

Numerous guidelines and frameworks are available for sustainability reporting, among them the UN Global Compact,[8] the Task

Force on Climate-Related Financial Disclosure (TCFD),[9] the UN Sustainable Development Goals (SDGs),[10] CDP,[11] and the OECD Guidelines for Multinational Enterprises,[12] just to name a few. But for the sake of reliability and uniformity, it is advisable to use a recognized reporting standard such as the international GRI Sustainability Reporting Standards[13] (a majority of the world's largest corporations and public institutions now report in accordance with these) or the U.S. SASB Sustainability Accounting Standards.[14] The last two recently increased their mutual cooperation perhaps to develop a merged framework. These guidelines require each reporting organization to provide coherent and reliable information on: economic activity, social involvement, organizational structure, ethical code, and environmental compliance. They provide a reliable structure that simplifies the process for both writers and readers, which can be divided into chapters based on a set of indicators (see the "Report structure" section later in this chapter).

Another option is the innovative Integrated Report methodology,[15] which combines the corporate responsibility report with the financial one. It enables organizations to report on operations in relation to six types of capital – financial, manufactured, intellectual, human, social, and natural – in order to offer a fuller understanding of the extent to which the organization depends on these capitals and the impact it has on them. An Integrated Report also details the company's relationships with its stakeholders, including employees, customers, suppliers, business partners, regulators, and the general public.

Each standard has its own set of principles, but the key principles of a balanced report are transparency, materiality, and inclusiveness, which can be further expressed as the following three criteria:

1 Information that is being reported: completeness, relevance, and the sustainability context.
2 Quality of the information: accuracy, neutrality, and comparability.
3 Accessibility of the information: clarity and timeliness.

252 *The good process*

Technology and reporting: interactive/online

We are witnessing a steady transition toward interactive reporting platforms, such as social networks and mini-sites, which facilitate stakeholder engagement. This is an intelligent course of action for both marketing and reputational purposes, but also self-evident when one accepts that the essence of a report is to strengthen dialogue, trust, and transparency with stakeholders. Technology enables companies and stakeholders to access, collate, check, analyze, and correlate data, and also allows companies to operate and report in a highly integrated way. Improvements that technologically enhanced CSR reporting can bring include:

- Real-time data "from sensor to report" with automated data collection processes: this facilitates real-time stakeholder scrutiny, with verifiable, regularly updated information.
- Innovative communication channels, such as VR. Brewing giant Heineken's interactive sustainability report presented key information as GIFs.
- More integrated sustainability practices, especially with regard to supply chain management. According to the GRI: "Data technology will enable companies to operate in an integrated way within and across sectors and regions, monitoring their impacts and supply chains."[16]

Companies have to adapt their reporting practices and methods of data collection to keep in step with the digital age. Software platforms already exist for managing organizational sustainability reporting, including SAP[17] and SoFi.[18] We predict that, in the near future, we will see greater use of big data and machine learning applications and online reporting, for example, for audiences such as the stock exchange as well as for the wider public. At least part of most reports will soon be updated online.

Report structure

For most corporate responsibility reports the analytical basis comes from the material issues chosen by the reporting companies. These are selected in a formal process in collaboration with stakeholders. Organizations wishing to explore issues beyond their comfort zone can complete a process called a materiality analysis. Below is a quick overview of a recommended structure:

1 Company profile and strategy

This chapter includes a letter from the CEO, the organizational profile, its vision, corporate responsibility policy, corporate strategy and governance, a performance summary, and a short review of the company's products.

2 Business/economic impact

This chapter includes the organizational structure and its operational channels, mapping the value chain, products and services, and compliance with relevant standards. In addition, it reviews marketing across the board: policies, communications, awards and achievements, public affairs, and complaints. It also includes stakeholder engagement (i.e. with customers, suppliers, agents, regulators, and so on). It summarizes essential issues relevant to the actual reporting, such as new standards. This is where we will also find the corporate governance structure, including ownership, legal form and board of directors, legal compliance, regulations, and so on. It also includes disclosures pertaining to the organizational supply chain, a description of the supply chain, the procurement process, and the management of socially sustainable procurement.

3 Environmental impacts

This chapter discloses the organization's environmental policy and maps environmental impacts and environmental activity (procedures, assignments of responsibility), with reference to various material topics such as energy consumption, carbon footprint, water consumption, and waste disposal. It also makes reference where applicable to standards such as ISO 14000.

4 Social impacts

The final chapter provides disclosures about employment and social standards. It begins with a review of the company's social policy and maps social impacts. It addresses labor–management relations with regard to employee rights, employment conditions, training and education, diversity and equal opportunity, occupational health and safety, work–life balance, intra-organizational communication, accessibility, and so on.

It details the organization's community involvement on such topics as: the community involvement policy (methodologies, community projects, and volunteer work), measurement and evaluation, and the community contribution budget. Also important to disclose here is ethics: the organizational code, implementation, documentation, ethical violations, etc. The report concludes with a review of assurances and alignments under GRI or SASB standards.

Finally, including an index is recommended.

★ ★ ★

Reporting is never a goal in itself. It is a tool to help observe a company from new angles, to build internal and external communication, to integrate siloed functions, and to update the management vision. It is the process itself that is important, and so beneficial that we recommend it to all companies.

Notes

1 Rory Sullivan, *Valuing Corporate Responsibility: How Do Investors Really Use Corporate Responsibility Information?* Sheffield: Greenleaf Publishing, 2001.
2 "Directive 2014/95/EU – also called the non-financial reporting directive (NFRD)." https://ec.europa.eu/info/business-economy-euro/company-reporting-and-auditing/company-reporting/non-financial-reporting_en.
3 Claire Jeffery, *Comparing the Implementation of the EU Non-financial Reporting Directive in the UK, Germany, France and Italy*. Frank Bold, November 2017. http://www.purposeofcorporation.org/comparing-the-eu-non-financial-reporting-directive.pdf.

4 "Directive 2014/95/EU – also called the non-financial reporting directive (NFRD)." *op. cit.*
5 https://www.accountability.org/standards.
6 https://www.iaasb.org/publications/international-standard-assurance-engagements-isae-3000-revised-assurance-engagements-other-audits-or-0.
7 https://docs.wbcsd.org/2019/11/WBCSD_ICAEW_A_buyers_guide_to_assurance_on_non-financial_information.pdf.
8 https://www.unglobalcompact.org.
9 https://www.fsb-tcfd.org.
10 https://sustainabledevelopment.un.org/.
11 https://www.cdp.net/en.
12 https://www.oecd.org/corporate/mne/.
13 www.globalreporting.org.
14 https://www.sasb.org/.
15 http://integratedreporting.org/.
16 Inna Amesheva, "Five technology trends defining the future of corporate sustainability." *Eco-Business*, August 28, 2017. https://www.eco-business.com/opinion/five-technology-trends-defining-the-future-of-corporate-sustainability/.
17 https://www.sap.com.
18 https://insights.spherasolutions.com/sofi-software/building-ppc.

Afterword: take the lead and go beyond

I began this book by urging you to "dream big." Dreams about our children and grandchildren inheriting a world with sufficient drinking water, clean air, a world that values nature and people and protects the weak.

Those with a dream – the people with good vision – are often those who bring about change. Shimon Peres, my mentor and one of the greatest visionaries of the modern era, once said,

> It doesn't matter what degree you earned or who you are. What's important is what you do, and if you do it well, you're an entrepreneur, if not, then you're not. A man is measured by his actions not by his degree. A degree is meaningless.

He went on to say, "If you look towards the future, you're an entrepreneur. If you look back on the past, you're wasting your time."

We can see these philosophies in action right now, in real time. All around the world political and business leaders go beyond and are taking the future into their own hands. Net profit is no longer the be-all and end-all under the realization that wealth is meaningless in a polluted world. No one wants their grandchildren growing up in a dystopian reality, even if they are the ones holding the bigger guns.

Economic leaders across the globe are starting to appreciate the *real* profit that is there to be made. Profit for themselves, their grandchildren, and the society in which they live. Here is where their leadership is measured. The greatest leaders are not and go beyond short-term opportunists: they are those who look ahead with the aim of making a positive impact on the future.

Anybody reading these lines can be a leader and a visionary, whether in their company or in their own household. A small business manager in charge of several employees has a greater influence on that business than any government authority. Such managers are the undisputed leaders of their realms, and every decision they make, large and small, impacts the lives of many others.

Global change occurs only when local leaders join global leaders. This is not straightforward – but it is much simpler to go beyond than you think.

In this book, I have tried to describe the background to the current changes in the economy, the environment, and society and, more importantly, draw a working roadmap toward a better future.

Throughout the book I have identified concrete actions to fulfill the good vision and to help companies and the world around go beyond to a better place: a world in which corporate responsibility is a necessary investment and not an expense. Many people have contributed to this book, but any mistakes that remain are my responsibility alone. In the spirit of stakeholder dialogue – the importance of which we have discussed at length – I will be more than happy to receive your feedback about the book. Contact me at ivri.verbin@goodvision.co.il, www.Goodvision.co.il, www.GrantThornton.global.

About Good Vision

Good Vision, part of the Grant Thornton Group with more than 55,000 employees, is a firm that specializes in planning and managing corporate responsibility and sustainability processes.

Since its inception, the company has operated as a one-stop shop for corporate responsibility. It takes an holistic approach to all areas of corporate responsibility and the interfaces between them. The company offers a wide variety of services, having managed hundreds of projects for dozens of customers operating in all sectors of the economy; we specialize in, inter alia, strategically planning social, environmental, and ethical projects, and executive project management and process integration within organizations.

In 2016, the company merged with the Grant Thornton Fahn Kanne to allow greater financial and accounting synergies and to improve the international presence. The shift from an independent private company to a collaboration with a leading global accounting firm was a foregone conclusion as the topic of corporate responsibility became a core function of business strategy. Revolutions, as we know, begin from within.

Our purpose

We aim to support companies in discovering and fulfilling their potential for sustainability.

Our vision

We strive to integrate issues of corporate responsibility within the strategic thinking and work plan of each corporation. As a business consulting firm, we focus on the company's business objectives and values. As such, we advise and accompany our clients with a vision that supports and leverages the company's values, needs, positioning, and branding.

Our mission and values

Our mission is to lead our clients to comprehensive and accountable corporate responsibility in a manner that best serves their objectives.

We focus on our clients and their needs, striving to provide them with knowledge and advanced solutions drawn from various sources around the world. We are committed to maintaining a professional, proactive, attentive, and ongoing relationship with our clients.

Our team

Our company consists of account managers and internal and external consultants, who offer personal support and attention to each client. We integrate our business-strategic experience and our experience with nonprofit organizations with a profound understanding and practical knowledge of various issues relating to corporate responsibility. All these elements translate into innovative thinking and effective operations at the interface between business, community, and the environment. The team presents multidisciplinary and multi cultural experience with a strong desire to create added value for our clients. We invest in learning and specializing, providing our clients with a dependable foundation while operating proactively and discretely.

Ivri Verbin, founder and CEO of GoodVision and a partner at Grant Thornton Fahn Kanne, has been active in the field of corporate responsibility for over 15 years and is a featured speaker on the subject. In addition, he is a team member of Grant Thornton's global corporate responsibility center of excellence. Prior to his sustainability career, he served as an advisor to the Israeli Foreign Minister, Shimon Peres.

Index

AA1000 AccountAbility Assurance Standard 247
AA1000 Stakeholder Engagement Standard (SES) 147–148
AccountAbility 148, 247
Accountable Capitalism Act (ACA) 106
Acumen Fund 79
Adama 218
AIDS epidemic 119
Airbnb 59, 60, 61
AirShield 37
Alibaba 61, 92
Alon, Gal 144
ALYN Pediatric Rehabilitation Hospital 36
Amazon 92, 99–101
Amdocs 9–10
American Leadership in Energy and Environmental Design (LEED) system 203
Ant Forest 77–78
Apple 62, 92, 93, 94, 167, 190
Applied Materials, Inc., 191
Ariely, Dan 151, 153
artificial intelligence (AI) 40–41, 213
Assicurazioni Generali 139
Australian Green Star standard 203
Australian Workplace Equality Index (AWEI) 155
Authenticitys 52

Bain 122
B Corporations (B Corps) 79, 80–81
"Be My Eyes" app 73
Bebchuk Lucian Prof 13
BenAmi, Eitan 192
Ben and Jerry's PartnerShop® 73
Bergkamp, Claire 50
Better Cotton Initiative (BCI) 49
Beyond Meat 53–54
Bezos, Jeff 100
Bezos Earth Fund 100
Birnbaum, Daniel 116
Bitcoin 59
Black Lives Matter campaign 236
BlackRock 83, 84
blockchain 59, 91, 168, 213
Bloomberg 83, 124, 248
BNP Paribas 79
Boston Consulting Group 48
Bottom of the Pyramid (BOP) concept 74
#boycottpepsi 236
Brandeis, Louis 84
Brand-Levine, Dalit 39
Branson, Sir Richard 80
Braungart, Michael 69
Breathe 164
BreezoMeter 36–37
British Building Research Establishment Environmental

Assessment Method (BREEAM) 203
British Business in the Community (BITC) 153, 230
Brundtland Commission 71
B Team 31
Built to Last (Collins) 8
Burberry 49, 50
business: bulletproofing your reputation 103–104; change in 90–91; climate change and impact on 26–30; corporate responsibility of 89–90; ethics 130–131; future-proofing your 94; making progress in 91–94; observing 99, 101–102; regulation 89–90; responsibility for innovation and learning 104–105; responsibly managing risks 96–98; social license to operate 94–96; staying ahead of regulation 106; *see also* organizations
business ethics *see* ethics
business judgment rule 112
Business Roundtable 12, 13

C40 City Solutions Platform 192
CAL Fire 28
Cambridge Analytica 240
Cambridge Sustainability Network 64
Campaign (magazine) 236
capitalism 58; maximizing shareholder wealth 129; unethical 129–130
carbon footprint 183–186, 190
Carbon Trust 184
Cassiopeia 162
CDP (Carbon Disclosure Project) 29, 31, 185, 251
Cemex 82–83
Chalabi, Mona 38
Chandiok, Vishesh 168

charity: crowdfunding for 215; JGive 215–216; *see also* volunteering
Chernow, Beverly Goodman 199
chief sustainability officer 117
Chouinard, Yvon 173
ChowNow 22
Chr. Hansen 38
circular economy: cradle to cradle 69–71; definition of 65; industrial symbiosis 71; LOOP™ 68–69; Nespresso 65–66; Switch 67
Circularity Gap Report 66
Citi Bike 189
clean air 5, 99, 187, 204, 256
climate: Ant Forest application 77–78; justice 6, 100; leadership 31–32
climate change 6; 2° challenge 30–31; impact on business 26–30; investor relations 83, 84; supply chains and 167–168
Clooney, George 169
Coca-Cola 103
code of ethics *see* ethics
coffee, Nespresso 65–66, 169
Cohen, Liat 140
Cohen, Sir Ronald 62, 63
Collins, Jim 8
Committee of Sponsoring Organizations of the Treadway Commission (COSO) 97–98
community: 360Giving 216; collaborations in 226–228; corporate culture 227–228; cross-sectoral alliances 226–228; engagement/relations strategy 213; Google Foundation 214; issues and dilemmas for 214–216; JGive 215–216; social contribution as management tool 214–216; as stakeholders 211–212; sweetgreen 233; third

sector 225–226; *see also* flagship community projects
companies: directors of the future 113–115; *see also* business; organizations
Competitive Advantage model 8
Cone Communications 11, 231
Conscious Hotels 52
construction *see* green construction
corporate events: going green 191–193; principles for green 192–193
corporate governance, organizations 111–113
Corporate Knights Global 100 Index 38
Corporate Leaders Network for Climate Action (CLN) 31
corporate responsibility 116–119; assessment of 124; business 90, 91; chain of events in 121–122; chief sustainability officer 117; decision-making 123; definition of 2, 13; directors of the future 113–115; establishing administrative infrastructures 118; gap analysis 123–124; integrating organizational vision 122–123; inter- and intra-organizational partnerships 119; investment 83–84; leading and managing 118; managing risks 96–98; personal 109–110; process of 126; reporting in 245–249; reputation and 103–104; roadmap to 123–124; senior management and 117; setting timetables for 125–126; strategy 124; sustainability and 115; taking the lead 256–257; Unilever 110–111; work environment for employees 152–154; work plan 124

Corporate Social Responsibility (Kotler and Lee) 212
corporations: capitalism and 129–130; corporate responsibility 121–122; *see also* business; organizations
cotton: supply chain 168
COVID-19 1, 7–8; Amazon and 100; business after 89; changing workplace 9–12; corporate governance 112; crisis 19–24; digital marketing 239–241; employees during 149; environmental impact 180; future work predictions 164–165; green business model 193–195; online volunteering 224–225; responsibility of pandemic 109; technology and 33–35; tourism and 50–51; transportation 187
Cradle to Cradle (C2C) model 69–70
Creator: San Francisco 34
Credit Suisse 79
crowdfunding 215
customer relationship management (CRM) 3
customs barriers 58
cyber-security 114

Danone 22
Danziger, Avi 146
DaSilva, Alison 11
Daveu, Marie-Claire 38–39
Davis-Peccoud, Jenny 122
Delivering Happiness (Hsieh) 163
Delta Galil 48, 67
Dentsu Aegis Network 241
Derek Handley 81
dialogue: applying AA1000 standard 147–148; attention and 144–145; Negev Energy 144–145; platform for stakeholder

Index 263

143–144; tools for successful 145–147
"Dieselgate" scandal, Volkswagen 27
digital era, corporate responsibility 2–4
digital marketing 239–241
Digital Revolution 1
Digital Smart Traceability 168
digital technology, sustainability and 3–4
Dilemma Café 139–140
disabilities: workplace diversity 157–158
diversity *see* workplace diversity
DonorsChoose 223
downcycling 70
Drucker, Peter 141, 245
Dynamic Crop Models 201

Easterbrook, Stephen 161
eBay 92
economics: circular economy 64–72; COVID-19 crisis 19–24; discourse 58; impact economy 62–63; from pipeline to platform 61–62; sharing economy 59–61; social enterprises 72–74
Economist's Brands and Branding, The (Gibbons) 239
EcoVadis 178
Elkington, John 45–46
employees: Cassiopeia 162; changing patterns in green business model 194–195; disabilities of 157–158; diversifying recruitment 156–157; engagement in transportation policy 189–190; future of work predictions 164–165; gender 158–162; happy 150–151; inclusive organizations 155; investing in accessibility 158; outsourced workers 158; responsibility to 149–150, 165; retraining and upskilling 163–164; sexual harassment and 159–162; training 161–162; training on energy management 196; work environment for 152–154; work–life balance 162–163; workplace diversity 154–158; of Zappos 151–152
energy efficiency: control and measurement 195; energy-efficient devices 196–197; five R' of sustainable consumption 197; reducing consumption 195–196
Energy Star label 196
Enron 112, 129
enterprise resource planning (ERP) 3
Enterprise Risk Management (ERM) 97
environment: BreezoMeter 36–37; management system 209–210; plastic problem and 47–48; sustainability 44–45; triple bottom line (TBL) 45–46
environmental responsibility: carbon footprint 183–186; Carbon Trust 184; CDP 185; Citi Bike 189; corporate 180; creating policy and goals 180–183; energy efficiency in 195–197; GHG protocol 185–186; going green for corporate events 191–193; green construction 202–207; green office concept 193–195; green teams and committees 207–209; Interface 182–183; management system 209–210; NetBeat™ by Netafim 200–201; plastic war 198–200; Pukka 181–182; setting goals 183; sustainable transportation

186–191; UK legislation 188; water conservation 200–202; *see also* green construction
Environment Journal 67–68
ESG (environment, social, and governance) investment 78; criteria 96–97; disclosures and regulation 84–85; *see also* investment
ethics: code approval and launch of 137–138; continuous process of renewal of 141–142; corporate codes of 136; customized code of 137; diagnosis and analysis 133; formulating a code of 131–132, 134; formulating and writing 134–136; interviews 133–134; organizational code of 130–131; organized by organizational function 132; organized by stakeholders 132; organized by values 132; Saab 46–47; walking the talk 138–141; wording a code of 137; writing the code 132–136
Ettinger, Lia 44
European Union 65, 77; EMAS (Eco-Management and Audit Scheme) 209; non-financial reporting directive (NRFD) 85
Eurovision Song Contest 192
Extinction Rebellion (XR) 7

Facebook 38, 41, 60, 92, 103, 141, 153, 158, 241
FaceTime 241
Fair Trade 175–179; certification 177; Heineken and 172–173; joining the trend 177–179; Pukka Herbs 181; rapidly growing trend 176–177; social contract 178; supply chain 102
fake news 241
Farrow, Joel 164
fashion, sustainable 48–50

Fast Company (Kohnke) 10
finance: global economy 77; *see also* investment
Financial Times (newspaper) 1, 89
Fink, Larry 83, 84
First Industrial Revolution 1
Fiverr.com 12
flagship community projects: choosing 217–218; cross-sectoral steering committee 223; DonorsChoose 223; employee compensation 221–222; employee training and orientation 221; employee volunteering and engagement 219–221; engagement termination 218–219; Friends for Health project 219; GiveGab 224; leading by example 221; measurement and evaluation 218; online volunteering 224–225; strategic planning 217; volunteerability 222; volunteer database 222; volunteering for companies 222–223; VolunteerMatch 225; *see also* community
Flint (MI) water crisis 94–95
food industry, sustainable 53–55
food waste 54–55
Forbes (magazine) 110
Ford, Henry 211
Ford Foundation 13, 81
Fortune (magazine) 125
Fourth Industrial Revolution 2, 61
Friedman, Milton 21, 89, 130
Friends for Health 219
FSC (Forest Stewardship Council) 178
Future Meat Technologies 54

gender: employees 158–162; sexual harassment 159–162
Generation Zs: values of 235; workplace 11, 20; work predictions 164

Gibbons, Giles 122, 239
Ginossar, Yossi 97
GiveGab 224
Glassdoor 164
global emissions 5, 53
Global Impact Investing Network (GIIN) 78, 82
global initiatives, plastic problem and 47–48
globalization 58, 112, 113, 239
global pandemic 1, 24, 187
Global Reporting Initiative 178
Global Risks Report 98
Global Sustainable Investment Alliance 78
Global Workplace Analytics and FlexJobs survey 10
GMO-Free USA 101
Gobbetti, Marco 50
GoFundMe 34
Goler, Lori 153
Good Business 122
goodhang 34
Goodvertising 238
Good Vision 30, 48, 136, 146; Friends for Health project 219; Greenhouse Gas (GHG) Protocol 185–186; identifying three stages 133–136; implementation model 139–141; mission and values 259; plastic war 198, 199; team 259; vision of 258–259; wording a code of ethics 137
Google 60, 92, 93, 190
Google Foundation 214
Google.org 214
Gorsky, Alex 12
Grant Thornton 19, 97, 105, 114, 155, 168
Grant Thornton Fahn Kanne 258, 259
Grant Thornton Group 258
green business model, turning green office concept into 193–195
green construction: benefits of 203; cost of green buildings 203–204; describing a green building 202–203; innovation of 206–207; in practice 204–206; *see also* environmental responsibility
greenhouse gas (GHG) emissions 49, 183, 184, 249; footprint 238; protocol 185–186; substitutions 198
green marketing: consumer and social marketing 237–239; strategy for 232–234
green procurement 172; in practice 172–175; responsible sourcing 174–175
green teams and committees 207–209; organizational and employee profit 208; tips 208–209
greenwashing 234–235
Greta Effect 7
Guardian (newspaper) 187
Guilherme Leal 81

Harel insurance 22
Harvard Business Review (journal) 22
Harvard Business School 13, 22, 64, 83, 111
Hazan, Eric 40–41
Heineken 172–173, 252
Hella Ventures 37
Henderson, Rebecca 13, 111
Heschel Center for Sustainability 44
Hibob 164
Home Depot 232
Home Exchange 59
Honda 27
HR chatbots 10
Hsieh, Tony 151
Hydrop 49

IFC (International Finance Corporation) 80
Impact (Cohen) 62
impact economy 62–63
impact investing 78–79, 82

266　*Index*

IMPACT week 64
Impact-Weighted Accounts Project 83
individualism, decline of 20
industrialized and developing countries 58
Industrial Revolution 5; First 1; Fourth 2, 61
industrial symbiosis 71; Kalundborg 71–72
information revolution: ICL ESG reporting 249–250; investors 248–249; mandatory reporting and assurance 247–248; practice of 250–252; report structure 252–254; social and environmental reporting 245–249; standards and frameworks 250–251; technology and reporting 252
innovation: business taking responsibility for 104–105; disruptive 39; green construction 206–207; sustainability as driver of 38–39; Tesla 39–40
INSEAD business school 49, 64
Instagram 141
Institute of Chartered Accountants in England and Wales (ICAEW) 248
Intel 191
Interface, carpet and floor tile company 182–183
International Auditing and Assurance Standards Board (IAASB) 248
International Labour Organization (ILO) 177
Internet of things (IoT) 2, 62, 91, 213
investment: B Corporations (B Corps) 79, 80–81; ESG (environment social and governance) 78; ESG disclosures and regulations 84–85; growth of impact investing 82; impact investing 78–80; improving investor relations 83–84
investors, sustainability reports 248–249
IPCC (Intergovernmental Panel on Climate Change) 6
iPhone 61–62, 91, 93, 94, 167
ISAE 3000, 247, 248
ISEP INSEAD Social Entrepreneurship program 64
Israel: Future Meat Technologies 54; Ministry of Environmental Protection 37; Nespresso 65–66; startup nation 35, 36
Israel Electric Corporation 137

Jackson, Mike 236
Jenner, Kendall 235
JGive 215–216
Jhaveri, Janvi 34
Joann McPike 81
Johnson & Johnson 13
Johnson, Boris 188
Journal of Sustainable Tourism 51
Jurassic Park (film) 40
Just Good Business (McElhaney) 149

Kalundborg 71–72
Kantar Futures 50
Kellogg's 101–102
Kemp, Nicola 236
Kering Group 81
Kessel, Anthea 123
Klein, Naomi 21
Kodak 90
Kolster, Thomas 238
Kotler, Philip 212
Kramer, Mark R., 22, 23
Kurzweil, Ray 33
Kyoto Protocol 180

leadership: climate 31–32; SodaStream 116
Leadership in Energy and Environmental Design (LEED) system 203

Lean In (Sandberg) 158
Leather Working Group 125
Lee, Nancy 212
Let My People Go Surfing (Chouinard) 173
Levy, Paul 22
LGBT+ community 155, 226, 239
liberalism 58
lifecycle assessment (LCA) 175, 196
London Stock Exchange 77
LOOP™ 68–69
L'Oréal 167
LVMH 22

Machine learning 10, 40
McDonald's 48, 161
McDonough, William 69
McElhaney, Kellie 149–150
McKinsey & Co. 3, 26, 41, 61–63, 154
management commitment 127
marketing: digital 239–241; green 237–239; greenwashing 234–235; practice of green marketing 236–237; social 239
Martinez, Eduardo 21
Mastercard 117
Materials Innovation Lab 39
Meisling, Annemarie 38
Mercer 30
#MeToo campaign 159, 239
Microsoft 93
Migdal Insurance Company 139
Millennials: environmental issues 194; spending power of 67–68; sustainability 237; values of 235; workplace 9, 11, 20, 35, 164
Miodownik, Gaby 201
Mission Zero® 182
Mobileye 188
Moovit 191
MSC (Marine Stewardship Council) 179, 233
MSCI 83, 248
Murphy, Colin 51
Musk, Elon 40

Narayanan, Arvind 35
natural resources 5, 47, 58, 68, 72, 181, 198, 201, 202, 232
Nature Climate Change 51
Enlight Energy 144–145
Nespresso 65–66, 169
NetBeat™ by Netafim 200–201
Netflix 39
New York Stock Exchange (NYSE) 250
New York Times (newspaper) 89
Nike 167, 238
Nissan 117
Nokia 90, 91, 93, 94
North Star Alliance 119
Novogratz, Jacqueline 79
Novo Nordisk 72

Ocean Works 48
OECD 52, 180, 251
One Young World 81
organizations: corporate governance of 111–113; corporate sustainability of 229–231; COVID-19 implications 231–232; customers as real shareholders of 229–231; digital marketing 239–241; Goodvertising 238; green consumer and social marketing 237–239; greenwashing 234–235; integrating vision 122–123; P&G 234; Pepsi 235–236; reporting structure 252–254; social marketing 239; strategy of socially responsible (green) marketing 232–234; sweetgreen 233; target audiences 241–242; TOMS 237; *see also* business
Our World Data 53
outsourced workers 158
Oxford Saïd Business School 64

Paris Climate Agreement 6, 30
Parkinson's disease 64

Patagonia 173–174
Patel, Neil 232
PayPal 92
Pepsi 116, 235–236
Peres, Shimon 64, 256
PG&E (Pacific Gas and Electric Company) 28–29
plastic war: benefits of 200; disposable *vs* reusable 198–199; environment and 47–48; single use *vs* multi-use 198–199; substitutions 198
Platform as a Service (PaaS) 62
platform businesses 61–62
Pole, Sebastian 181
Policy Institute for Energy, Environment and the Economy 51
Polman, Paul 110–111
Pololikashvili, Zurab 51
Porter, Michael 8, 74
#POURITFORWARD campaign 227
PRI (Principles for Responsible Investment) 23
Princeton University 35
PRISM network 155
Procter & Gamble (P&G) 234
Pukka 181–182
Pulse of the Fashion Industry 48

Rainforest Alliance 178
Ralph Lauren 117
Recreational Equipment Inc. (REI) 124–125
recycling 175
Reddit 35
reporting 254; business strategy for 245–249; common format 246; ICL ESG 249–250; investors in sustainability reports 248–249; mandatory 247–248; structure of 252–254; *see also* information revolution
reputation: Amazon 99–101; bulletproofing 103–104; Goodvertising 238; Kellogg's 101–102; risk 29
Reputation Institute 103
responsibility: revolution 12–14; technology and 40–41; *see also* environmental responsibility
Responsible Wool Standard 125
Richards, Jonathan 164
Ritson, Mark 232
Roadster 40
Robèrt, Karl-Henrik 70
Roche Pharmaceuticals 146
Rockefeller Foundation 78, 81
Ross, Marina 49
Roundup 101

S2G Ventures 54
Saab 46–47
Samsung 93
Sandberg, Sheryl 158
Sano Brunos Enterprises 39
SAP 41, 64, 141, 252
Sarbanes-Oxley Act (SOX) 138
Schwab Klaus 163
Science (magazine) 71
Science Based Targets 49
Serafeim, George 83
Shared Value model 212
sharing economy 59–61
Sharing Economy, The (Sundararajan) 59
Shvartz, Eitan 192
Siemens 62
Sivan, Yesha 3
social contribution, management tool 214–216
social enterprises 63, 72–74, 235
Social Impact Bonds 79
socialism 58
social license 94–96
social media 92
social-washing 235
SodaStream 116
SoFi 252
Stahl, Walter 69

Stakeholder Engagement Standard (SES) 147–148
stakeholders 143; platform for dialogue 143–144; tools for successful dialogue 145–147
Staples 171
Starbucks 48, 225, 232
startup nation, Israel 35, 36
Stella Artois 227
Stella McCartney 50
Strive Masiyiwa 81
Sullivan, Rory 246
Summersalt 241
Sundararajan, Arun 59
supply chain 167–169; building a responsible 169–171; cotton 168; EcoVadis 178; Fair Trade and 175–179; green procurement 172; green procurement in practice 172–175; Heineken 172–173, 172–175; Patagonia 173–174; responsible sourcing 174–175; TerraCycle 170–171
sustainability: description of 44–45; digital technology and 3–4; driver of innovation 38–39; fashion 48–50; food 53–55; management 127; organizations 229–231; responsible supply chain 169–171; tourism 50–53; vision and working plan 127
Sustainable Apparel Coalition 48
sustainable development, definition of 45
Sustainable Development Goals (SDGs) 4, 8, 14, 38, 51, 183, 251
sweetgreen 233
Switch (Sustainable Waste into Textiles Creates Harmony) 67

Tahini El Arz 226
Tarki, Atta 22
Task Force on Climate-Related Financial Disclosure (TCFD) 250–251
Tech4Good 35, 73
technology: ALYNovation 36; BreezoMeter 36–37; COVID-19 and 33–35; IMPACT at INSEAD 64; for planning and monitoring 212–213; responsibility and 40–41; role of 33; Siemens 62; Tech4Good 35; tech giants and 37–38; Tesla 39–40; Zoom software 34–35
Tel Aviv College 3
Tel Aviv Stock Exchange 250
TerraCycle 170–171
Tesla 39–40
The Natural Step (TNS) 70, 71
third sector 225–226
360Giving 216
Thunberg, Greta 6–7
Tiffany and Co. Foundation 81
TikTok 38
TOMS 237
tourism, sustainable 50–53
Tourism4SDGs.org 52
Toyota 27
Toyota Prius 40
transportation: Citi Bike 189; employee engagement 189–190; implementation of procedures 190; reducing fuel dependence and demand 191; sustainable 186–191
Travelers Companies, Inc 30
TRIP (Technology, Resource availability, Impact and Policy) 30
triple bottom line (TBL) 45–46
Troughton, Wayne 52
Turo 59
Twitter 35, 38
Tyson Foods 117

Uber 59, 60, 61, 188
UK legislation 188
Unilever 81, 110–111, 168, 234, 238; LOOP™ 68–69

United Nations (UN) 77, 177; Climate Change Conference 7; Food and Agriculture Organization (FAO) 53, 54; Global Compact 178, 250; Sustainable Development Goals (SDGs) 4, 8, 14, 38, 51, 183, 251; World Food Program (WFP) 119; World Tourism Organization (UNWTO) 50–52
universal basic income 21
University of California, Davis 51
University of Michigan 104
upcycling 70
UPS Foundation 21
U.S. Cone Communications 11, 231
U.S. SASB Sustainability Accounting Standards 251, 254

Valuing Corporate Responsibility (Sullivan) 246
vegan food 53–54
Verbin, Ivri 259
Viarco 64
Virgin Atlantic 22
Virgin Unite 81
Virtual Dining Chicago 34
Volkswagen 27
volunteering: companies and 222–223; database 222; DonorsChoose 223; employee engagement in 219–221; Friends for Health initiative 219; GiveGab 224; online 224–225; volunteerability 222; VolunteerMatch 225; *see also* flagship community projects
VolunteerMatch 225

Walgreens 22
Walker, Darren 13
Walmart 23, 41, 232
Warren, Elizabeth 106
Wasteless 54
water conservation 200–202; adopting conservation culture 202; changing wasteful habits 201; mechanical measures reducing use 201
water crisis, Flint, Michigan 94–95
Water.org 227
Waze 188, 191
Waze Carpool 191
Weidberg, Roy 250
Weinstein, Harvey 159
Weiss, Jeff 22
We Mean Business 31–32
Western Digital 191
Westwell, Tim 181
Wharton School of Business 100
Whole Foods 48, 233
Wikipedia 130
woke-washing 235
work-life balance, employees 162–163
workplace diversity: creating 154–158; disabilities 157–158; recruitment 156–157; *see also* employees
Workplace Diversity (Esty, Griffin and Schorr) 155–156
World Bank 51, 53, 77, 80
World Business Council for Sustainable Development (WBCSD) 65, 211, 248
World Conference on Smart Destinations 51
World Economic Forum 4, 7, 26, 51, 66, 98, 163
World Food Program (WFP) 119
World Health Organization 36
World Travel and Tourism Council 51

YouTube 35

Zadek, Simon 121, 123
Zappos 151–152
Zoombombing 35
Zoom software 34–35
Zoref, Lior 146
Zuckerberg, Mark 38